D1826725

*Resistance and Visions –
Postcolonial, Post-secular and Queer
Contributions to Theology and the
Study of Religions*

*Resistencias y visiones –
contribuciones postcoloniales,
postseculares y queer a la teología y
a los estudios de las religiones*

*Widerstand und Visionen –
der Beitrag postkolonialer,
postsäkularer und queerer Theorie
zu Theologie und
Religionswissenschaften*

Journal of the European Society of Women in Theological Research

Anuario de la asociación europea de mujeres para la investigación teológica

Jahrbuch der Europäischen Gesellschaft für theologische Forschung von Frauen

Volume 22

Bibliographical information and books for review in the Journal should be sent to:
Sigríður Guðmarsdóttir PhD.,
Kirdjustett 7a, 113 Reykjavík, Iceland

Articles for consideration for the Journal should be sent to:
Sigríður Guðmarsdóttir PhD.,
Kirdjustett 7a, 113 Reykjavík, Iceland

Resistance and Visions – Postcolonial, Post-secular and Queer Contributions to Theology and the Study of Religions

Resistencias y visiones – contribuciones postcoloniales, postseculares y queer a la teología y a los estudios de las religiones

Widerstand und Visionen – der Beitrag postkolonialer, postsäkularer und queerer Theorie zu Theologie und Religionswissenschaften

Editors:
*Ulrike Auga, Sigríður Guðmarsdóttir,
Stefanie Knauss, Silvia Martínez Cano*

PEETERS
LEUVEN – PARIS – WALPOLE, MA
2014

Journal of the European Society of Women
in Theological Research, 22

© 2014, Peeters Publishers, Leuven / Belgium
ISBN 978-90-429-3173-2
ISSN 1783-2454
eISSN 1783-2446
D/2014/0602/103
Cover design by Margret Omlin-Küchler

CONTENTS – INHALT – ÍNDICE

Journal of the European Society of Women in Theological Research 22 (2014) 1-4.
doi: 10.2143/ESWTR.22.0.3040787

Introduction

The fifteenth international conference of the ESWTR took place in Dresden, Germany, in August 2013. We would like to thank all – organizers, sponsors, assistants, participants – who helped realize this conference and make it a memorable event.

The title of the conference was *New Horizons: Resistance and Visions*. The location for this conference on resistance, vision and women's scholarship on gender and theology was no coincidence. Dresden, the former capital and royal residence of Saxony, known for its baroque and rococo splendor, stands as a symbol of the destruction of WWII, Cold War politics, dissidence protest against the socialist regimes, powerful restorations, and the revivals of protest movements in the past few decades. This beautiful city by the Elbe thus served as an important background to the theological musings that took place during the conference, a witness to resistance, catalyst for visions, and inspiration to new horizons.

The goal of this conference in Dresden, 25 years after the *Wende*, was to inquire about the importance of the political and theological efficacy of the dissidence in eastern Europe which led to the peaceful revolutions around 1989, and which serves as a role model for current resistances and new social movements. Many of the resisting persons, many of the dissident political, religious, and artistic mobilizations imagined an open radical, democratic, and solidary society not only beyond existing fake socialism but also beyond existing limited democracy with its capitalism.

An important part of the conference was thus a panel with women from different eastern European backgrounds who gave intimate insight into the experience, rationale, and theologies in the context of political transitions. Additionally, film screenings and guided tours to historical sites of struggle, like the former East German political prison in Dresden, made the context of resistance and vision palpable.

Thus the conference underlined the inseparability of the personal, the political, and the theological, and the conference call for papers posed its theological questions accordingly:

In our world coined by globalisation and neoliberalism a commodification of the whole life has emerged. In consequence, poverty, (hetero-)sexism, homophobia, racism, fundamentalism and nationalism (including right-wing extremism) are producing violent exclusions instead of inclusive ideas of community. What answers can theological perspectives of different religions offer to sustainably decrease economic and epistemic violence?

Especially liberationist, intersectional, feminist, and gender-sensitive approaches have proved to be very conscious of these issues and have contributed immensely to their analysis in theology and religious studies. More recently, postcolonial, post-secular and queer theories have furthered the critical debates in cultural and social analysis and enriched previous approaches. Whereas often only one of these theoretical approches is used to frame the analysis, this conference provided the opportunity to discuss the contributions to theology and the study of religions of all three approaches together.

The articles collected in this volume were all presented at the Dresden conference. They were discussed in companionship and solidarity, and then turned from conference papers into peer-reviewed articles. All of the articles offer their own unique vision and partial answer to the questions of resistance and visions. Consequently, the editorial team has chosen to organize the entire volume around the conference theme instead of dividing it up into the traditional sections.

The volume opens up with *Ulrike Auga*'s article which provides a framework for the following papers by introducing postcolonial, post-secular and queer methodologies and their contributions to theological and religious studies reflections on resistance and visions, using as her starting point the dissident movements in former East Germany.

The next papers focus on resistance movements in various forms and queer visions of alternative societies of justice and solidarity. *Anne-Marie Korte*'s paper proposes a European feminist and public theology, drawing like Auga on a case study from the context of former Eastern bloc states, namely the Pussy Riot feminist *Punk Prayer* event in 2012, in order to analyze hybrid and ambiguous performances of feminist public theology in Europe which offer the possibility of resistance against antidemocratic and corrupted powers. *Teresa Forcades i Vila* then directs our attention to structures of "fake democracies" which operate under the pretension that the people rule, while in fact they are powerless. Forcades i Vila proposes four principles of Christian theology as indispensable tools in dismantling fake democracies, namely the notion of a creation which is still ongoing and human participation in co-creation, queer notions of unity in diversity, the inseparability of love and freedom, and finally the importance of metanoia, or conversion. *Janet Jakobsen* then introduces alternative queer economies and visions of justice, with a special emphasis on domestic work. For Jakobsen, such a vision of justice can never be monolithic or uniform, but is instead connected, engaged, and achieved in solidarity through analyses that take the intersecting categories of gender, sexuality, race, nation, class, age, ability, etc. seriously. As for Jakobsen, alternative notions of economies are at the heart of Kwok Pui-lan's and Joerg Rieger's articles. Their papers represent companion pieces, as they were presented together at the Dresden conference. *Kwok* argues that the Occupy movement with its protest against the growing disparity between rich and poor requires us to rethink the relation between God and politics. Drawing on the insights of *minjung* theology (the theology of the multitude), she exposes the limits of a masculinist and heterosexist portrayal of God. *Rieger* also focuses on the Occupy movement and its critique of not just dominant power in politics and economics, but also as it is embodied in religion. As with the other contributions to this volume, his paper moves beyond critique, however, in pointing out alternative experiences of power in Jewish and Christian traditions that enable a new understanding of solidarity. *Julia Enxing*'s contribution also focuses on a protest movement and its visions of a different reality, namely guerilla gardening and its parallels with resistance movements within the churches. This form of "green" resistance, working with flowers, plants, seeds, and soil, is a call against the oppression of the environment and persons, using forms of communication and protest that question borders and differences, and cultivate them colorfully.

The next set of papers focuses on issues of postcoloniality and World Christianity from different perspectives. *Musa Dube*'s contribution provides an introduction to postcolonial biblical exegesis and a powerful critique of traditional forms of biblical studies with their inherent colonial presumptions. Dube then goes beyond her critique by discussing her current research in which she reads letters from the modern colonial context, seeking to identify strategies of domination, resistance, collaboration, and the emergence of hybridity in the modern colonial contact zone. *Andrea Taschl-Erber*'s text also focuses on the Bible and its potential for resistance. Her intertextual reading of the opening of the Gospel of Luke discovers the subversive memory, rooted in traditions in the First Testament, of prophetic social criticism and political resistance by women. Especially the Magnificat becomes a document of resistance against social oppression and the experience of violence perpetrated by the Roman colonial power, a messianic vision of political freedom and socio-economic justice. *Eleonora Hof*'s article explores and critiques prevalent

3

imaginaries of World Christianity. Using gender as a critical category, she challenges tropes of imagining World Christianity, shifting attention from notions of travelling and exploration towards storytelling because it provides room for ambivalence, displacement, rupture, continuity, and the strategies of identity negotiation.

The two papers that conclude our volume present the maybe newest approaches to the issues discussed here going beyond body and developing new ways of thinking – and critiquing – concepts of materiality, vulnerability, and personhood. In her article, *Mayra Rivera* bridges the gap between liberation and postcolonial theology, calling for theologies of the body to examine social-material incarnations, social inequality, pain, and desire. She argues that the challenge now is to think corporeality in a way that refuses objectifying knowledge and idealizations that deny vulnerability, suggesting the concept of flesh as a possibility to further develop the accounts of the relationships that constitute life. In their paper, *Montserrat Escribano-Cárcel* and *Neus Forcano i Aparicio* bring together queer and postcolonial theologies with the insights of neurosciences, thus opening up a new perspective in theological thought. They show how the combined insights of neurosciences and Christian theology on the concept of "subject" help to question the epistemic pillars sustaining our perception of reality, and at the same time, to think of the possibility of making each and every human life better.

The papers collected here show the surplus of the synergy between the postcolonial, post-secular and queer approaches they apply, and we hope that they may inspire further interdisciplinary research and activism in theology and the study of religions. The section ESWTR Members in Action, founded in Dresden, also calls for stronger connections between activism, theory, and theology linked to global debates, to further develop the visionary contributions of theology to a more just society.

Journal of the European Society of Women in Theological Research 22 (2014) 5-30.
doi: 10.2143/ESWTR.22.0.3040788

Ulrike Auga

Resistance and the Radical Social Imaginary: A Genealogy from Eastern European Dissidence to New Social Movements: Connecting the Debates between Activism and Postcolonial, Post-secular and Queer Epistemology and Theology

> "Imagine it is socialism and nobody leaves."
> (Christa Wolf)[1]

Introduction

Centuries of world-wide resistance against patriarchal behavior in societies, symbolic orders and not least dominant theologies have brought about certain improvements. Only standing on the shoulders of feminist (liberation) theologies, Black theologies, Womanist theologies, Chicana theologies, etc. have we been able to develop our current perspective.[2] However, up until today racism, sexism, homophobia, transphobia, nationalism, classism, fundamentalism, etc. have not disappeared from our societies and churches. It also has to be acknowledged that some resistance theories, practices and theologies remain violent. Furthermore, with globalization and neoliberalism we face an even more toxic cocktail of economic, sovereign, and epistemic violence.

Therefore, critical theology has begun to look beyond established liberation theology for new perspectives on resistance and for new visions of improved and less exclusive ways of living together. In the last decades, postcolonial, post-secular and queer theories have begun to play a role in the study of "religion". All focus on a poststructuralist understanding of power and mechanisms of the production of truth, and the analysis of how in discourses

---

[1]   Thus the well-known East German writer Christa Wolf in her address to the people at Alexanderplatz in Berlin on November 4, 1989: Christa Wolf, *Auf dem Weg nach Tabou: Texte 1990-1994* (Kiepenheuer & Witsch: Köln 1994), 13 (my translation).

[2]   See for instance the 14th International ESWTR Conference "Feminist theology: listening, understanding and giving answer in a secular and plural world," Salamanca 2011.

(including state institutions like universities, etc.) a particular kind of knowledge is held to be true.

To avoid some pitfalls I find it important to use all three theories together. Postcolonial theory underlines the complex efficacy of epistemic violence and emphasizes that we all live in a world affected by colonialism and under neo-colonial conditions. From the critique of the construction of the "oriental Other" an interdependent approach to the critique of the essentialization and naturalization of the categories of knowledge, "gender", "race", "class", "nation", "ability" and "religion" emerges. Post-secular theory overcomes the Kantian division between reason and irrational faith. It underlines the importance of religious practices for subject formation, agency, and human flourishing. However, in consequence a de-essentialized category of "religion" is needed for non-faith-based and faith-based approaches to the study of religions. Queer theory underlines that on the one hand the interdependence of nation state, capitalism, and heteronormativity should be considered in the critique of patriarchy and symbolic gender orders. On the other hand, the queering of categories or sites of analysis is a complex epistemological enterprise which tries to revolutionize the (self-)study of the marginalized by undoing those epistemic structures that keep subjects in (universalistic) objectified positions. Queer theory also discusses possible concepts of resistance and futurity.

If we look at more recent resistance theories, it is clear that they are connected with social movements and various activist approaches but in different forms than earlier rights or identity based struggles. Following the crisis of social justice since the financial crisis 2007-2008, the "Arab Spring", and the Occupy movement, several hundred protest movements have emerged in the last few years in order to protest against increasing economic, social, political, and cultural exclusion. Many of these resistance movements understand themselves to be in the tradition of the dissidence movements in "eastern European" countries.

However, the relationship between protest in eastern European socialist countries and these current protest movements is rarely investigated. It appears to me that dissidence in eastern Europe and its connection with theology, the church, and "religion" is a useful, yet neglected issue, not only for elaborating resistance and vision in (feminist) theology and religious studies, but also for insights into the further development of postcolonial, post-secular and queer theory.

In the peaceful revolutions around the year 1989, the discursive character of resistance and vision becomes obvious, and with it, the need for the historicization and diversification of the understanding of resistance and the danger of epistemic violence within certain resistance discourses. Furthermore, in the dissidence to totalitarian socialism one could find new alliances among activist groups as well as between activism and theory, and, in a post-secular gesture, alliances between faith-based and non-faith-based protest.

In this essay I will take a closer look at the genealogy of recent forms of resistance and the role of faith-based protest in new social movements. Then I will develop ways to apply postcolonial, post-secular, and queer approaches to theology and religious studies.

The Dissident Protest of 1989: Resistance, Vision, and Theology

The notion of dissidence gained a new political and theoretical momentum with the intensification of the political resistance which emerged in Poland, which was connected with the Perestroika and Glasnost of Mikhail Gorbachev in the Soviet Union and eventually reached all socialist eastern European countries. Dissidence means political resistance within a political system against an elected government (an authoritarian regime, but also "fake democracies")[3] often envisioning a society shaped by greater solidarity.[4] Some reasons for resistance were the political violence of the totalitarian socialist regimes, the lack of representation, freedom of speech, freedom to travel, governmental accountability, and economic hardships. The methods of resistance vary in different historical epochs and countries and include civil disobedience, peaceful marches, but also the power of the masses of bodies, as in the Occupy movement, or what was later named the "swarm logic" of the multitude.[5]

During the time of eastern dissidence the western democratic states applauded the protest because the socialist states counted as regimes with totalitarian tendencies. The Arab Spring was welcomed in a similar manner in the beginning. In contrast, in western states with their framework of nation statehood, market economy, and a representative democracy, radical, dissident protest has so far been seen as unnecessary because this system was understood as the best possible, in need only of slight improvements which could

---

3 See Teresa Forcades i Vila's contribution to this volume.
4 See Ulrike Auga, *Intellektuelle – zwischen Dissidenz und Legitimierung: Eine kulturkritische Theorie im Kontext der Transition Südafrikas* (LIT: Münster 2007); Dietrich Beyrau, *Intelligenz und Dissens: Die russischen Bildungsschichten in der Sowjetunion 1917-1985* (Vandenhoeck & Ruprecht: Göttingen 1993). See also Sabine Hark, *Dissidente Partizipation: Eine Diskursgeschichte des Feminismus* (Suhrkamp: Frankfurt 2005).
5 See Michael Hardt / Antonio Negri, *Multitude: War and Democracy in the Age of Empire* (Penguin: London 2004).

be brought about through an elected multi-party system of government and slight interventions by civil society. The new resistance underlines that the liberal idea of the self-regulation of the market in today's societies is false and democracy limited because of capitalism and the exclusive form of the nation state. Furthermore it has been shown that today political transformation towards a just democracy can only be brought about by new social movements.

The shared goal of resistance movements is to overcome the current government. However, the visions of a new collectivity differ greatly. This is a challenge which remains present in current political uprisings. Facing political oppression and economic hardship in East Germany, for example, some aimed for a representative democracy with market economy as in the "West". So the movement turned from chanting "We are *the* people" at demonstrations – a claim to take the power from the regime – to "We are *one* people", implying the goal of reunification. However, numerous others aimed at a society characterized by greater solidarity, going beyond the "actually existing socialism" with planned economy, but also beyond capitalism and the "limited democracy" of the West. Some people, among them theologians such as Wolfgang Ullmann, worked on a new constitution for a more just German state.

When talking about the role of churches, theology, and faith-based organizations in the peaceful revolutions of 1989, it is necessary to differentiate between individual churches and theologians and their involvement in supporting or critiquing the socialist totalitarian governments. Differences among the events in Eastern Bloc countries should be also taken into account.[6] Generally speaking, a more or less violent secularization was forced onto the churches because of the Marxist-Leninist philosophy which understands religion as "the opium of the people".[7]

I draw on the example of the Protestant Church in East Germany I belong to in order to illustrate how churches and theology were involved in defining the heritage of resistance I alluded to. To oversimplify, one could say that after the Second World War, when two German states had emerged, and after 1961, when

---

[6] See Hendrik Bispinck / Jürgen Danyel / Hans-Hermann Hertle / Hermann Wentker (eds.), *Aufstände im Ostblock: Zur Krisengeschichte des realen Sozialismus* (Christoph Links Verlag: Berlin 2004); Detlef Pollack, *Politischer Protest: Politisch alternative Gruppen in der DDR* (Leske und Budrich: Opladen 2000).

[7] Karl Marx, "Debatten über Preßfreiheit und Publikation der Landständischen Verhandlungen," in: *Rheinische Zeitung* nr. 130, 10 May 1842, Marx-Engels-Werke vol. 1, 47. http://www.mlwerke.de/me/me01/me01_041.htm, 15 May 2014.

the Wall was built and the existence of the two states was considered a fact, the life of the different strands of the church became politically increasingly separated from each other but never split. Some theologians and church officials supported the highly controversial notion of "the Church in Socialism", which meant a gradual establishment within the state. This approach with its consequently positive attitude toward the fake socialism of East Germany was defended with the pretence at legitimizing East Germany as a truly anti-Fascist and anti-capitalist state.[8] However, for many, the oppressive and totalitarian character of the East German regime became ever more visible and unbearable. Because the freedom of speech was limited, yet the right to religious freedom was maintained, churches became the only places where it was possible to express one's opinion.[9] Some members of the church founded the "Church from below" in order to distance themselves from the church that supported the system. Furthermore, many pastors (also beyond the Church from below) opened their doors for prayers, services, and concerts which were indeed political gatherings. Christa Wolf remembers: "November 4 [1989] on Alexanderplatz – the day of the closest approximation between artists, intellectuals, and other people – was by no means [...] a contingent product of a lucky moment. It was the culmination and climax of a previous history in which authors, theater people, peace groups, and other groups had come into contact and conversation with each other under the roof of the church [...]".[10] Members of the church encouraged people who were victims of the secret police and state violence.[11] Large parts of the Protestant Church in East Germany became the umbrella organization for peaceful resistance. It was in churches where the marches with candles started which brought about the "velvet revolution".

It is important that this dissidence is seen as resistance *and* vision because bare resistance is in danger to be also violent. The authoritarian self-proclaimedly socialist countries based their education on their interpretation of a Marxist

---

8   See Erhart Neubert, *Geschichte der Opposition in der DDR 1949-1989* (Bundeszentrale für politische Bildung: Bonn 1997); Anette Emtmann, *Zivilgesellschaft zwischen Revolution und Demokratie: Die 'samtene Revolution' im Lichte Antonio Gramscis Kategorien der 'società civile'* (Argument: Berlin 1998).

9   See Claudia Lepp / Kurt Nowak (eds.), *Evangelische Kirche im geteilten Deutschland 1945-1989/90* (Vandenhoeck & Ruprecht: Göttingen 2001).

10 Christa Wolf, "Zwischenrede, 1990," in: Christa Wolf, *Auf dem Weg nach Tabou: Texte 1990-1994* (Kiepenheuer & Witsch: Köln 1994), 18 (my translation).

11 See Marianne Subklew, *Der Pankower Friedenskreis: Geschichte einer Ost-Berliner Gruppe innerhalb der Evangelischen Kirchen in der DDR 1981-1989* (Der Andere Verlag: Osnabrück 2004).

model of society's natural development from capitalism via socialism to an as yet unrealized communism where injustice would be abandoned. There was certainly some influence on the emergence of solidary individual and collective social imaginaries via living in an atheist utopian state of hope. Even though many people denounced the reality of socialism and many of the doctrinal teachings of the ruling party, the visionary, almost salvational utopian promise for a more just society left some imprints in many people. Additionally, limited access to goods and the danger of resistance brought people closer. However, the openly visionary element was also strong beyond dictated ideologies. People read philosopher Ernst Bloch or the utopian dissident writer and Nobel Prize laureate (1970), Alexandr Solzhenitsyn. The role of the arts was very important. Literature and theater performances were a place of resistant and openly visionary knowledge production. As public intellectuals, artists put pressure on the regime and offered alternative ways of representation.[12] Gestures of solidarity and protest were clearly present in everyday life. The achievement of a more just society for all, not the increased consumption of goods, was at the center of the philosophy of life of many. There is a fundamental difference between the dictated communist futurities and the vision of the peaceful revolution. The former is a closed, naturalized idea of socialism/communism, whereas the vision of parts of the dissidence is an open contribution to the radical social imaginary.[13]

Some aspects of dissidence in East Germany are worthwhile remembering for today's resistance movements. Political transitions show the discursive character of resistance. Some protagonists, and this is also true for the theologians that were involved, remained dissident in the post-transitional society; others became part of the new dominant discourse. Another important observation is the following: in a kind of postcolonial and post-secular gesture people formed surprising alliances between faith-based and non-faith-based belongings. They made astonishing post-identitarian compromises to form alliances against political oppression where gender hierarchies were (provisionally) undone. This even changed feminist theology in East Germany.[14] But there are also some regrets. The hierarchy

---

[12] See for example the performances of dissident artists Freya Klier and Stephan Krawczyk in GDR churches.

[13] See Cornelius Castoriadis, "Radical Imagination and the Social Instituting Imaginary," in: David Curtis (ed.), *The Castoriadis Reader* (Blackwell: Oxford 2011), 319-337.

[14] See Ulrike Auga, "'Stiefschwestern': Zum Verhältnis feministisch-theologischer Ansätze in Ost- und Westdeutschland," in: Ulrike Auga / Claudia Bruns / Levke Harders / Gabriele Jähnert

in the symbolic gender order was not undone in a lasting fashion even though in East Germany gender equality was instituted much earlier than in West Germany and women were economically independent because nearly all women were employed and earned their own income. This underlines furthermore that resistance needs to go beyond the rights discourse to undo the "glass ceilings" and "walls in our heads". The experience of the eastern dissidence protest also emphasizes that resistance discourses and practices need to overcome epistemic violence. This fact is most regrettably true for some churches which supported the protest but then became violently patriarchal or homophobic, such as the Catholic Church in Romania, Hungary, Croatia, and the Orthodox Church in Russia. However, one of the most important points to remember is the attempt at radical democracy and the contribution to the radical social imaginary of an open visionary element that is necessary for the self-constitution of a society.

New Resistance, "New, New" Social Movements and "Religion"
At present the world is facing an enormous crisis of social, political, and economic justice for a number of reasons: ever greater inequalities within and among societies with growing economic, social, political, and cultural exclusion. Many people feel a lack of governmental accountability and perceive the state of representative democracy as unsatisfactory and/or no longer achievable. The United Nations prove unable to develop effective measures against poverty, hunger, and the environmental breakdown.[15] Whereas Claude Lefort calls the actually existing democracy a "limited democracy",[16] Teresa Forcades i Vila speaks in this volume about "fake democracy". Butler, Laclau, and Žižek call for a "radical democracy".[17]

Protest movements that have appeared over the last few years underline that the social consequences of the neoliberal empire call for new resistances and new visions of solidarity. Even though it might be more appropriate to speak

---

(eds.), *Das Geschlecht der Wissenschaften: Zur Geschichte von Akademikerinnen im 19. und 20. Jahrhundert* (Campus: Frankfurt 2010), 303-326.

[15] See Sara Burke, "Time to Press the Reset Button on Representative Democracy? Or Do We Need a Whole New Operating System?," in: Werner Puschra / Sara Burke (eds.), *The Future We the People Need: Voices from New Social Movements in North Africa, Middle East & North America* (FES: Berlin / New York 2013), 5-13.

[16] See Claude Lefort, *The Political Forms of Modern Society: Bureaucracy, Democracy, Totalitarianism* (MIT Press: Cambridge 1986).

[17] See Judith Butler / Ernesto Laclau / Slavoj Žižek, *Contingency, Hegemony, Universality: Contemporary Dialogues on the Left* (Verso: Brooklyn / London 2011).

about "decolonization" instead of "occupation" (as in "Occupy Wall Street") the focus of their critique is justified.[18] The emerging violence is the result of an interplay between economic, sovereign, and epistemic violence.

There are many "new, new social movements",[19] but the Occupy movement underlines visibly the reinvention of politics, revolution, and utopia in the twenty-first century and is therefore used as an example here. The Occupy movement is an international protest movement against social and economic inequality. The movement was clearly inspired by the Arab Spring, especially the Tahrir Square protests in Cairo, and the "Arab Spring" can be related to the "Prague Spring" in 1968 with its protest against the socialist regime, one of the earliest significant protests in eastern European countries.[20] A further influence was the Democracy Village set up outside the British Parliament in London in 2010. Another inspiration was the Spanish Indignados ("the outraged") movement, which started in May 2011 with camps in Madrid and in a few weeks spread all over Spain and across the world.[21]

The methods and structures of the protests are closely linked to the possibilities of communication in the contemporary network society of the information age. Protesters use internet technologies and social media to organize locally and establish links with other Occupy groups around the globe. Their means of protest, which are peaceful, are participatory democracy, non-violence, civil disobedience, occupation, picketing, demonstrations, internet activism, general strikes, and various forms of direct action.

The slogan "We are the 99%" captured public attention first through a tumblr weblog entry and became the main feature, a summary of the movement's demands.[22] Overall the aims of the resistance are in development but

---

[18] The usage of the term "occupy" as in the Occupy Wall Street movement was critiqued by several "First Nations" activists as too closely connected with the colonizing past of the U.S.

[19] See Janet Jakobsen's contribution to this volume.

[20] See Lauren Frayer, "Inspired by Arab Protests, Spain's Unemployed Rally for Change," in: *Voice of America*, 18 May 2011. (http://www.voanews.com/content/inspired-by-arab-protests-spains-unemployed-rally-for-change-122237154/139615.html, 15 May 2014).

[21] See Manuel Castells, "The Long and the Quick of Revolution (2011)," OpenDemocracy.net. http:// Anthony-barnett/long-and-quick-of-revolution, 15 May 2014.

[22] See Adam Weinstein, "We Are the 99 Percent Creators Revealed: Mother Jones and the Foundation for National Progress." (http://www.motherjones.com/politics/2011/10/we-are-the-99-percent-creators, 15 May 2014). The slogan refers to the concentration of wealth among the top 1 percent of income earners compared to the other 99 percent. In the U.S., the top 1 percent of income earners has more than doubled their after-tax income over the last 30 years according to the 2011 Congressional Budget Office report (see Robert Pear, "Top Earners Doubled Share

the vision for a just society remains an open vision. Kwok Pui-lan and Joerg Rieger's volume *Occupy Religion: Theology of the Multitude* (2012) argues that there is a growing role for religion in the Occupy movement. Their starting point is the historical role the churches played in social movements, and they question how people of faith can work for social justice.[23]

Jesse Jackson – in accordance with Dietrich Bonhoeffer's "Church for the Others"[24] – sees the Occupy movement as a descendent of the Civil Rights Movement involving personalities like Mohandas "Mahatma" Gandhi, Martin Luther King Jr., and Nelson Mandela:

> They are all exalted now but they were rejected as occupiers, as protesters, as radicals, called terrorists by governments [...] The occupiers' cause is a just cause, a moral cause. They should not be dismissed but heard [...] the church should be the headquarters for the Occupy Movement. In a sense, the occupiers represent the conscience of the church.[25]

In my own research I noticed the diversity of the movement in terms of class or education, "nationality" or "ethnicity", "gender", "race", "age", "ability" and "religion". It is important to underline that it is a non-identitarian form of resistance. Overall the Occupy movement is a non-religious form of mobilization with varying perceptions of religion in different parts of the world. Some strands which are influenced by (neo-)Marxist atheist philosophy are skeptical about religion. Others have been influenced by the (feminist) liberation theology pre-conferences to the World Social Forums. Furthermore, numerous theologians and students of theology, who are active in the Green Movement and Anti-atomic Power Movement, now also join Occupy in Europe.[26]

---

of Nation's Income, Study Finds", in: *The New York Times*, 25 October 2011. (http://www.nytimes.com/2011/10/26/us/politics/top-earners-doubled-share-of-nations-income-cbo-says.html/?_r=0, 15 May 2014).

[23] See Kwok Pui-lan / Joerg Rieger, *Occupy Religion: Theology of the Multitude* (Rowman & Littlefield Publishers: Lanham 2012).

[24] See Ulrike Auga, "Decolonizing Public Space: A Challenge of Dietrich Bonhoeffer's and Gayatri Ch. Spivak's Concepts of Resistance, 'Religion' and 'Gender'," in: *Feminist Theology* (forthcoming).

[25] See Peter Walker, "Jesse Jackson Cheers on Occupy London Protesters," in: *The Guardian*, 15 December 2011. (http://www.guardian.co.uk/world/2011/dec/15/jesse-jackson-occupy-london-protesters, 15 May 2014).

[26] See Ulrike Auga, "Imagine the Future! A Critical Transreligious Bio-theology of 'the 99 Percent'," in: *Feminist Theology* 22.1 (2013), 20-37.

The Pussy Riot performance became an icon of new resistance against the state in the context of religion. The Russian band Pussy Riot performed a *Punk Prayer* to Mother Mary to end the regime of Putin. Three members of the band, Nadezhda Tolokonnikova, Maria Alyokhina and Yekaterina Samutsevich, were imprisoned and only much later released.[27] The Russian Orthodox Church has played a questionable role by supporting Putin's power claims, which were accompanied by new bills amending the existing federal law to support homophobia.[28]

Postcolonies, Modern Empires, and the "Others"

Postcolonialism serves as a label for many different approaches which share the critique of the empire and colonialism. Postcolonialism is also about the opening up of new spaces to investigate colonial, anti-colonial, and neocolonial phenomena.

"[P]ostcolonialism [...] has been primarily concerned to examine the processes and effects of, and reactions to, European colonialism from the sixteenth century up to and including the neo-colonialism of the present day."[29] Achille Mbembe coins the term "postcolony" for all the "cultures" affected by the imperial process and underlines the necessity of postcolonial epistemologies that reach beyond colonialism. He studies colonial, post-, and neocolonial interactions of colonizing societies with formerly economically, culturally, and territorially colonized populations. The critique of all forms of violence of colonialism must also include a self-critique of anti-colonial resistance because

---

[27] See Anne-Marie Korte's contribution to this volume.

[28] As an amendment to the federal law "On the protection of children from information harmful to their health and development", the so-called "blasphemy bill" and the "gay propaganda bill" were passed unanimously by the Russian State Duma on June 11, 2013 and signed by President Vladimir Putin on July 2, 2013. They legitimize "legislative acts of the Russian Federation aimed at protecting children from information which propagandizes the rejection of traditional family values", and ban the distribution of "propaganda" in support of "non-traditional relationships" to minors. "Public actions expressing obvious disrespect toward society and committed to abuse the religious feelings of believers" will be severely punished. (http://pravo. gov.ru/proxy/ips/?docbody=&vkart=card&nd=102337335&rdk=&intelsearch=135-%D4%C7, 15 May 2014). See also Alec Luhn, "Russian Anti-gay Law Prompts Rise in Homophobic Violence," in: *The Guardian*, 1 September 2013, 3.

[29] Bill Ashcroft / Gareth Griffiths / Helen Tiffin, *Post-colonial Studies: The Key Concepts* (Routledge: London 2007, 2nd ed.), 169. For the study of postcolonial theory see also Reina Lewis, *Feminist Postcolonial Theory: A Reader* (Routledge: London 1999).

some national liberation projects were also nationalist and maintained a hierarchical symbolic gender order.[30]

Historically this critique is rooted in European colonialism including the occupation of the Americas, slave trade, etc., accompanied by Enlightenment ideas, the emergence of universalist thought under the premises of a European notion of progress, and the anti-colonial resistance of national liberation projects. Postcolonial critique extends anti-colonial critique and draws on a) poststructuralism with its deconstruction of the constellations of power, knowledge, and truth; b) psychoanalysis with the question of subjectivation and reconsiderations of subject formation; and c) Marxism with its critique of capitalism and hegemony.

Postcolonial thought emerged with Edward Said's study *Orientalism*. Influenced by Michel Foucault and Antonio Gramsci he showed how imperial power, the production of literature, and the perception of tradition interact.[31] He re-read texts of the "western" literary canon (e.g. Joseph Conrad's *Heart of Darkness* [1899]) for its colonial intentions. Said also analyzed the work of European Orient Studies. He concluded that the "western" gaze at the geographical "East" produces the "Orient" as the exotic "Other". Another new perspective of postcolonial thought is the concept of "hybridity" which Homi Bhabha develops in his highly influential book *The Location of Culture*.[32]

I would like to look at two central concepts of postcolonial theory. The deciphering of epistemic violence and with it the de-essentialization of categories is a crucial task for Said and Gayatri Chakravorty Spivak and a major strategy in postcolonial theory. Said criticizes the construction of the essentialized "Other" as a violent act called "Othering". Essentialism reduces and "others" the subject.[33] It presumes an (inferior) ontological a priori. "By Othering we mean imagining someone as alien and different to 'us' in such a way that 'they' are excluded from 'our' 'normal', 'superior' and 'civilized' group. Indeed, it is by imagining a foreign 'Other' in this way that 'our' group can become more confident and exclusive".[34]

---

[30] See Achille Mbembe, *On the Postcolony* (University of California Press: Berkeley 2001).

[31] See Edward Said, *Orientalism* (Pantheon Books: New York 1978).

[32] See Homi Bhabha, *The Location of Culture* (Routledge: New York / London 1994).

[33] For wider debates see Lisa Isherwood / David Harris, *Radical Otherness: Sociological and Theological Approaches* (Acumen: Durham 2013); Luis Quiros, *An Other's Mind* (Author House: Bloomington 2011).

[34] Adrian Holliday / John Kullman / Martin Hyde, *Intercultural Communication: An Advanced Resource Book* (Routledge: London 2010), 2.

This essentialization is often connected with categories of knowledge through which "nation", "ethnicity", "race", "class", "gender", "ability", and "religion" are characterized as homogenizing descriptions of a group. Notions of group "identity" are in danger to fall into the trap of "Othering" and to become essentializing concepts.[35] This can also happen if intersectionality, that is the taking into account of several overlapping categories, is applied in a superficial manner,[36] as the critique of "queers of color" shows; their strategies will be discussed below.[37]

A second important concept addressed in postcolonial theory is that of individual and collective representation. Spivak discusses the position of the subaltern (woman), who cannot speak and represent herself because of the epistemic violence of the colonial discourse that is, for example, implied in legal structures and in patriarchal formations of local traditions. However, to speak for somebody can be an act of objectivation if the agency of the oppressed subject is not acknowledged. Saba Mahmood's understanding of resistance led postcolonial, post-secular theory to shift from representation to the analysis of subject formation, agency, and human flourishing.[38]

---

[35] Spivak playfully uses the phrase "strategic essentialism". She is aware of essentialisms of gender, class, etc., but she argues that at times one has to allude to "oppressed identities" in order to build political alliances. Spivak has often been misunderstood as if she would support the essentialized identitarian categories of "nation", "race", and "class". This misunderstanding has consequences for some postcolonial theologies which rely uncritically on Spivak. However, as a Marxist she retains an essentialized notion of "religon". See Auga, "Decolonizing Public Space".

[36] See Kimberlé Crenshaws, "Demarginalizing the Intersection of Race and Sex: A Black Feminist Critique of Antidiscrimination Doctrine, Feminist Theory, and Antiracist Politics," in: Anne Phillips (ed.), *Feminism and Politics: Oxford Readings in Feminism* (Oxford University Press: Oxford 1998), 314-343, and my critique: Ulrike Auga, "Geschlecht und Religion als interdependente Kategorien des Wissens: Dekonstruktion, Diskursanalyse und Intersektionalitätsdebatte und die Kritik antiker Texte", in: Ute E. Eisen / Christine Gerber / Angela Standhartinger (eds.), *Doing Gender – Doing Religion: Zur Wechselwirkung von Geschlechterkonzepten und religiöser Identitätsbildung in Antike und frühem Islam* (Mohr Siebeck: Tübingen 2013), Wissenschaftliche Untersuchungen zum Neuen Testament I 302, 37-74.

[37] See Roderick A. Ferguson, *Aberrations in Black: Toward a Queer of Color Critique* (University of Minnesota Press: Minneapolis 2003); José Esteban Muñoz, *Disidentifications: Queers of Color and the Performance of Politics* (University of Minnesota Press: Minneapolis 2007).

[38] See Saba Mahmood, *Politics of Piety: The Islamic Revival and the Feminist Subject* (Princeton University Press: Princeton 2012, 2nd ed.).

Queer Epistemological Critique and the Biopolitical Perspective

The previous reflections have shown the need for an interaction between queer and postcolonial critique. Queer critique is not an identitarian approach. It is a critique of the essentialization of gender and sexuality and of heteronormativity, and implies a consequent epistemological critique, which allows new perspectives on minority discourses. One of the most important aspects of queer analysis is its potential for the deconstruction and destabilization of categories.[39]

Queer concepts developed out of the poststructuralist critique of gender, especially Judith Butler's deconstruction of the notion of gender. Butler showed that "[t]here is no gender identity behind the expressions of gender; […] identity is performatively constituted by the very 'expressions' that are said to be its results."[40] Equally, categories of gender, nation, race, etc. are shown to be constructed and to emerge performatively. Queer critique is "a point of departure for a broad critique that is calibrated to account for the social antagonism of nationality, race, gender, and class as well as sexuality".[41]

A number of ideas of queer theory can usefully be applied to theology and religious studies: a) the new focus on subject formation and agency; b) the disidentification of violent concepts of identity of which José Esteban Muñoz writes that "[d]isidentification is meant to be descriptive of the survival strategies the minority subject practices in order to negotiate a phobic majoritarian public sphere that continuously elides or punishes the existence of subjects who do not conform to the phantasm of normative citizenship."[42] c) With Gilles Deleuze and Félix Guattari, queer assemblage (and related concepts such as networks and tensities) goes beyond collectivities with their exclusions.[43] d) The concept of "queer collectivity" and its political potential is

---

[39] See Gabriele Dietze / Elahe Haschemi Yekani, "'Checks and Balances': Zum Verhältnis von Intersektionalität und Queer Theory," in: Katharina Walgenbach / Gabriele Dietze / Lann Hornscheidt / Kerstin Palm (eds.), *Gender als interdependente Kategorie: Interventionen und neue Perspektiven auf Intersektionalität, Diversität und Heterogenität aus den Gender Studies* (Budrich: Opladen 2007), 107-139.

[40] Judith Butler, *Gender Trouble: Feminism and the Subversion of Identity* (Routledge: New York 1990), 25.

[41] Anne McClintock / Phillip Brian Harper / José Esteban Muñoz / Trish Rosen (eds.), *Queer Transexions of Race, Nation, and Gender* (Duke University Press: Durham 1997), Social Text 52-53 (Book 15), 90.

[42] See Muñoz, *Disidentifications*, 4.

[43] See Jasbir Puar, *Terrorist Assemblages: Homonationalism in Queer Times* (Duke University Press: Durham 2007).

interlinked with the idea of queer utopia. Drawing on Ernst Bloch, José Esteban Muñoz claims that "queer is not yet there", and describes as queer the open futurity without violence to which he aspires. e) Queer of color concepts (Roderick Ferguson) and queer diaspora approaches (José Esteban Muñoz) harshly criticize capitalism. Ferguson laments the blind spots in Marxist thinking regarding gender, sexuality, and race. He writes: "Queer of color analysis extends women of color feminism by investigating how intersecting racial, gender, and sexual practices antagonize and/or conspire with the normative investments of nation states and capital."[44] He draws on Adrienne Rich's early queer of color critique and learns from Aihwa Ong's analysis of capital and transnationalism that "[t]he reproduction of racialized gender and sexual regulations [...] facilitate the production of global capital."[45]

I suggest taking this kind of critique even further. Not only gender and sexuality are regulated, but everybody's life is affected by regulations through the nation state and capital. I argue for the integration of the critique of biopolitical effects and their counter-discourses into queer critique. Michel Foucault used the concept of biopower/biopolitics to describe a competitive life-or-death rationale in the biopolitically regulated state, which claims that either "we" or the "others" (but not both) could survive. This counts for both capitalist and socialist competitive regimes.[46] Consequently, in such a society only the body that makes profit has a value. The weak or ill body as well as dissident sexuality count as risk and are enemies within the own collective body. Individual and collective reproduction are thought of as intertwined. The other human body is understood as a racialized, essentialized "Other". Adriana Petryna speaks of biological citizenship when people face biopolitical regulations or exclusions.[47] This is especially precarious in the case of non-citizen citizens.

In combination with globalization processes, exploitative capitalism becomes even harsher. The neoliberal empire expands in a different fashion than former imperialism with new forms of work and new forms of regulating

---

[44] Ferguson, *Aberrations in Black*, 4. See also Roderick A. Ferguson, "Racing Homonormativity: Citizenship, Sociology and Gay Identity," in: E. Johnson Patrick / Mae G. Henderson (eds.), *Black Queer Studies: A Critical Anthology* (Duke University Press: Durham 2005), 52-67.

[45] Ferguson, *Aberrations in Black*, 136.

[46] See Michel Foucault, *Il faut défendre la société: Cours au Collège de France 1975-1976* (Seuil: Paris 1997).

[47] See Adriana Petryna, *Life Exposed: Biological Citizens after Chernobyl* (Princeton University Press: Princeton 2002).

populations. Michael Hardt and Antonio Negri underline new forms of resistance and individual and collective subject formation/mass formation, representation.[48] They speak of the multitude instead of the working class. Their critique of the neoliberal empire remains seminal. However they underestimate the biopolitical regulations and the diversity of new empires beyond western neoliberalism which might work quite differently in Russia, for example.

Certain categories seem in certain contexts more useful for biopolitical regulations: today the category "religion" is at the center of public discourse.

The Importance of the Post-secular Turn for Critical Theology and Religious Studies

Several historical events have influenced the shift in debates about the notion of "religion". The year 1989 brought about the end of many violently atheist socialist totalitarian states. September 11, 2001 with the Islamist terrorist attacks in the U.S. on the one hand underlined religious fundamentalism. On the other hand, the "Arab Spring" showed the importance of faith-based protest for resistance and furthered debates about the possibility of different forms of relationship between democracy, state form, and religion.

I can here only briefly and in an oversimplifying manner mention some of the shifts in these debates.[49] a) The postcolonial term "neorientalism" (Occidentalism) describes how the "West" instrumentalizes outbursts of Islamic fundamentalism to criticizes Islam as such and to depict the self-imagination of the "West" as more enlightened or Christianity as more rational. However, this also means that the analysis focuses more strongly on "religion" as a category now. b) We speak of the end of the traditional secularization thesis because despite certain secularization phenomena in societies, "religion" is not fading; instead a new perception of the concept of "religion" and faith-based practices emerges. c) Overwriting former prejudices in critical and feminist theory towards "religion" as oppressive and patriarchal, it is now possible to show the importance of subject formation, agency, and human flourishing also within and through religious practices.[50] d) "Religion" appears

---

[48] See Michael Hardt / Antonio Negri, *Empire* (Harvard University Press: Cambridge 2002); Hardt / Negri, *Multitude*.

[49] For a longer summary see Auga, "Decolonizing Public Space".

[50] See Mahmood, *Politics of Piety*. Saba Mahmood undertook an ethnographic study of a grassroots women's piety movement in Cairo. With her results she challenges secular-liberal principles as goals of resistance. She showed how female participants gain subject formation, agency and

as a site where new knowledge can emerge. e) The perception of the role of religion in the public sphere has shifted. This new importance of religion had previously been posited by post-secular scholars but gained broader attention when Jürgen Habermas, who in the past understood the public sphere as secular, insisted that it is necessary to focus attention on religion in a diversified society. He argued for religion's importance to correct capitalism. However, the contributions of religious persons would have to be "translated" for the non-religious. Thus for Habermas "religion" remains the "Other" of society. Charles Taylor contributes to this debate with his understanding of the public sphere as a realm of creativity and social imaginaries through which citizens give form to their lives together, and he seeks for overlaps in shared values of solidarity or social projects among diverse population groups.[51] Regrettably, he underestimates the conditions of capitalism and biopolitical regulations. f) In contrast to essentialist fundamentalism, identitarian conservative theories or previous identitarian liberation theology, there is a turn to de-essentialize or disidentify the category "religion". This does not mean to take away the character of faith, but to illuminate the constructions of the relationships between power, knowledge, and truth that are attached to essentializing epistemologies. In the debate about the public sphere, Judith Butler claimed that religious cohabitation in a globalized world is only possible with de-essentialized concepts of religion.[52] But also and especially the fields of religious studies, interreligious studies, comparative theology and neighboring fields are making an effort to elaborate the constructed, performative, and imagined character of "religion".[53]

---

human flourishing beyond "western" (feminist) values of freedom and autonomy. She extends Foucault's notion of resistance discourses and Butler's notion of performativity: agency is also to be found in the inhabiting of norms (not only in resisting dominant discourses). Religion is opening up possibilities, is enabling agency. See also the review of the new edition in this volume.

[51] See Judith Butler / Jürgen Habermas / Charles Taylor / Cornel West, *The Power of Religion in the Public Sphere* (Columbia University Press: New York 2011).

[52] See Butler / Habermas / Taylor / West, *The Power of Religion.*

[53] See Tomoko Masuzawa, *The Invention of World Religions: Or, How European Universalism Was Preserved in the Language of Pluralism* (The University of Chicago Press: Chicago 2005); David Chidester, *Empire of Religion: Imperialism and Comparative Religion* (The University of Chicago Press: Chicago 2014); David Chidester, *Savage Systems: Colonialism and Comparative Religion in Southern Africa* (University of Virginia Press: Charlottesville 1996); Richard King, *Orientalism and Religion: Postcolonial Theory, India and 'The Mystic East'* (Routledge: London 1996); Michael Bergunder, "Was ist Religion? Kulturwissenschaftliche

Aspects of Postcolonial and Public Theologies after Empire and the Biopolitical Turn

For theology, religious studies, and neighboring fields it is high time to rethink those disciplines which are obviously shaped by a colonial heritage such as missionary studies and reinvent them as postcolonial intercultural theology.[54] Furthermore, we also need postcolonial theologies of religions for a pluralist world.[55]

It is highly important to show the interdependence between traditional theological disciplines and colonial discourses because they still influence the canon of research and teaching in large parts of the world and – via ethics commissions – contribute directly to the dominant discourses in societies.[56]

Exegesis
Postcolonial exegesis is critical towards the historical-critical method especially as taught in the German tradition. The achievement of the historical-critical method as resistance against magisterial truth claims and against violent evangelical interpretations is acknowledged. However, Kwok Pui-lan argues that this approach is determined by "western", white, male perceptions of the "correct" understanding of the text.[57] The relationship between Europe's colonial expansion and the historical-critical method is not made transparent.[58]

Some critics claim that the historical-critical method especially oppressed the "local" readings of biblical texts which are based on different understandings of history or a different relationship between politics and religion. An example for a contextual approach is the *minjung* theology which uses as a hermeneutic key the experience of the *minjung* (the people). Thus *minjung* is understood to refer to the *ochlos* in the gospel of Mark, and the identification

---

Überlegungen zum Gegenstand der Religionswissenschaft", in: *Zeitschrift für Religionswissenschaft (zfr)* 19.1-2 (2011), 3-55.

54 See Marion Grau, *Rethinking Mission in the Postcolony: Salvation, Society and Subversion* (T&T Clark International: London 2011); Mark J. Cartledge / David Cheetham (eds.), *Intercultural Theology* (SCM Press: London 2011). See also Eleanora Hof's article in this volume.

55 See Jenny Daggers, *Postcolonial Theology of Religions: Particularity and Pluralism in World Christianity* (Routledge: London 2013). See the review of Jenny Daggers's book in this volume.

56 See Fernando F. Segovia / Stephen D. Moore (eds.), *Postcolonial Biblical Criticism* (T&T Clark: London 2005).

57 See Kwok Pui-lan, *Discovering the Bible in a Non-biblical World* (Orbis: Maryknoll 1995), 40.

58 See Kwok Pui-lan, *Postcolonial Imagination and Feminist Theology* (John Knox Press: Louisville 2005), 62.

of Jesus with the suffering *minjung/ochlos* is underlined.[59] The *han* exegesis of Wonhee Anne Joh or Rey Chow starts with the experience of ethnical or class exclusion (*han*).[60] Fernando Segovia argues that because historical criticism adheres to positivistic prejudices which only allow for an "informed", academic reader, neglect the context of the reader, and pretend scientific objectivity, it is today obsolete.[61] The most radical position is taken by R.S. Sugirtharajah who criticizes historical-critical exegesis as Eurocentric and serving colonial aims. Shaped by the emerging rationalism and historical understanding of the Enlightenment, the method pretended to be "scientific" and "objective", but instead it was clearly connected with orientalist philologies, race theories and an evolutionist understanding of religions.[62] Elisabeth Schüssler Fiorenza argues along the same lines writing that the battle surrounding this method is a battle about domination in an as such unjust academic system.[63]

In her book *Toward a Postcolonial Feminist Interpretation of the Bible*, Musa Dube underlines:

> In view of the fact that Christian biblical religion has been "unique in its imperial sponsorship", in ancient and current times and over different people and different places, the Bible is also a colonizing text: it has repeatedly authorized the subjugation of foreign nations and lands. Further, in view of the fact that the New Testament and many other Hebrew Bible books were born in imperialist settings, they are post-colonial books.[64]

---

[59] See Byung-Mu Ahn, "Jesus und das Minjung im Markusevangelium," in: Jürgen Moltmann (ed.), *Theologie des Volkes Gottes in Südkorea* (Neukirchener Verlag: Neukirchen-Vluyn 1984), 110-132.

[60] See Wonhee Anne Joh, *Heart of the Cross: A Postcolonial Christology* (John Knox Press: Louisville 2006). See also Rey Chow, *The Protestant Ethic and the Spirit of Capitalism* (Columbia University Press: New York 2000), 19-50.

[61] See Anna Runesson, *Exegesis in the Making: Postcolonialism and New Testament Studies* (Brill: Leiden 2010), 59.

[62] See R.S. Sugirtharajah, *Postcolonial Criticism and Biblical Interpretation* (Oxford University Press: Oxford 2002); R.S. Sugirtharajah (ed.), *Voices from the Margin: Interpreting the Bible in the Third World* (Orbis Books: Maryknoll / New York 2006, rev. and exp. 3rd ed.); R.S. Sugirtharajah (ed.), *Still at the Margins: Biblical Scholarship Fifteen Years After the Voices from the Margin* (T&T Clark: London 2008).

[63] See Elisabeth Schüssler Fiorenza, *But She Said: Feminist Practices of Biblical Interpretation* (Beacon: Boston 1992), 180.

[64] Musa W. Dube, *Postcolonial Feminist Interpretation of the Bible* (Chalice Press: Atlanta 2000), 15.

In Dube's understanding the Bible emerged in a colonial context and has been used for purposes of subjugation up until today, but it also contains anti-colonial strands that go beyond its colonializing elements. Dube also discusses postcoloniality, ethics, and feminism. She shows the influence of religion and biblical interpretation on African women and their oppression. Together with indigenous religions, Christianity in Africa still supports patriarchal systems. Dube tries to decolonize religious practices with hybrid strategies and hybrid spaces.[65]

Dube's work is an important achievement; however, the deconstruction of categories seems sometimes in danger to get lost. How can feminist biblical exegesis react even better to postcolonial challenges between materiality and epistemic violence?

Several postcolonial exegetes have used the historical-critical method in an "integrative" or "inclusive" way in correlation to other methods. They always take into account the reader's context and experience in the widest sense and do not disqualify reading strategies that arise from local knowledge production or local archives.[66]

Constructive Theology, Feminism, New Social Movements after Empire
The field of systematic or dogmatic theology is criticized because as a coherent dogmatic system it too often carries universalist exclusive structures. Today, these fields are further developed as "constructive theology" by theologians like Sallie McFague, Catherine Keller, Serene Jones, Stefanie Knauss and others.[67] Their focus reaches beyond truth claims about the interpretation of dogmatic sentences, looking at theological and ethical issues from an individual perspective and experience, and discussing issues such as the question of the survival of the world facing environmental problems, the question of love under globalized conditions, the question of trauma in a violated world,

---

[65] See Musa W. Dube, "Postcoloniality, Feminist Spaces, and Religions," in: Laura Donaldson / Kwok Pui-lan (eds.), *Postcolonialism, Feminism and Religious Discourse* (Routledge: New York / London 2002), 100-120. See also Dube's contribution to this volume.

[66] See Stephen D. Moore, *Empire and Apocalypse: Postcolonialism and the New Testament* (Phoenix: Sheffield 2006). See also Ulrike Auga / Bertram Schirr, "'Do Not Conform to the Patterns of This World': A Postcolonial Investigation of Performativity, Metamorphoses, and Bodily Materiality in Romans 12," in: *Feminist Theology* 22.4 (2014), 1-18.

[67] See Serene Jones / Paul Lakeland (eds.), *Constructive Theology: A Contemporary Approach to Classical Themes* (Fortress Press: Minneapolis 2005).

or the inclusion of visual arts in systematic theological approaches in search of new, open (poetic) languages.

In this context, the inter- and transdisciplinary debate between theologians and Gayatri Ch. Spivak was especially prominent and is recorded in the volume *Planetary Loves* (2011). This debate represents the attempt at the postcolonial deconstruction of the universal presumptions of theology and was a great achievement because Spivak's critique of epistemic violence in terms of "race", "class", and "nation" is highly relevant for theology.[68] However, Spivak's essentialist notion of "religion" remains problematic.[69] The question remains, how it is possible to deal better with these categories of knowledge in theology?

Postcolonial Imagination, Multitude, and the Critique of Neoliberalism

Kwok Pui-lan has been an important voice since the beginnings of postcolonial theology. She stresses the necessity of postcolonial imagination also and especially in theology.[70] Already in her earlier writings she uses Hardt's and Negri's critique of the neoliberal empire. In *Occupy Religion*, co-authored with Joerg Rieger, mentioned above, they look at the new social movement Occupy Wall Street and use the notion of the multitude for the elaboration of their theology.[71] The questions they share with the work of Janet Jakobsen and and Teresa Forcades i Vila (in this volume) are: how do we deal in theology and ethics with neoliberalism in a postcolonial world in the future? What are our societal visions?

Today, the perception of the public sphere and resistance within it changes in decisive ways.[72] This has influenced the emergence of the field of public theology as a further development of political and liberation theology. Here faith-based protest is an issue as well as biopolitics and counter-discourses to empire. Trygve Wyller, for example, analyzes new concepts of solidarities in

---

[68] See Stephen Moore / Mayra Rivera (eds.), *Planetary Loves: Spivak, Postcoloniality, and Theology* (Fordham University Press: New York 2011).

[69] See my critique in: Auga, "Decolonizing Public Space".

[70] See Kwok, *Postcolonial Imagination and Feminist Theology*; Kwok Pui-lan (ed.), *Hope Abundant: Third World and Indigenous Women's Theology* (Orbis Books: Maryknoll 2010).

[71] See Rieger / Kwok, *Occupy Religion*.

[72] See Partha Chatterjee, *The Politics of the Governed: Reflections on Popular Politics in Most of the World* (Columbia University Press: New York 2004). See also Arjun Appaduraj, *The Future as Cultural Fact: Essays on the Global Condition* (Verso: London 2013).

non-legalized Swedish communities;[73] William Storrar studies non-citizen citizens as a challenge for public theology.[74]

Beyond the Body

Postcolonial theology is based on questions arising with and within liberation theologies.[75] However, because of the emergence of postcolonial theory in different geographical and philosophical contexts, there seemed to be a slight divide between postcolonial and liberation theologies in the past. This gap is elegantly overcome in Mayra Rivera's work drawing on Latin American Studies and poststructuralism.[76] Her essay "A Labyrinth of Incarnations: The Social Materiality of Bodies" (in this volume) connects traditional (feminist) liberation theologies with insights from poststructuralist philosophy and postcolonial theory. Furthermore, it draws on the most current theoretical turns towards materiality and affect and applies them for the development of a theology of corporality beyond the "body". Rivera suggests that the explorations of social-material incarnations should characterize a new phase in theologies of the body. She develops concepts for future interpretations which allow to overcome the epistemic violence attached to notions of the "body", which used to be a sexualized, racialized, and perfectionized able body in dominant societal and theological discourses. Rivera innovatively suggests using the notion of "flesh" instead of "body" to achieve a new understanding of bodily materiality. However, the notions of "flesh" and "materiality" also must be rethought.

---

[73] See Trygve E Wyller, "The Undocumented Embodied: Shaping the Space Where the Sacred and the Secular Intertwine," in: Trygve E. Wyller / Rosemarie Van Den Breemer / José Casanova (eds.), *Secular and Sacred? The Scandinavian Case of Religion in Human Rights, Law and Public Space* (Vandenhoeck & Ruprecht: Göttingen 2014), 221-236.

[74] See William F. Storrar, "Non-citizen Citizens: A Challenge for Public Theology," paper presented at "Postcolonial Theory as a Challenge for Theology," Faculty of Theology, Humboldt University Berlin, 31 May 2013. See also William F. Storrar / Andrew R. Morton (eds.), *Public Theology for the 21st Century: Essays in Honour of Duncan B. Forrester* (T&T Clark: London 2004).

[75] See Ivan Petrella, *Beyond Liberation Theology: A Polemic* (SCM Press: Norwich 2008).

[76] See Mayra Rivera, *The Touch of Transcendence: A Postcolonial Theology of God* (John Knox: Westminster 2007). See also Cathrine Keller / Michael Nausner / Mayra Rivera (eds.), *Postcolonial Theologies: Divinity and Empire* (Chalice Press: Atlanta 2004); Enrique Dussel / Eduardo Mendieta / Carmen Bohórquez (eds.), *El pensamiento filosofico latinoamericano, del Caribe y latino (1300-2000): Historia, corrientes, temas y filosofos* (Siglo XXI: Mexico City 2009).

Queer Theology and Precarious Postcolonial Sexualities

Queer theology scrutinizes societal discourses to overcome heteronormativity and epistemic violence in the broadest sense in dominant and liberation theologies and in society influenced by symbolic orders.

Queer theology is especially connected with the late Argentinian theologian Marcella Althaus-Reid.[77] Althaus-Reid works in the footsteps of classical theories of liberation in Latin America, challenging them and going beyond them, and combines them with queer theory. She applies Paulo Freire's pedagogy of the oppressed, which gives agency to marginalized people in grassroots communities in Latin America, to theology and uses this approach in marginalized contexts in Scotland. She claims that queer theology is an undertaking oriented toward base communities, be it in dissident medieval women's communities or in soup kitchens in Brazilian Favelas staffed by transvestites. Queer theology analyzes how throughout the history of Christianity excluded subjects try to achieve agency and self-representation, and how they actualize the Christian narrative in that. Althaus-Reid writes: "It is a fight for representativity, for a person reading theology to be able to be interpellated by the text, that is, by saying 'it is me; I recognise myself in this situation.'"[78]

Queer theology works with the notions of performativity (Judith Butler) or transgression (Georges Bataille). Transgression includes the symbolic transgression of inscribed gender differences and heteronormative symbolic orders especially in church and tradition, and the rereading of classical Christian texts through the eyes of invisible, marginalized, stereotyped, stigmatized, "othered" subjects.

Another important representative of queer theology is the Welsh theologian Lisa Isherwood. In her study *The Fat Jesus: Christianity and Body Image*, Isherwood deals with marginalized bodies: the overweight, poor, persons of color, or with the body of the planet itself. She focuses on conservative Christian eschatologies and how they form alliances with neoliberal exploitation.[79] She responds with creative resistance by rereading forgotten theologoumena such as *energeia*, *dynamis*, and *emanatio*. With Isherwood, it becomes clear

---

[77] See Marcella Althaus-Reid, *Indecent Theology: Theological Perversions in Sex, Gender and Politics* (Routledge: London 2000). See also Marcella Althaus-Reid, *The Queer God* (Routledge: London 2003).

[78] Althaus-Reid, *Indecent Theology*, 89.

[79] See Lisa Isherwood, *The Fat Jesus: Christianity and Body Image* (Seabury Books: London 2008).

again that queer theology has an interest in embodiment theory as well as in ecological and cosmological questions.

For Patrick S. Cheng, "radical love", as he describes it in his book *Radical Love*, is "a love so extreme that it dissolves our existing boundaries, whether they are boundaries that separate us from people, that separate us from pre-conceived notions of sexuality and gender identity, or that separate us from God".[80] This book is a good introduction to important aspects in queer theology, which does consider the regulation of sexuality, but fails to understand it in terms of biopolitics and regulations of life. This biopolitical critique is necessary to overcome inherent violence, as postcolonial theory has shown: radical democracy needs radical love needs radical theologies of life.

Critical, Feminist/Queer, Postcolonial, Post-secular Theology of Life as Invention and Intervention

What are the challenges that arise for dominant and resistance theologies from activism and theory? They question notions of universalist truth claims, notions of individual and collective "identity", notions of representation, democracy, freedom, and autonomy. They also challenge the violence present in economy, the precariousness of life, and the search for the good life. Therefore, we need responsible theologies which adequately respond to this crisis.

The subject of theologizing cannot be homogenized, but emerges from a complex interference of different, appearing, and disappearing subject formations through temporary alliances. Agency and human flourishing have to be understood in their particular contexts. Theological approaches can therefore only be seen as "minor theologies" (particular theologies) based on particular experiences.[81]

For the future of theology the following elements from postcolonial, post-secular and queer theories are particularly useful. 1) The fundamental insight into the interdependence between epistemic, sovereign, and economic violence. 2) It is important to understand the discursive character of resistance in contrast to dominant discourses in society. Political dissidence is resistance that is open to a new vision or project. 3) The aim of resistance is to remove all kinds of violence, which means that self-definition via the exclusion of the "Other" is inacceptable in theology. In order to disentangle violence from the

---

[80] Patrick S. Cheng, *Radical Love: An Introduction to Queer Theology* (Seabury Books: New York 2011), x.

[81] See Auga, "Decolonizing Public Space".

context of religion it is necessary to critique the production of knowledge. This entails the critique of the violence in/of religions, a turn to non-essentialized ideas of religion, and the acceptance of religion as a sphere of "emancipatory" new knowledge productions. 4) Feminist theology and the studies of religions has to include the critique of economic and biopolitical violence. 5) The focus should shift from identity and representational politics to performativity, subject formation, agency, and human flourishing also in the religious sphere. 6) Cornelius Castoriadis writes that "society is creation, and creation of itself: self-creation [... and thus] self-institution".[82] Consequently, I would like my theology to contribute to the radical social imaginary which enhances not only the self-institution of society but promotes agency and human flourishing. Everybody can participate in the imagining of new, open, inclusive social imaginaries in the quest for cohabitation without exclusion.[83]

Already practiced and possible interventions for theologians might be the following: The extension of the notion of individual freedom to human flourishing. The formation of new alliances among activist movements and groups, and between activism and theory. The practice of (new) gestures of solidarity. The practice of new forms of representation. Rethinking economy and the triad of nation state – market economy – democracy. The (re-)formulation of notions of democracy and emancipation. To join new social movements. To call for actions. To decolonize/pray/act/perform/translate/queer.[84]

Los enfoques intersectorial, feminista, con perspectiva de género, queer, postcolonial y postsecular son visiones especialmente sensibles a la violencia de los órdenes políticos y simbólicos de la sociedad, también del hablar teológico y religioso de los mismos. Simplificando mucho, se podría decir que la teología y la crítica de la religión subrayan, en común con la histórica liberación de contexto post- secular y queer y las teologías postcoloniales, la resistencia, la curación de carácter visionario de los textos y las prácticas religiosas. Sin embargo, a veces se proyectan críticas agresivas identitarias y esencialistas de la ideología, que aplican una epistemología postestructuralista y crítica de la ciencia y el cambio de la representación a la acción. El texto pretende introducir estos enfoques para promover el debate que podría ayudar a conducir a nuevas perspectivas en la teología feminista, teología crítica y los estudios religiosos.

---

[82] Castoriadis, "Radical Imagination," 323.

[83] See Judith Butler in: Judith Butler / Jürgen Habermas / Charles Taylor / Cornel West, *The Power of Religion in the Public Sphere* (Columbia University Press: New York 2011), 70-91.

[84] See http://www.queer-theological-college.weebly.com for an initiative started by Ulrike Auga, Teresa Forcades i Vila and Lisa Isherwood.

Además, al conectar el debate con la ubicación de la Alemania Oriental (del congreso) el texto trata de poner de relieve la acción de la disidencia de Europa del Este que llevó a la revolución pacífica de 1989 y que influyó en la resistencia a la Primavera Árabe en 2011 y heredan el Movimiento Occupy y la protesta de Pussy Riot. El artículo se pregunta cómo un deseo de una sociedad más solidaria podría dar cuenta de la búsqueda actual de una sociedad más justa.

Muchos movimientos y movilizaciones políticas, religiosas y artísticas resistentes imaginaron una sociedad democrática y solidaria abierta, radical, no sólo más allá del socialismo real, sino también más allá del capitalismo y su democracia limitada. Estas movilizaciones mostraron actuaciones sorprendentes como alianzas entre mujeres laicas y religiosas, la paz y los movimientos ambientales y no menos importante el proceso ecuménico. Debido a que la experiencia y los conceptos de la disidencia del Este europeo casi no están presentes en los debates teóricos y teológicos postcoloniales, post- seculares y queer, así como en sus aplicaciones como, por ejemplo, el auto-imaginario político y cultural de Europa o en las ideas extendidas de colectividad como nuevos conjuntos, entonces pretendemos elaborarlas aquí.

Intersectional, feminist, gender-sensitive, queer, postcolonial and post-secular approaches are especially sensitive for the violence of societal or global political and symbolic orders and not least of theological and religious "speaking" itself. Oversimplifying, one could say that postcolonial, post-secular and queer theology and critique of religion, together with historic contextual liberation theologies, underline the resistant, healing, visionary character of religious texts and practices. However they expand this sometimes violent, essentialist identitarian critique of ideology applying a poststructuralist epistemology and critique of science and shift from representation to agency. The text introduces these approaches to further a debate which might help to lead to new perspectives in feminist theology, critical theology and religious studies.

Furthermore, connecting the debate with the situation of East Germany, this paper highlights the agency of eastern European dissidence which lead to the peaceful revolution in 1989 and which offered its idea of resistance to the Arab Spring in 2011, and then to the Occupy movement and the Pussy Riot protest. This paper asks how their urge for a more solidary society can inform the current search for a more just society. Many resistant political, religious, and artistic movements and mobilizations imagined an open, radical democratic and solidary society not only beyond the actually existing socialism but also beyond capitalism and its limited democracy. These mobilizations showed surprising performances and alliances between secular and religious women's, peace and environmental movements and not least the ecumenical process. Because the experience and the concepts of eastern European dissidence are almost not present in postcolonial, post-secular and queer theoretical and theological debates as well as in applications, for instance the political and cultural self-imagination of Europe or in extended ideas of collectivity like new assemblages, they are elaborated here.

Intersektionale, feministische, genderbewusste, queere, postkoloniale und postsäkulare Ansätze zeigen eine besondere Sensibilität für die Gewaltförmigkeit gesellschaftlicher oder globaler politischer und symbolischer Ordnungen und nicht zuletzt auch des theologischen und religiösen "Sprechens" selbst.

Vereinfachend lässt sich sagen, postkoloniale, postsäkulare und queere Theologie und Religionskritik unterstreichen gemeinsam mit den historischen kontextuellen Befreiungstheologien den widerständigen, "heilenden" und visionären Charakter religiöser Texte und Praktiken, erweitern jedoch deren bisweilen selbst gewaltvoll bleibende essentialistische identitäre Idelogiekritik um eine (poststrukturalistische) Wissens- und Wissenschaftskritik und bewegen sich von einer Repräsentationskritik zur Frage nach Handlungsfähigkeit (*agency*). In diese Ausrichtungen möchte der Text einführen, um auch mittels dieser Debatte zu einer breiteren Neujustierung feministischer theologischer Forschung und kritischer Theologie und Religionswissenschaft zu gelangen.

Darüber hinaus soll mit dem lokalen Bezug zu Ostdeutschland die politische und theologische Wirkkraft der Dissidenz Osteuropas, die mit zu den friedlichen Revolutionen 1989 führte und die Gedankengeberin für den Arabischen Frühling 2011 war, für die gegenwärtige Suche nach solidarischem Zusammenleben in der einen Welt fruchtbar gemacht werden, deren Genealogie sich über Occupy Wall Street zu Pussy Riot fortsetzt.

Zahlreiche widerständige politische, religiöse und künstlerische Mobilisierungen imaginierten eine offene, radikal demokratische und solidarische Gesellschaft, nicht nur jenseits des real existierenden Sozialismus, sondern auch jenseits des Kapitalismus und seiner begrenzten Demokratie. Diese Mobilisierungen wurden getragen von überraschenden Performanzen und Allianzen aus säkularen und religiösen Frauen-, Friedens- und Umweltbewegungen und nicht zuletzt vom ökumenischen Prozess.

Da die Erfahrungen und Konzepte osteuropäischer Dissidenz sowohl in den postkolonialen, postsäkularen und queeren theoretischen und theologischen Debatten, als auch in Umsetzungen wie der politischen und kulturellen Selbstimagination Europas oder erweiterter neuer gemeinschaftlicher Assemblagen bisher nicht ausreichend diskutiert wurden, sollen sie hier zur Sprache kommen.

Ulrike Auga was born in East Berlin and participated in the struggle of the peaceful revolution in 1989. She worked for several years in Johannesburg, Bamako and Jerusalem before she became Professor of Theology and Gender Studies at Humboldt University Berlin and Dietrich Bonhoeffer Visiting Professor at Union Theological Seminary, New York. Her research focuses on the intersection between religious studies, the philosophy of religion and gender, queer, postcolonial and post-secular theory.

Journal of the European Society of Women in Theological Research 22 (2014) 31-53.
doi: 10.2143/ESWTR.22.0.3040789

Anne-Marie Korte

Pussy Riot's *Punk Prayer* as a Case of/for Feminist Public Theology

Introduction

In this contribution I aim to discuss the goals and contours of a contemporary, Europe-based feminist public theology. In the first part of this contribution, I will explicate my interest in this position in conversation with earlier and recently emerging debates on public theology. Then, in the second part, I will relate my interest for a contextual feminist public theology to some significant biographical aspects of my life as a feminist theologian and a researcher in the field of religion and gender. As will become clear, to me this means more – and is also more complicated – than giving an account of my own context, position, interests, and limitations as a researcher, which is generally regarded as an indispensable part of feminist methodology. The question of why, but also of where and when to engage with feminist public theology is also at stake here.[1] In the third part of this text I will present an analysis of Pussy Riot's *Punk Prayer* and the reactions and comments that it has elicited. In February 2012, this Russian feminist formation did a "political art performance" in Moscow's central Russian Orthodox Christ the Saviour Church, which was followed by extremely critical and unprecedented repressive reactions by the leading figures of the Russian government and the Russian Orthodox Church. Through this case study I attempt to make my theoretical and personal reflections on feminist public theology more concrete, suggesting how and to which

---

[1] See the feminist epistemologist positions of Donna Haraway and Karen Barad who argue that (feminist) researchers are not only situated in, but also part of the reality that they investigate, and should therefore reflect their moral responsibilities for the networks, processes, and relations in which they are involved as researchers. Donna Haraway, "Situated Knowledges: The Science Question in Feminism and the Privilege of Partial Perspective," in: Donna Haraway, *Simians, Cyborgs, and Women: The Reinvention of Nature* (Routledge: New York 1991), 183-201; Karen Barad, *Meeting the Universe Halfway: Quantum Physics and the Entanglement of Matter and Meaning* (Duke University Press: Durham 2007), esp. 393.

ends Pussy Riot's *Punk Prayer* could be interpreted as a case of and for feminist public theology.

Feminist Public Theology in Discussion
In 1981 American theologian David Tracy introduced his famous threefold typology of the main "publics" to which theological reflection should be directed: the academy, the church, and the (larger) society as different (though interrelated) publics. Tracy stated that every theologian "must face squarely the claims to meaning and truth of all three publics" and address each accordingly. For all theological reflection, whether it be fundamental, systematic or practical (to use Tracy's categories), is "determined by a relentless drive to genuine publicness to and for all three publics."[2] Tracy's call for "publicness" conveyed, in a passionate but also rather general way, the task for theologians to be more engaged and to speak in a relevant manner in and for the public domains and circuits of modern secularizing societies, in which theological reflection has increasingly lost its status and self-evidence.

According to Tracy's typology, "public theology" – in its current manifestations – is sometimes cast as a separate branch of theology, namely as a form of theological reflection that primarily responds to societal developments and questions (as distinguished from internal ecclesial or academic ones).[3] But according to Scottish theologian Duncan Forrester, public theology is characterized by more complex dynamics. He affirms that public theology often takes "the world's agenda", or parts of it, as its own agenda, but states that it does so in order to deploy and develop theology in and for the public debate. "[It] seeks to offer distinctive and constructive insights from the treasury of faith to help in the building of a decent society, the restraint of evil, the curbing of violence, nation-building, and reconciliation in the public arena."[4] Forrester

---

[2] David Tracy, *The Analogical Imagination: Christian Theology and the Culture of Pluralism* (SCM Press: London 1981), 29.

[3] See Max L. Stackhouse, "Public Theology and Political Economy in a Globalizing Era," in: William Storrar / Andrew Morton (eds.), *Public Theology for the 21st Century: Essays in Honour of Duncan B. Forrester* (T&T Clark: London 2004), 179-194; Max L. Stackhouse, "Civil Religion, Political Theology and Public Theology: What's the Difference?," in: Len D. Hansen (ed.), *Christian in Public: Aims, Methodologies, and Issues in Public Theology* (African Sun Media: Stellenbosch 2007), 78-95; Ernst M. Conradie (ed.), *Collected Essays in Public Theology – Dirk Smit* (Sun Press: Stellenbosch 2007).

[4] Duncan B. Forrester, "The Scope of Public Theology," in: *Studies in Christian Ethics* 17.2 (2004), 6.

also notes an increasing interest among theologians and scholars of religion in public theology, related to the post-9/11 awareness of the changing public role of religion in contemporary societies, in particular in those societies that are perceived as secularized or secularizing.

Generally speaking, contemporary public theology seeks to reflect on practices of faith and on faith-related questions in their specific relation to the public domain and people's social, political, and communal lives. Public theology aims at contributing to this communal life, in particular to the furthering of social justice and human dignity that this communal life both depends on and gives rise to. Public theology does so by performing critical interventions, both theoretical and practical.[5] It acknowledges as foundational the need for theology to interact with public issues of contemporary society, issues, I would like to emphasize, that also encompass questions and concerns with strong personal and private dimensions.

Philosopher Jürgen Habermas's reflections on the political, social, and cultural role of the public domain in modern societies are foundational for numerous examples of public theology.[6] His 2008 manifesto "Notes on Post-secular Society", in which he revised his view on the public role of religion, stimulated these debates in important ways.[7] He argues that the role of religion in the contemporary public domain is characterized by the new visibility and

---

[5]   See William F. Storrar / Andrew R. Morton (eds.), *Public Theology for the 21st Century: Essays in Honour of Duncan B. Forrester* (T & T Clark: London 2004); Gavin D'Costa, *Theology in the Public Square: Church, Academy and Nation* (Blackwell: Oxford 2005); Hent de Vries / Lawrence E. Sullivan (eds.), *Political Theologies: Public Religions in a Post-secular World* (Fordham University Press: New York 2006); Graham Ward / Michel Hoelzl (eds.), *The New Visibility of Religion: Studies in Religion and Cultural Hermeneutics* (Continuum: London 2008); Michael S. Hogue, "After the Secular: Toward a Pragmatic Public Theology," in: *Journal of the American Academy of Religion* 78.2 (2010), 346-374; Christopher Baker / Justin Beaumont (eds.), *Postsecular Cities: Space, Theory and Practice* (Continuum: London 2010); Aloys Wijngaards, *Worldly Theology: On Connecting Public Theology and Economics* (PhD thesis, Radboud University Nijmegen 2012); and the *International Journal for Public Theology* published by Brill, Leiden.

[6]   Besides Habermas, in particular Jürgen Moltmann, José Casanova, and Charles Taylor have contributed to the current rise of interest for these topics in the field of theology and the study of religion. José Casanova, *Public Religions in the Modern World* (University of Chicago Press: Chicago 1994); Jürgen Moltmann, *God for a Secular Society: The Public Relevance of Theology* (SCM Press: London 1999); Charles Taylor, *A Secular Age* (Harvard University Press: Cambridge 2007).

[7]   See Jürgen Habermas, "Notes on Post-Secular Society," in: *New Perspectives Quarterly* 25.4 (2008), 17-29.

transformed presence of religions. The term "post-secular" does not denote an actual change of status or condition of European countries, but the awareness of change and transition. "Today, public consciousness in Europe can be described in terms of a 'post-secular society' to the extent that at present it still has to adjust itself to the continued existence of religious communities in an increasingly secularized environment."[8]

Habermas takes a critical position towards modern self-evidently secularist understandings of the public sphere as the place and forum of the formation of public opinion. He pleads to recognize and value the contribution of religious utterances and stances within this political public sphere. He argues that "[p]articularly with regard to vulnerable social relations, religious traditions possess the power to convincingly articulate moral sensitivities and solidaristic intuitions".[9] Habermas's observations have been met with critical responses, but his insistence that religious worldviews and the moral teachings of religions should be welcomed, rather than feared and excluded, with their contributions to the public debate has definitely inspired the interest in and further development of public theological views.

Public theology in its current forms has its roots in the political, liberation, and contextual theologies of the twentieth century.[10] I will analyze this interrelationship in more detail below. There are two other characteristics of public theology that I find important to mention here, because they have directly stimulated my own current interest in public theology. First, public theology is based predominantly – but certainly not only – in Europe and connected to the long history, current developments and ongoing fierce debates about the role of religion in the public domain in many European societies.[11] Second, up until now, feminist theologians and scholars of gender and religion have not very actively taken part in the articulation of and debates on public theology. There are, however, a few notable exceptions, whose contributions I will discuss here.[12]

---

[8]   Habermas, "Notes on Post-secular Society," 19.

[9]   Habermas, "Notes on Post-secular Society," 29.

[10] See also Stackhouse, "Civil Religion, Political Theology and Public Theology".

[11] A lively interest in public theology is also noticeable in South Africa, Canada, New Zealand, and in circles of Lutheran and Calvinist theologians (see note 4).

[12] See Marcella María Althaus-Reid, "In the Centre There Are No Fragments: *Teologías Desencajadas* (Reflections on Unfitting Theologies)," in: William F. Storrar / Andrew R. Morton (eds.), *Public Theology for the 21st Century: Essays in Honour of Duncan B. Forrester* (T&T Clark: London 2004), 365-384; Mary C. Grey, "Living Without Dreams: Is There a Spirituality

As the point of departure for this exploration I have taken a recent publication by Rosemary Radford Ruether, one of the founding mothers of Christian feminist theology, who has contributed substantially to this field for more than forty years now and who can be called one of its most eminent, constant and well-known public voices. In 2010 the fairly new, Europe-based *International Journal of Public Theology*[13] published a special issue on feminist theology, in which Ruether wrote the opening article under the heading "Feminist Theology: Where Is It Going?". Without defining public theology as such, Ruether claims here that "[f]eminist theology is one of the major forms of public theology that has developed over the last forty years".[14]

Interesting for my argument here is Ruether's portrayal of feminist theology as public theology. Using a genealogical approach she sketches forty years of feminist theology as "a trajectory of development in terms of continual expansion and diversification, across race and ethnic groups, across nations and continents and across faiths".[15] Beginning with the feminist critique and revision of Christian and Jewish theology at seminaries and universities in the U.S.A. in the 1960s and 1970s, Ruether discerns five stages in this trajectory of development:

- *Feminist Theological Awakenings*: the impact of the civil rights and feminist movements at the seminaries and universities in the U.S.A. in the 1960s and 1970s;
- *Ethnic and Sexual Diversity*: the critique of feminists of color, LGBT scholars and new generations in the feminist movement and at the seminaries and universities in the U.S.A. in the 1980s and 1990s;

---

for Justice in a Globalized World?," in: William F. Storrar / Andrew R. Morton, *Public Theology for the 21st Century: Essays in Honour of Duncan B. Forrester* (T&T Clark: London 2004), 231-249; Rosemary Radford Ruether, "Feminist Theology: Where Is It Going?," in: *International Journal of Public Theology* 4 (2010), 5-20; Heather Walton, "You Have to Say You Cannot Speak: Feminist Reflections Upon Public Theology," in: *International Journal of Public Theology* 4 (2010), 21-36.

13 Edited by Sebastian Kim (York St John University, UK). Its mission statement reads: "Public theology is the result of the growing need for theology to interact with public issues of contemporary society. It seeks to engage in dialogue with different academic disciplines such as politics, economics, cultural studies, religious studies, as well as with spirituality, globalization and society in general. The *International Journal of Public Theology*, affiliated with the Global Network for Public Theology, is a platform for original interdisciplinary research in the field of public theology." (http://www.brill.com/international-journal-public-theology, 27 May 2014).

14 Ruether, "Feminist Theology: Where Is It Going?," 6.

15 Ruether, "Feminist Theology: Where Is It Going?," 6.

- *International Reach*: the critical contributions of Two Thirds World feminisms and non-western Christianities from the 1990s onwards;
- *Interfaith Expansion*: the rise of cooperation and exchange among feminists across religions;
- *Transnational Feminism*: the rise of international feminist politics in United Nations settings, human rights movements and eco-justice movements as the common ground for feminist-theological cooperation across nations, cultures, and religions.

For each stage, Ruether identifies the social movements that initiated action and reform. She mentions the actual locations and institutions involved, the leading authors, and the results of their activities. In particular, Ruether names the networks and organisations that have been the result of these stages. Consistent with her own life-long, outspoken political interests and her activist stances in feminist movements within and across religions, Ruether highlights the role of movements for social justice and of faith-based organisations that engage with these movements, seeing them as the instances that have given decisive new impulses to feminist theology. She thus equates this particular social embedding with the public position and relevance of feminist theology.

I do think that Ruether rightly sees the listed social movements and organisations as the social texture and constitutive for the political dynamics of classic feminist theology. However, I also think that she fails to reflect upon some critical aspects and crucial questions that feminist public theology faces today.[16] It is important to acknowledge how deeply Ruether's understanding of feminist theology as public theology is informed by the goals and suppositions of twentieth-century political theology as developed in the 1960s by German theologians Johann Baptist Metz and Dorothee Sölle.[17] These theologians aimed to withstand both the modern tendency towards the privatization of faith and the traditional hegemonic politicization of religion, and they strove to make theological reflection contribute to a critical-political discourse in the

---

[16] Ruether's genealogical sketch of feminist theology also has a remarkable blind spot because it does not consider the European situation, developments, and influences as one of its locations and sources. Pioneering feminist theologians from the first generation came from Europe or studied in Europe (Elisabeth Schüssler Fiorenza, Mary Daly) and in western Europe since the mid-1970s, authors such as Elisabeth Moltmann, Catharina Halkes, and Elisabeth Gössmann have published very influential texts in this field.

[17] See Johann Baptist Metz, *Theology of the World* (Herder & Herder: London 1968); Dorothee Sölle, *Political Theology* (Fortress Press: Minneapolis 1974).

public realm, on the basis of the social implications of the Christian message. More recently German theologian Jürgen Moltmann, one of the most influential spokespersons of this political theology, has summarized its aims and suppositions by arguing that Christian theology has at its core a concern for the coming of God's kingdom in human history:

> Its subject alone makes Christian theology a *theologia publica*, a public theology. It gets involved in the public affairs of society. It thinks about what is of general concern in the light of hope in Christ for the Kingdom of God. It becomes political in the name of the poor and the marginalized in a given society. Remembrance of the crucified Christ makes it critical towards political religions and idolatries. It thinks critically about the religious and moral values of the societies in which it exists, and presents its reflections as a reasoned position.[18]

This generation of Christian political theologians has been able to connect the Enlightenment social and political ideals of freedom, autonomy, and equality to the origins of the biblical and Christian traditions, and to present Christianity's core message as an emancipatory model of faith that could be reasonably expressed and discussed. They were fully convinced that this political theology could play a substantial and critical role in the socio-political realm, because of its dual mission of offering hope and expressing critique founded in the eschatological vision of the coming of God's kingdom. However, no critical account was given of the rationalized concept of religious faith that this emancipatory model rests upon, a model which moreover hardly acknowledges the material, ritual, communal, and institutional aspects of religions as parts of the public domain. Faith here comes close to one's innermost personal convictions as an independent citizen, a rather confined, Protestant and modern western view, as postcolonial anthropologists such as Talal Assad, Saba Mahmood, and Nilüfer Göle have argued.[19] When Dorothee Sölle, in the later part of her

---

[18] Moltmann, *God for a Secular Society*, 1.

[19] See Talal Asad, *Formations of the Secular: Christianity, Islam, Modernity* (Stanford University Press: Stanford 2003); Mahmood, Saba, "Religious Reason and Secular Affect: An Incommensurable Divide?," in: Talal Asad / Wendy Brown / Judith Butler / Saba Mahmood, *Is Critique Secular?: Blasphemy, Injury and Free Speech* (Townsend Center for the Humanities: Berkeley 2009), 64-100; Nilüfer Göle / Ludwig Ammann, *Islam in Public: Turkey, Iran and Europe* (Istanbul Bilgi University Press: Istanbul 2006); Nilüfer Göle, "The Civilizational, Spatial, and Sexual Powers of the Secular," in: Michael Warner / Jonathan Vanantwerpen / Craig Calhoun (eds.), *Varieties of Secularism in a Secular Age* (Harvard University Press: Cambridge 2010), 243-264.

life, turned to an exploration of the spiritual sources of this emancipatory model of faith – and, therefore, turned to study the mystical schools and practices of the great world religions – many politically engaged Christians thought she had lost her interest in political theology.[20]

This modern emancipatory model of faith that bolsters political theology also pervades Ruether's overview of feminist theology as public theology that I presented earlier. Typical of all feminist theology, Ruether states, is its dual mission that can be shared and sustained by feminists across nations, ethnic differences, and religions in an "interfaith dialogue":

> On the one hand, it would seek to see how each of the world's religious traditions is contributing to the problem with its traditional teachings of the subordination of women, of ethnic minorities and of nature. On the other hand, it would seek to lift up the positive traditions of each religious tradition that can contribute to justice between men and women, between ethnic groups and towards a sustainable relationship between humans and the rest of nature. It would seek to diffuse hostility and violence based on religious exclusivism and negation of other religions and to create an environment for ecumenical cooperation toward a peaceful, just and sustainable world.[21]

Both Heather Walton and Marcella Althaus-Reid have taken a sceptical position towards a public theology that like Ruether's so clearly speaks of liberatory hope and that is based on an emancipatory model of faith that could be shared across national, ethnic, and religious differences. Walton, a practical theologian at the University of Glasgow, states that it is feminist theology itself that has provided her with both reservation and antidotes towards these ambitions. Her engagement with feminist theology during her daily struggles with the ambiguity of faith, the shortcomings of religious communities, and the complexities of critical gender analyses,[22] has taught her, first, to "cherish particularity, location and diversity in theological reflection rather than the

---

[20] See Dorothee Sölle, *Mystik und Widerstand: 'Du stilles Geschrei'* (Hoffmann und Campe: Hamburg 1997).

[21] Ruether, "Feminist Theology: Where Is It Going?," 19.

[22] "The ambiguities of gender and power are clearest within the heterogeneous terrain of religious practice. Churches, mosques, shrines and cult gatherings are sites in which normative ideals are ever more deeply embedded, and arenas from which women can appropriate moral, emotional and material resources to pursue their own projects" (Andrea Cornwall, *Readings in Gender in Africa* [James Currey: Oxford 2005], 11).

construction of new grand narratives."[23] Secondly, Walton expresses the need for feminist public theology to include much more than rational discourse if it is to approach the unbearable mystery of human suffering of which religious faith tries to speak. And a third reservation that Walton has concerns the observation that public theologians often employ the gendered conventions by which the public sphere is differentiated from the feminized "private" environment of both local churches and the domestic sphere. As feminist critique has demonstrated, Habermas's conception of the public sphere risks privileging certain understandings of rational communication over others, and reifying the distinctions between private and public, reinscribing the gendered binaries on which this distinction rests. Walton points to the necessity to deconstruct gendered public/private distinctions as a requirement for feminist public theology to engage with the most pressing social needs of women in everyday life.[24]

Marcella Althaus-Reid, originating from Argentina and working for the Queer Theology Project at the University of Edinburgh until her untimely death in 2009, speaks from a feminist postcolonial perspective, and has questioned even more radically the ambitions of public theology as represented by Jürgen Moltmann, Duncan Forrester, and Max Stackhouse. She states that instead of globalizing theological discourse and speaking in generalizing and moralizing terms of and to the "most excluded", public theologians should engage with the subversive voices, unfitting theological fragments and indecent longings that already "are speaking back to the Empire", to use Gayatra Spivak's well-known postcolonial metaphor.[25] Althaus-Reid wants us to turn to the "real praxis of living theology" and to the "theology in action" that comes to us in these voices, fragments and longings "from below", as she has tried to do exemplarily in her *Indecent Theology* project.[26]

For Althaus-Reid, the objectives of revolt against the crushing neoliberal market system should be constitutive parts of any radical public theology, and they include a self-critical stance of theologians regarding their own position and praxis.[27] In her witty and provocative style she offers a glimpse of what this could mean:

---

[23] Walton, "You Have to Say You Cannot Speak," 26-27.
[24] See Walton, "You Have to Say You Cannot Speak," 31.
[25] See Gayatri Chakravorty Spivak, *Can the Subaltern Speak?* (Macmillan: Basingstoke 1988).
[26] See Marcella Althaus-Reid, *Indecent Theology: Theological Perversions in Sex, Gender and Politics* (Routledge: London 2000).
[27] See Althaus-Reid, "In the Centre There Are No Fragments," 377.

> We are doing political theology in times of desperation. Baring our bums in public has become a gesture of thinking people and perhaps of thinking theologians too. We need a political theology much more disruptive in thinking but also in writing. Or in not writing, but joining rebellious people. A political theology the aim of which is to destabilize the status quo, and to destabilize itself.[28]

Despite their differences these various stances in and towards public theology all demonstrate a deep concern to keep feminist theologians unconditionally focused on today's most pressing social questions and needs. In my view it is important to reconsider these profound ambitions in the light of post-secular awareness and critical thought, because these perspectives can help to acknowledge and address the significant institutional changes and intellectual challenges in which theology and religious studies are involved in contemporary Europe.[29]

Shifts and Challenges to Address

Currently there are three important shifts that I see as refractions of the post-secular situation that affect feminist theology and should be confronted:

(1) the rise of international and interfaith feminisms (and their impact on the academic study of religion and gender);[30]
(2) the significant changes of the position and intellectual agenda of theology and religious studies in western universities, which in Europe are strongly interconnected with both secularizing and reconfessionalizing tendencies;[31]
(3) the increased presence of religion(s) in the public domain as "medium" or "arena" of political and cultural conflicts.[32]

---

[28] Althaus-Reid, "In the Centre There Are No Fragments," 375.
[29] See José Casanova, *Religion, Politics and Gender Equality: Public Religions Revisited* (United Nations Research Institute for Social Development [UNRISD], Draft, April 2009); Rosi Braidotti, "In Spite of the Times: The Postsecular Turn in Feminism," in: *Theory, Culture and Society* 25.6 (2008), 1-24; Sarah Bracke, "Conjugating the Modern/Religious, Conceptualizing Female Religious Agency: Contours of a 'Post-secular' Conjuncture," in: *Theory, Culture and Society* 25.6 (2008), 51-67.
[30] See Dawn T. M. Llewellyn, "Secular and Religious Feminisms: A Future of Disconnection?," in: *Feminist Theology* 21.3 (2013), 244-258.
[31] See Maaike de Haardt, "Expanding the Concepts and the Field: Feminist Liberation Theology and Beyond," in: *Journal of Feminist Studies in Religion* 27.1 (2011), 114-118.
[32] See Anne-Marie Korte, "Openings: A Genealogical Introduction to Religion and Gender," in: *Religion and Gender* 1.1 (2011), 1-17.

In my own history as a teacher in feminist theology and a researcher in the field of religion and gender I have been involved in these shifts in a very profound way, which has caused me to reflect upon both their practical and theoretical implications. In 2006, I was suddenly confronted with the end of my appointment as Associate Professor of Theological Women's Studies at a Roman Catholic Theological Faculty in the Netherlands, where I had been teaching for two decades. My subject, theological women's studies, had been removed from the academic theological curriculum and my authorization to teach at a Roman Catholic Theological Faculty where priests are trained was withdrawn. I was transferred several times to various teaching and research positions outside the Roman Catholic theological education programmes, until after three years I obtained a chair for Religion and Gender at the Faculty of Humanities of a large state university in the Netherlands, a chair that is now incorporated in the Department of Philosophy and Religious Studies.

From the moment that I started working outside a primarily theological academic setting, I realized that I had to rearrange my theoretical frameworks and scholarly networks in substantial ways. In this constellation I started a series of new projects, founded an international and interdisciplinary journal, obtained the funding for an international cooperation project, designed new courses and gathered new research groups, all under the heading of "Religion and Gender", now conceived as an interdisciplinary field of studies within the humanities, in which students and scholars from a great variety of disciplines participate. I came to see feminist theology as one of the contributors to this field of studies, alongside the increasing number of scholars in gender studies who study religion from the perspective of many disciplines within the humanities and the social sciences.

This change in my position compelled me to rethink my relation to what I call "classic" feminist theology and to confront my smouldering worries about its position and relevance in contemporary society. For quite some time my greatest concern has been that classic feminist theology and its most direct successors, as mapped by Rosemary Radford Ruether, hardly engage with the many questions posed by the transformations of religion and the new visibility and controversiality of religions, nor with the problematization of the western secularization paradigm and the western conception of religious faith, nor with the rise of a post-secular critical awareness, at least as an epistemological stance.

For instance, for me the most critical public issue to address is why gendered corporeality and normative sexuality figure so prominently in many contemporary public conflicts over religion in modern and modernizing societies.[33] Recent developments, summarized as the de-privatization of religion and the (re-)turn to religion as a political mobilizer in modern societies, show that this fascination for dis/closed female corporeality is more than a remnant of an almost overcome androcentric worldview. Close attention to the correct appearance, positioning, and use of women's bodies forms a substantive way to perform collective and individual religious identity in and towards modern western society. Moreover, this modeling of female – and in some cases also male – corporeality establishes and represents religious change and renewal in a modern, globalized, and multi-religious culture. And finally, these developments show that women are not only to be thought of as objects of these processes of religious profiling, but also as agents and initiators, who create public religious presence by modelling their bodies. This is a vast, complex array of questions that are of utmost relevance for gender studies in theology and religion, for which the more classic feminist theological approaches, in my opinion, do not offer analytical tools or insights.

I directed my research to projects that center on the questions outlined above. The summer of 2006 became memorable: pop star Madonna caused great agitation by performing a crucifixion scene in her *Confessions on a Dance Floor* show, and I realized that the worldwide commotion and controversies that this performance evoked, revealed the seismographic status of female corporeality and normative sexuality at the shifting fracture lines of religion versus secularity. I started studying this case, discovered more cases and came to focus my research on contemporary feminist art and performance projects accused of blasphemy.[34] I will now turn to one of these cases and discuss Pussy Riot's *Punk Prayer* as a case of/for Feminist Public Theology.

---

[33] See for an example from India: Veena Das, "The Figure of the Abducted Woman: The Citizen as Sexed," in: Hent de Vries / Lawrence E. Sullivan (eds.), *Political Theologies: Public Religions in a Post-secular World* (Fordham University Press: New York 2006), 427-443.

[34] Anne-Marie Korte, "Madonna's Crucifixion and the Female Body in Feminist Theology," in: Rosemarie Buikema / Iris van der Tuin (eds.), *Doing Gender in Media, Art and Culture* (Routledge: New York 2009), 117-133; Anne-Marie Korte, "Madonna's kruisigingscène: Blasfemie of theologische uitdaging?," in: *Tijdschrift voor Theologie* 49 (2009), 125-140; Anne-Marie Korte, "Blasphemous Feminist Art: Incarnate Politics of Identity in Post-secular Society" (forthcoming).

Pussy Riot's *Punk Prayer* as a Case of/for Feminist Public Theology

Virgin Mary, Put Putin Away
(Punk Prayer)

Virgin Mary, Mother of God, put Putin away,
Put Putin away, put Putin away!
(End chorus)

Black robe, golden epaulettes
All parishioners crawl to bow
The phantom of liberty is in heaven
Gay pride sent to Siberia in chains

The head of the KGB, their chief saint,
Leads protesters to prison under escort
In order not to offend His Holiness
Women must give birth and love

Shit, shit, the Lord's shit!
Shit, shit, the Lord's shit

(Chorus)
Virgin Mary, Mother of God, become a feminist
Become a feminist, become a feminist!
(End chorus)

The church's praise of rotten dictators
The cross-bearer procession of black limousines
A teacher-preacher will meet you at school
Go to class – bring him money!

Patriarch Gundyaev believes in Putin
Bitch, better believe in God instead!
The belt of the Virgin can't replace mass meetings
Mary, Mother of God, is with us in protest!

(Chorus)
Virgin Mary, Mother of God, put Putin away,
Put Putin away, put Putin away!
(End chorus)[35]

---

[35] Authorized lyrics in: Pussy Riot, *Pussy Riot! A Punk Prayer for Freedom: Letters from Prison, Songs, Poems, and Courtroom Statements, Plus Tributes to the Punk Band That Shook the World* (The Feminist Press at the City University of New York: New York 2013), 13-14.

On February 21, 2012, five female members of the Russian feminist punk formation Pussy Riot (an art collective consisting of about a dozen young Russian men and women based in Moscow) performed an unexpected, but well-prepared "political gesture" in the center of Moscow. They introduced a novel element to the series of political protests in urban guerrilla style that they had been practicing in the previous two years in the wake of the Arab Spring in 2011.[36] This time they addressed the renewed and tightening relationship between church and state in contemporary Russia, performing a (self-designated) *Punk Prayer* in the Russian Orthodox Christ the Saviour Church near the Kremlin. At the beginning of carnival, a week before Eastern Christianity's Great Lent, they walked into the cathedral. Four of the female members took off their winter gear and pulled brightly colored balaclavas over their heads. Dressed in short dresses, leggings and boots, they advanced toward the iconostasis and started jumping around, punching and kicking the air, singing and shouting, kneeling and crossing themselves, while being videotaped from several angles by other group members. Within less than a minute they were apprehended by security guards and removed from the sanctuary.

On the very day of the curtailed performance the group released a video clip on the internet in which both the act and its termination were shown. This clip also included the full version of the anti-Putin *Punk Prayer*, which is partly performed in the style of a solemn hymn to the Virgin Mary, and partly in the form of a shouted punk rap. The song, called "Mother of God, Put Putin Away", condemns the Russian Orthodox Church's ties to the Putin regime, calls its teaching that women must "know your place in the birthing ward" "holy shit", states that "the most holy Mother of God is at the rallies with us", and implores the Virgin Mary to chase Putin out of her church. The chorus sounds: "Virgin Mary, Mother of God, put Putin away, Virgin Mary, Mother of God, put Putin away."

On the evening after Pussy Riot's protest performance in the Christ the Saviour Church, Archpriest Vsevolod Chaplin condemned it on national

---

[36] "After the Arab Spring, we had come to understand that Russia needed political and sexual emancipation, audacity, the feminist whip and a feminist president" (Pussy Riot, "The History of Pussy Riot," in: Emily Neu / Jade French with Pussy Riot (eds.), *Let's Start a Pussy Riot* (Rough Trade: London 2013), 22; Pussy Riot, "Art or Politics?," in: Pussy Riot, *Pussy Riot! A Punk Prayer for Freedom: Letters from Prison, Songs, Poems, and Courtroom Statements, Plus Tributes to the Punk Band That Shook the World* (The Feminist Press at the City University of New York: New York 2013), 15-16.

television and called for the persecution of the group's members. The next day he posted a blog on the *Orthodox Politics* website in which he argued that the art collective had violated statutes on anti-extremism, that their action was criminal, and that they had offended the feelings of believers. His comments were soon followed by a fast growing amount of official complaints against the group.[37]

On March 3, the very day before the controversial re-election of Vladimir Putin as president of Russia, two members of the group who had actually performed in the Christ the Saviour Church, were arrested. Maria Alyokhina (24) and Nadezhda Tolokonnikova (22) were charged with "hooliganism (that is, undermining civil order) motivated by religious hatred".[38] Yekaterina Samutsevich (29), a group member who had not participated in the performance, was arrested on March 15. On August 17 all three women were convicted and sentenced to two years of imprisonment in a penal colony. On October 10, 2012, this sentence was partly confirmed after an appeal to higher court by the accused women. This Moscow court upheld the two-year prison terms for Alyokhina and Tolokonnikova, but ordered Samutsevich freed with a suspended sentence. On December 29, 2013 the two imprisoned women were released under a general amnesty marking the twentieth anniversary of Russia's post-Soviet constitution.[39] This amnesty was proposed by President Putin several weeks before the start of the Olympic Games in Sochi in 2014 and was immediately confirmed by the Russian parliament. Their liberation came four months before the women were due to be released.

The severe condemnations of the female performers of the *Punk Prayer* are obviously related to the sharp criticism that their act expressed with regard to the complicity of the Russian Orthodox Church in the authoritarian regime in

---

[37] See Rachel L. Schroeder / Vyacheslav Karpov, "The Crimes and Punishments of the 'Enemies of the Church' and the Nature of Russia's Desecularising Regime," in: *Religion, State and Society* 41.3 (2013), 284-311.

[38] Indictment expressed by Judge Marina Syrova of the Moscow Khamovniki District Court. Cited in: Olga G. Voronina, "Pussy Riot Steal the Stage in the Moscow Cathedral of Christ the Saviour: Punk Prayer on Trial Online and in Court," in: *Digital Icons: Studies in Russian, Eurasian and Central European New Media* 9 (2013), 72-75.

[39] In a gesture to mark the two decades since Russia adopted a new constitution in 1993, President Vladimir Putin announced a bill offering amnesty to people convicted of non-violent crimes (which actually concerned many persons of the political opposition). Political observers have regarded this as an attempt to appease the critics of Russia's human rights record before the Winter Olympics in Sochi in early 2014.

Russia, and to the fact that it referred to a series of high-profile incidents and public issues at that moment. The *Punk Prayer* act denounced corruption in the church, ridiculed the luxurious lifestyle of Patriarch Kirill, and decried the close connections between church and state security. It pointed to the dire consequences of the current repressive regime for women, LGBT persons, and those who take part in political opposition, groups who are all bereft of their freedom of speech, action and choice. This harsh criticism is articulated in lines shouted in punk style, alternated by a high-pitched, sung chorus consisting of the intercession of Mary as Mother of God, using Rachmaninoff's *Mary Vespers* so cherished by many Russians. In the chorus Mary is asked to "become a feminist", "join our protest" and "drive Putin away".

At their trial the women were accused of intending to openly express "disrespect for the Christian world and church canons", to "desecrate" the church and to "inflict deep wounds on Orthodox Christians". They were literally accused of committing a "maliciously conscious and thoroughly planned action of humiliation of the feelings and beliefs of multiple adherents of the Orthodox Christian confession and diminishment of the spiritual foundation of the state".[40] Further, according to the prosecutors, the offensive lyrics and indecent performance rendered the women's behavior "vulgar, impudent and cynical", which supported the charge of hooliganism.[41] The witnesses for the prosecution (church personnel, guards, and visitors) all attested that they felt hurt, outraged, or threatened by the shouting, movements, clothing, and gestures of the three women and by their appearance on the soleas, the space in front of the iconostasis.[42]

The three Pussy Riot members responded in much detail to the charges of religious hatred and blasphemy both in their speeches at their defence and in their open letters to President Medvedev and Patriarch Kyrill.[43] On the one hand, they rigorously denounced and ridiculed these charges and stated that the accusations as such reflected and affirmed the corrupt and intimidating Putin regime. On the other hand, they composed a series of refined arguments to prove that they had not intended to perform a blasphemous act at all. They claimed their act was not anti-religious, but a necessary critique of the abuse and corruption of the Russian Orthodox tradition through the new alliance between the Putin regime and the Russian Orthodox Church. Referring to

---

[40] Schroeder / Karpov, "The Crimes and Punishments of the 'Enemies of the Church'," 297.
[41] "Prosecutor's Statement," in: Pussy Riot, *Pussy Riot!*, 52-54.
[42] "Excerpts from the Court Transcript," in: Pussy Riot, *Pussy Riot!*, 49-52.
[43] See Pussy Riot, *Pussy Riot!*, 15-48; 87-118.

biblical texts as well as the works of philosophers, novelists, Russian dissidents, and contemporary feminist critics, they suggested that their own position might be more aligned with the original intentions and prophetic aspects of the Christian faith than that of their opponents. They expressed particular concern about the fact that core Christian values, such as love, justice, and selfless devotion, have been perverted by those in power and made an instrument of subordination, which turns "sons of God" into "slaves of God."[44]

The *Punk Prayer* case attracted huge international attention and outrage. It evoked condemnations of the sentencing as well as acts of support for the women from human rights organizations, politicians, scholars, and artists worldwide, in particular in western countries. Vigils, protest actions, conferences, and research groups have been organized in response to the case. As a recent research project shows, the western media coverage of this case outside Russia is strongly framed in terms of the accused and convicted women being victims of repressive state and religious regimes and courageous heroines defending the freedom of speech and human rights, in particular the rights of women and LGBT persons.[45] In this framework, the religious aspects of the *Punk Prayer* and the subsequent legal proceedings are hardly discussed as such. The fact that the Pussy Riot collective created a "political art performance" in the form of a punk *prayer* and that the women were charged of a type of hooliganism motivated by *religious* hatred (and acted out as blasphemy) have been perceived in these media as effective tools for rebellion as well as for repression, but not as intrinsicly meaningful gestures or stances.

For the Russian authorities who initiated the law suit and for the Church authorities involved, there never was any doubt that the Pussy Riot formation had seriously assaulted the Russian Orthodox faith and Church. The Russian media predominantly endorsed this perception and the majority of the Russian population affirmed that intolerable blasphemy had taken place.[46] The Russian state-related media even went so far as to report on a comparable blasphemous performance of Finnish Pussy Riot supporters in front of a cathedral in

---

[44] Reference to the Russian philosopher Nikolai Berdyaev, in: "Closing Courtroom Statement by Masha," in: Pussy Riot, *Pussy Riot!*, 106.

[45] See Tabitha M. van Zinnen, *Pussy Riot's Punk Prayer: Blasfemie, parrèsia en de strijd om vrijheid.* n.d. (http://igitur-archive.library.uu.nl/student-theses/2013-0905-200911/UUindex.html, 16 May 2014).

[46] See Schroeder / Karpov, "The Crimes and Punishments of the 'Enemies of the Church'," 292-298; Nicholas Denysenko, "An Appeal to Mary: An Analysis of Pussy Riot's Punk Performance in Moscow," in: *Journal of the American Academy of Religion* 81.4 (2013), 1061-1092.

Helsinki, Finland, that had resulted in a law suit and the conviction of the performers. This story was made up and circulated to legitimize the sentencing of the three members of the Pussy Riot formation.[47]

In the non-Russian western media a new interest in the religious aspects of the case emerged after the publication of the extensive and highly interesting texts that the accused women presented in court for their defence during their trial in August 2012. Now theologians also started to analyze the religious aspects of the performance, the law suit, and the defence. In particular the rich religious references and the high level of theological reflection in the women's self-defence were met with enthusiastic reactions. The women were praised for their nuanced views on religion and theology, and some theologians even recognized a kind of prayerfully radical sincerity in their performance and explanations. Professors of theology and philosophy publicly declared their admiration: Tom Beaudoin wondered whether the group was "intentionally or accidentally helping the church meet its own potential theological goals of distinguishing Christianity from state power".[48] Timothy Beal offered a refined analysis of the various types of theological argumentation (biblical, historical, and philosophical) the women deployed in their statements for the court and in other texts written during their imprisonment. According to Beal, "[t]aken together, these statements are nothing less than a radical theological apologia for Pussy Riot's media altar crash."[49]

However, returning to the critical remarks of Heather Walton and Marcella Althaus-Reid on the tendency among public theologians to globalize theological discourse and moralize specific theological agendas (including liberationist stances), I want to raise the question of whether reconstructions of Pussy Riot's statements for the defence in terms of their intentional or inadvertent contribution to established theological debates and goals help to understand, value, and support their act as feminist political protest. I doubt that this is the case, not only because, as these and other examples of theological interpretation show, no attention is paid at all to the gendered and feminist aspects of the *Punk Prayer* and its consequences. For instance, only female members

---

[47] See Teivo Teivainen, "Girls by the Church: Construction of a Pussy Riot Event in Finland as a Threat to Russian Gender Roles and Sexual Norms" (forthcoming).

[48] Tom Beaudoin, "'Punk Prayer Service' in Moscow Cathedral," posted in *Rock and Theology* on 10 April 2012. (http://www.rockandtheology.com/?p=5316, 16 May 2014).

[49] Timothy Beal, "Pussy Riot's Theology," in: *The Chronicle of Higher Education*, 17 September 2012. (http://chronicle.com/article/Pussy-Riots-Theology/134398/, 16 May 2014).

of the Pussy Riot formation were arrested and convicted, and the official charge of "hooliganism out of religious hatred" that was brought against them included gender specific accusations and argumentations concerning the three women's "vulgar, impudent and cynical" behavior.

But even more important is the fact that this (attempted) theological interpretation and recognition of the *Punk Prayer* act fails to acknowledge the deeply hybrid and ambiguous character of this act, which I consider constitutive of its aim and function as feminist political protest. This performance critically addresses the oppressive Russian regime (in the tradition of Russian dissident activism) and the new alignment with and legitimization by the Russian Orthodox Church that this regime seeks, showing in particular the intimidating consequences for "the others" of these patriarchal sovereigns: women, homosexuals, political dissidents, and people unable to appropriate the "grace" and favors of the neo-liberal economy in its corrupt manifestations. In this act of protest, political analysis and theological arguments, secular and religious points of view, public and private interests, and rational and affective interpellations, all come together and cannot be clearly separated from each other. Moreover, this complexity is underlined by the very style and composition of this gesture of protest, with its many deliberately chosen multi-media details of time, location, bodily appearance, and movements, arrangements of sound and music, and its ingenious ritual and symbolic allusions, all forcing the audience to distinguish between sincerity and deception.

It is precisely this deliberate entanglement of views, positions, and styles that should be acknowledged in the *Punk Prayer* protest, in the accusations that it gave rise to, and in particular in the defence of the Pussy Riot members in which they reflect on their performance, its original intentions, and its actual impact on Russian society and abroad. In her court statements Pussy Riot member Yekaterina Samutsevich refers explicitly to the fact that this entanglement is intended. She eloquently analyses Putin's "need to exploit the Orthodox religion and its aesthetics". "Apparently, [Putin] felt the need for more convincing, transcendental guarantees of his long tenure at the helm. It was here that the need arose to make use of the aesthetics of the Orthodox religion, historically associated with the heyday of Imperial Russia, where power came not from earthly manifestations such as democratic elections and civil society, but from God Himself."[50] According to Samutsevich,

---

[50] "Closing Courtroom Statement by Katya," in: Pussy Riot, *Pussy Riot!*, 88.

the authorities took advantage of a certain deficit of Orthodox aesthetics in Soviet times, when the Orthodox religion had the aura of a lost history, of something crushed and damaged by the Soviet totalitarian regime, and was thus an opposition culture. The authorities decided to appropriate this historical effect of loss and present their new political project to restore Russia's lost spiritual values, a project which has little to do with a genuine concern for preservation of Russian Orthodoxy's history and culture.[51]

Samutsevitch sees her performance in the Cathedral of Christ the Saviour with the song "Virgin Mary, put Putin away" not only as an act of protest against this manipulative turn to "Orthodox aesthetics" during election time. She also claims her performance to be an "unauthorized" alternative use of this Orthodox aesthetics. She states, "[i]n our performance we dared, without the Patriarch's blessing, to combine the visual image of Orthodox culture and protest culture, suggesting to smart people that Orthodox culture belongs not only to the Russian Orthodox Church, the Patriarch and Putin, that it might also take the side of civic rebellion and protest in Russia."[52]

To conclude, what is so challenging in Pussy Riot's criticism that this act could become a landmark in the history of the suppression of political opposition in Putin's Russia? The observation that with its *Punk Prayer* act the Pussy Riot formation has created disorder and has deliberately disturbed the peace, and that the persons present in the church at that instant, in particular the faithful, have been unsettled and shocked by this unexpected event, is certainly not incorrect or purely fictitious. However, the charge of hooliganism out of religious hatred and the indictment of blasphemy are unwarranted, and reflect a malign identification of the current political order and exercise of power with the defence of the sacredness of Russian Orthodox culture and tradition.

In my view the *Punk Prayer* performance is not born out of religious hatred – this act is too creative, too complex, and too elaborate regarding its religious content and meaning to be possibly reduced to "religious hate".[53] The rich speeches for the defence of the accused women, in which a nuanced discussion of religion and blasphemy is made part of their defence, supports this interpretation. But I also want to emphasize the hybridity and ambiguity of this performance. In the *Punk Prayer* an uncanny appeal to Russian Orthodox

---

[51] "Closing Courtroom Statement by Katya," in: Pussy Riot, *Pussy Riot!*, 88.

[52] "Closing Courtroom Statement by Katya," in: Pussy Riot, *Pussy Riot!*, 89.

[53] Voronina, "Pussy Riot Steal the Stage," 69-85.

ritual and aesthetics can be found. By its appeal to Mary, Russia's patroness and Holy Mother, to chase Putin away and join the feminists, this act forms a paradoxical and scandalous prayer indeed.[54] The enactment of this prayer in Moscow's most prestigious cathedral, directly in front of the iconostasis, in brightly colored clothes, with a confusing mixture of respectful and disrespectful gestures, of fitting and unfitting singing and shouting, reflects the deeply ambiguous status and meaning of this performance.

The *Punk Prayer* act is brave because it is ingeniously composed. By choosing to seek recourse to Mary with an explicit Hail Mary Prayer in the central Moscow cathedral, on the one hand, the women appropriated a traditional religious ritual (that women and lay people are allowed to perform in this church), while, on the other hand, they completely transformed this prayer and acted it out in a novel way by invoking Mary's help to chase Putin away and begging Mary to become a feminist. They confined their act just to this prayer to attract a maximum of attention. But they stayed anonymous and did not place themselves in the role of Mary or Jesus (which would be considered the central act of transgression in the allegedly blasphemous western feminist religious works of art and performances of the past decade).[55] Their most salient transgression was that they performed their prayer immediately in front of the iconostasis, where in religious services only priests and pastors are allowed. This, in my view, underscores that the invocation of Mary is pivotal to this act. The appeal to Mary is both an act of *parrhesia* (a venue to speak uncompromising truth about current affairs)[56] and an act of faith (a vision of hope expressed with a longing in which all the senses and means of expressions are involved).

La Europa del siglo 21 se ha enfrentado a desarrollos sociales y académicos sustanciales presentando serios desafíos a la teología feminista "clásica", que se ha establecido principalmente en contextos occidentales y predominantemente cristianos. Desafíos incisivos surgen de desarrollos tales como (1) el aumento de los feminismos internacionales e interreligiosos (y su impacto en el estudio académico de la religión y el sexo); (2) cambios significativos de la posición y la agenda intelectual de la teología y los estudios religiosos en las universidades occidentales, que están fuertemente interconectados con la secularización y reconfessionalizing tendencias en Europa; y (3) el aumento de la presencia de la religión(es) en el dominio público

---

[54] See Denysenko, "An Appeal to Mary," 1061-1092.
[55] Korte, "Madonna's Crucifixion"; Korte, "Blasphemous Feminist Art".
[56] Sergei Prozorov,"Pussy Riot and the Politics of Profanation: Parody, Performativity, Veridiction," in: *Political Studies* (17 June 2012), doi: 10.1111/1467-9248.12047.

como "medio" o "ámbito" de los conflictos políticos y culturales. Este trabajo consiste en un esfuerzo por esbozar los contornos de una teología pública feminista europea que tiene como objetivo hacer frente a estos desafíos. La primera parte de este trabajo se presenta la posición y las tareas de esta teología feminista pública en relación con las dos reflexiones (feminista-teológica) en teología pública y teoría crítica a la post-secular. La última parte de este trabajo es un ejemplo de estas consideraciones a través de un análisis de la Oración Punk ("performance arte político") de la formación rusa feminista Pussy Riot en la Iglesia de San Salvador, centro del cristianismo ortodoxo ruso, el 21 de febrero de 2012, que dio lugar a la acusación de "vandalismo motivado por el odio religioso" y el posterior enjuiciamiento y condena de las tres miembros del grupo en agosto de 2012. La atención se centra en la interrelación de los aspectos políticos, artísticos y teológicos, tanto en el desarrollo real y juicio correspondiente, en el cual una de las miembros acusados defendió su actuación diciendo: "En nuestra actuación nos atrevimos, sin la bendición del Patriarca, para combinar la imagen visual de la cultura ortodoxa y cultura de protesta, lo que sugiere que la gente inteligente que la cultura ortodoxa no pertenece sólo a la Iglesia ortodoxa Rusa, al Patriarca o a Putin, sino a ellos, que también podrían ponerse del lado de la rebelión cívica y protestar en Rusia."

21st-century Europe has faced substantial societal and academic developments that present serious challenges to "classic" feminist theology, which has been established mainly in western and predominantly Christian contexts. Incisive challenges emerge from developments such as (1) the rise of international and interfaith feminisms (and their impact on the academic study of religion and gender); (2) the significant changes of the position and intellectual agenda of theology and religious studies in western universities, which are strongly interconnected with both secularizing and reconfessionalizing tendencies in Europe; and (3) the increased presence of religion(s) in the public domain as "medium" or "arena" of political and cultural conflicts. This paper consist of an effort to sketch the outlines of a European feminist public theology that aims to address these challenges. The first parts of this paper discuss the position and tasks of this feminist public theology in relation to both (feminist-theological) reflections on public theology and to post-secular critical theory. The last part of this paper exemplifies these considerations through an analysis of the *Punk Prayer* ("political art performance") of the Russian feminist formation Pussy Riot in Moscow's central Russian Orthodox Christ the Saviour Church on February 21, 2012, which led to the accusation of "hooliganism motivated by religious hatred" and the subsequent prosecution and sentencing of three group members in August 2012. The focus is on the intertwining of political, artistic, and theological aspects in both the actual performance and the corresponding court case, in which one of the accused members defended their performance by stating: "In our performance we dared, without the Patriarch's blessing, to combine the visual image of Orthodox culture and protest culture, suggesting to smart people that

Orthodox culture belongs not only to the Russian Orthodox Church, the Patriarch and Putin, that it might also take the side of civic rebellion and protest in Russia."

Europa im 21. Jh. steht grundlegenden sozialen und akademischen Entwicklungen gegenüber, die eine ernsthafte Herausforderung für "klassische" feministische Theologie darstellen, die sich hauptsächlich im westlichen, christlichen Kontext entwickelte. Einschneidende Herausforderungen entstehen aus Veränderungen, wie (1) dem Entstehen von internationalen und inter-religiösen Feminismen (und ihrem Einfluss auf die akademische Forschung im Bereich Gender und Religion); (2) wichtigen Veränderungen in der Position und intellektuellen Agenda von Theologie und Religionswissenschaften an westlichen Universitäten, die sowohl mit säkularisierenden als auch rekonfessionalisierenden Tendenzen in Europa stark verbunden sind; und (3) die wachsende Präsenz von Religion(en) in der Öffentlichkeit als "Medium" oder "Arena" von politischen und kulturellen Konflikten. Dieser Beitrag versucht, die Umrisse einer europäischen feministischen *Public Theology* zu skizzieren, die darauf abzielt, diese Herausforderungen anzunehmen. Die ersten Abschnitte dieses Artikels diskutieren die Position und Aufgaben dieser feministischen *Public Theology* im Verhältnis zu (feministisch-theologischen) Reflektionen über *Public Theology* und zu postsäkularer kritischer Theorie. Der letzte Abschnitt dieses Artikels illustriert diese Überlegungen durch eine Analyse des *Punk Prayer* (eine "politische Kunstperformance") der russischen feministischen Formation Pussy Riot in der zentralen russisch-orthodoxen Christ-Erlöser-Kathedrale in Moskau am 21. Februar 2012, die zur Anklage wegen "Rowdytum motiviert von religiösem Hass" und der folgenden Anklage und Verurteilung von drei Mitgliedern im August 2012 führte. Der Fokus ist auf die Verbindung von politischen, künstlerischen und theologischen Aspekten in der Performance und der Gerichtsverhandlung gerichtet, in der eines der angeklagten Mitglieder ihre Performance so verteidigte: "In unserer Performance wagten wir es, ohne den Segen des Patriarchen visuelle Elemente der orthodoxen Kultur und der Protestkultur zu kombinieren und damit verständigen Menschen anzudeuten, dass die orthodoxe Kultur nicht nur der russisch-orthodoxen Kirche, dem Patriarchen und Putin gehört, sondern dass sie auch auf der Seite von bürgerlicher Rebellion und Protest in Russland stehen könnte."

Anne-Marie Korte is Professor of Religion and Gender at the Faculty of Humanities of Utrecht University, The Netherlands. She initiated the international research cooperation "Interdisciplinary Innovations in the Study of Religion and Gender: Postcolonial, Post-secular and Queer Perspectives" (2011-2014). She is the initiator and editor-in-chief of *Religion and Gender* (http://religionandgender.org).

Journal of the European Society of Women in Theological Research 22 (2014) 55-68.
doi: 10.2143/ESWTR.22.0.3040790

Teresa Forcades i Vila

Fake Democracies and the Political Consequences of the Christian Notion of Person

Within the larger question of whether religion can be useful in substantially diminishing economic and epistemic violence, I present a Christian notion of person able to unmask the fake democracies characteristic of western capitalist societies at the beginning of the 21st century in order to inspire a socio-political struggle for systems of governance that are more just and efficient. As the Christian theological tradition of liberation theology has clearly stated from its conception, far from being an accidental aspect of Christianity, the work for social justice and the preferential option for the poor are its criteria of authenticity (Mt 25:31-46).[1] Here, I do not assume that this potential of social transformation is exclusive of Christianity. I will develop the Christian perspective because it is the one I know and the one with which I identify, but I also wish to state that various perspectives of liberation theology do exist in other religious traditions (Hinduism, Buddhism, Judaism, and Islam).[2]

What is meant by the term "fake democracies" and what does it mean to consider them characteristic of western capitalist societies at the beginning of the 21st century? I have developed this topic in detail elsewhere;[3] here it will suffice to define the notion of "fake democracy" in a succinct way and to illustrate it with an example. By "fake democracy" I mean a political system that, despite calling itself democratic, allows the will of those who hold economic power be superior to the will of the people and places their interests above the interests of the majority. One example: in June 2009, Margaret Chan, then general director of the WHO, announced the maximal level of

---

[1]   See Gustavo Gutiérrez, *Hacía una teología de la liberación* (Perspectivas: Lima 1971).
[2]   See Christopher S. Queen / Sally B. King, *Engaged Buddhism: Buddhist Liberation Movements in Asia* (SUNY Press: Albany 1996); Hamid Dabashi, *Islamic Liberation Theology: Resisting the Empire* (Routledge: New York 2008); Marc H. Ellis, *Toward a Jewish Theology of Liberation: The Challenge of the 21st Century* (Baylor University Press: Waco 2004).
[3]   See Teresa Forcades i Vila, *És a les nostres mans: Crítica ètica al capitalisme* (Dau: Barcelona 2014).

international health alarm due to the swine-flu pandemic;[4] at the same time, the WHO and the governments that are part of it accepted that the commercialization of the pandemic flu vaccine be restricted to four pharmaceutical companies and warned that there might be a shortage of the vaccine due to the fact that these four companies could not be expected to meet the needs of the international demand.[5] In the context of such an international health alarm, why were not all laboratories allowed to manufacture a vaccine that could save – so we were told – millions of lives? If more laboratories had been granted the right to manufacture the vaccine, there would have been no shortage. The four companies that were granted the exclusive commercialization of the pandemic flu vaccine are part of the elite of the most prosperous businesses in the world.[6] How is it possible that the financial interests of these four companies be valued more than the life of millions of people?[7] The governments that allowed this to happen are "fake democracies" because, despite defending in word the people's sovereignty and the notion of the common good as their goal, in practice, their decisions are subservient to the interests of big transnational companies.[8] This example affords the opportunity to highlight the association between economic violence and democratic discourse that characterizes contemporary societies: elected politicians defend democracy and human rights as the most important national values while at the same time establishing and sustaining alliances with forces that render their words empty.

---

[4] See Margaret Chan, "World at the Start of 2009 Influenza Pandemic: Statement to the Press by WHO-Director General," in: *WHO Official Webpage*, 11 June 2009. (http://www.who.int/mediacentre/news/statements/2009/h1n1_pandemic_phase6_20090611/en/index.html, 9 August 2013).

[5] See Michael D. Shear / Rob Stein, "Administration Officials Blame Shortage of H1N1 on Manufacturers, Science," in: *The Washington Post*, 27 October 2009. (http://www.washingtonpost.com/wp-dyn/content/article/2009/10/26/AR2009102603487.html?hpid=topnews, 27 October 2009).

[6] See Matthew Herper, "The Most Productive Drug Companies of the Past 10 Years," in: *Forbes*, 15 April 2013. (http://www.forbes.com/sites/matthewherper/2013/04/15/the-most-productive-drug-companies-of-the-past-10-years/, 15 April 2013); Bruce Japsen, "Obamacare Will Bring Drug Industry $35 Billion in Profits," in: *Forbes*, 25 May 2013. (http://www.forbes.com/sites/brucejapsen/2013/05/25/obamacare-will-bring-drug-industry-35-billion-in-profits/, 25 May 2013).

[7] See Bernard Munos, "We the People vs. the Pharmaceutical Industry," in: *Forbes*, 29 April 2013. (http://www.forbes.com/sites/bernardmunos/2013/04/29/the-pharmaceutical-industry-vs-society/, 29 April 2013).

[8] See Teresa Forcades i Vila, *Els crims de les grans companyies farmacèutiques* (Ed. Cristianisme i Justícia: Barcelona 2006), Quaderns Cristianisme i Justícia 141; translated into Spanish (2006) and English (2006).

Confronted with such epistemic and structural violence, let us turn to a notion of "person" rooted in the Christian tradition able to help us overcome such violence. In what follows, I will analyze four basic categories of Christian theology and will draw for each of them some consequences for the notion of person, with particular attention to its political implications. The four theological categories I will analyze are: co-creation, unity in diversity, inseparability of love and freedom, and metanoia.

Co-creation

According to classical Christian theology, the world has been created by means of a free act of love and it is not yet complete.[9] It will attain completion only when all creatures who are part of this creation will reach their fullness and this, in the case of the human being created in the image of God, amounts to divinization by means of free acts of love, by means of acts of creation able to interrupt the causal chain to give rise to something "new".[10] The notion of co-creation is united to the notion of "personal freedom" without which the structural injustice present in the world would be impossible to overcome. If the subject were not able to create, that is, to imagine and to realize something truly "new", it would then be possible to manipulate her until her capacity for resistance was completely annulled. However, this is not the case. Despite it being painfully obvious that people can be manipulated, subjective freedom manifests itself time and again in human history in the fight for justice and in the enduring hope for a better world. Personal freedom has not been annulled, and according to Christian belief, it will never be, as it is an essential component of being human.

---

[9] The notion of *creatio continua* (continous creation) appears, among others, in the writings of Maximus the Confessor and Hildegard von Bingen. S. Maximi Confessoris, *Orationes Dominicae brevis expositio*. PG 90, 884. Hildegard of Bingen, *Commentary on the Johannine Prologue*, translated and introduced by Barbara Newman, in: *Theology Today* 60 (2003), 16-33. Cf. also for the biblical foundations of the notion of *creatio continua* Jon Levenson, *Creation and the Persistence of Evil* (Princeton University Press: Princeton 1994).

[10] In the words of Saint John of the Cross: "Y no hay que tener por imposible que el alma aspire en Dios, como Dios aspira en ella, por modo participado. Porque, dado que Dios le haga merced de unirla en la Santísima Trinidad, en que el alma se hace deiforme y Dios por participación, [...] esto es, transformada en las tres Personas en potencia y sabiduría y amor, y en esto semejante el alma a Dios, y para que pudiese venir a esto la crió a su imagen y semejanza" (cf. *Cántico* B 39,4).

The fight for greater social justice is not a utopian struggle, because all those who undertake it experience a "realized eschatology": the reality of the fullness of life is already anticipated in the fight itself at a subjective level – life has meaning, has an inner fullness –, and at the objective level as well – you live with others, you fight side by side, you share and you celebrate. Existential solitude gives rise to communion.

In addition to being inseparable from personal freedom, the notion of co-creation is intimately linked to the notion of providence, that is, God's promise that human life, no matter how violent its circumstances might be, remains always open to the possibility of expressing itself in a free act of love.[11] Such an act cannot be judged at the human level; only God can know to what extent a given action is truly a free act of love. For instance, the free act of love that was possible to Jesus while on the cross was not to come down from it and it was also not to accept the cross as inevitable or as wanted by his Father; it was something much deeper than that, something that went unnoticed by the majority, even though in this event all the love and all the sovereign freedom of the creator God were concentrated.[12] Providence so understood has nothing to do with "providentialism", that is the idea that at the end of the day, God's plans do always prevail. No. God's plans do not always prevail, because God's will is that there be no pain and no tears. But the pain and the tears which God does absolutely *not* want, did occur during the life of Jesus, and continue to occur around the world in our time.

This understanding of providence rules out the possibility of taking refuge in the notion of a God that is able to magically solve all problems, and confronts the person in her existential freedom. Instead of waiting for a savior, we are invited to acknowledge that salvation is in our hands and that God, far from being a substitute for individual freedom, is its ultimate warrant. Salvation is in our hands: not in our individual hands, but in our collective

---

[11] Teresa Forcades i Vila, "La Providencia como comunión," in: *Iglesia Viva* 254 (April-June 2013), 49-60.

[12] "San Juan de la Cruz afirma que Jesús en toda su vida no realizó obra mayor que cuando quedó inmóbil, clavado en la cruz, sin poder hacer nada absolutamente, en total desamparo de soledad y abandono. '[…] en él hizo la mayor obra que en toda su vida con milagros y obras había hecho […] que fue reconciliar y unir al género humano por gracia con Dios' (2 Subida 7,11). En este momento es cuando el Espíritu brota del costado abierto de Jesús en forma de agua y de sangre que nos arrastra como un torrente de vivificación hacia el centro de nosotros mismos, hacia la unificación de nuestro ser en el misterio de muerte y resurrección" (Cristina Kaufmann, *La transparència de l'invisible* [Ed. Claret: Barcelona 2007], 110).

hands.[13] Against the capitalist individualism that isolates the human person and makes each one separately responsible for her individual destiny, emerges the notion of collective responsibility: "Cain, where is your brother?" (Gen 4:8-10). Rut understood this responsibility and thanks to her the people of ancient Israel had a future.[14] Thanks to all the anonymous Ruts of history people of all nations continue to have a future. Nobody can substitute or take away my personal responsibility for my own actions, but the social determinants of one's happiness and wellbeing and, specifically, the social determinants of the happiness and the wellbeing of those most vulnerable among us, are a collective responsibility.

Unity in Diversity

"Queer" originally meant "strange" and was used in the 1990s in Great Britain to stigmatize homosexuals. In response, some homosexual activists appropriated the word to show that what was particularized in them and denounced as something negative, was in reality a positive singularity of all free human beings.[15] Queer was then defined as "unclassifiable". Thus, the supposed insult implicit in the fact of not fitting within heterosexual categories, was turned into an opportunity to analyze critically the criteria of social normalization: what is the origin of the social categories used to classify people sexually? Beyond the sexual domain, what is the origin of the social categories used to classify people in general? Is it desirable that people who do not fit into these categories finally be re-inscribed in them? Isn't it more desirable that those who do fit come to acknowledge their own uniqueness, and the irreducibility that identifies them and everyone else as "free beings beyond all labels"?

The notion of the person as articulated in classical trinitarian theology distinguishes itself precisely because it emphasizes the unique and irreducible character of personal identity, and because it develops a notion of unity inseparable

---

[13] "For where two or three are gathered in my name, I am there among them" (Mt 18:20).

[14] But Rut said, "Do not press me to leave you or to turn back from following you! Where you go, I will go; Where you lodge, I will lodge; your people shall be my people, and your God my God" (Rut 1:16).

[15] One of the most famous attempts by the LGBT community to re-claim the term "queer" was through an organisation called Queer Nation, which was formed in March 1990; a few months later, in June 1990, an influential though anonymous flier was distributed at the New York Gay Pride Parade entitled "Queers Read This". (http://en.wikipedia.org/wiki/Queer, 11 August 2013).

from diversity.[16] In the West (Parmenides, Plato) as well as in the East (for example in the Hindu notion of *maya* as illusion or delusion),[17] classically dominant philosophical currents have tended to conceive of the diversity of the world as "suboptimal", as a superficial expression of a deeper unitarian truth that only the wise person is able to grasp. Wisdom has consequently been defined as the capacity of perceiving the truth of unity behind the misleading appearance of multiplicity. This dominant idealistic trend has co-existed together with counter-discourses that have elevated diversity to the highest ontological degree and have considered unity to be illusory.[18]

In this context, the Christian theological notion of the triune God affirms the simultaneity of unity and diversity and their mutual implication.[19] Diversity cannot be a suboptimal category for Christian thought because it is present in God. Divine perfection and truth, far from being incompatible with diversity, are in fact intrinsically linked to it. The only perfection praised in the Gospels is that of love, and love cannot subsist in uniformity.[20] Love needs difference to exist. There is a "no" in God the Trinity; it is not the "no" of negation, but the "no" of irreducible otherness:[21] the Father is *not* the Son and

---

[16] For a thorough discussion of the notion of "person" in classical Trinitarian theology and of its relatioship to the modern notion of "freedom" as self-determination, cf. Teresa Forcades i Vila, *Ser persona, avui* (Publicacions de l'Abadia de Montserrat: Barcelona 2011).

[17] See Sukumari Bhattacharji, *The Indian Theogony: A Comparative Study of Indian Mythology from the Vedas to the Purāṇas* (Cambridge University Press: Cambridge 1970), 35: "*Maya* means 'wisdom, extraordinary or supernatural power' (only in earlier language), but later it comes to mean 'illusion, unreality, deception, fraud, trick, sorcery, witchcraft and magic'."

[18] Heráclito de Éfeso (544-484 a.C): "Lo contrario se opone de acuerdo; y de lo diverso la más hermosa armonía pues todas las cosas se originan en la discordia" (*Sobre la naturaleza, referencia a los contrarios*, 8).

[19] Thomas Aquinas: "Unum non est remotivum multitudinis, sed divisionis" (unity does not exclude diversity, but division, *Summa Theologica*, pars prima, q.30, a.3 ad3).

[20] Richard of Saint Victor: "Thus, who has an incommunicable difference has equally an incommunicable existence. As a consequence, in the divinity there are as many persons as incommunicable existences" (*De Trinitate*, 4.17).

[21] "In den differenten Personen der Trinität ist ein wirkliches Nicht- und Anderssein immer schon mitgegeben; es gehört zum 'inneren' Selbstvollzug Gottes: Gott, der Schöpfer und Urgrund allen Seins, enthält als der Eine ebenso ursprünglich Differenz und Vielheit in sich, die dann in der Pluriformität der Schöpfung ihre 'Verlängerung' und 'Abbildung' findet. Gott ist nicht nur Prinzip der Einheit der Schöpfung, sondern auch ihrer Vielheit; er ist nicht nur Quelle und Ursprung von Homogenität, sondern von Besonderheit und Vielfalt. So empfängt die Schöpfung vom trinitarischen Gott ihre einzigartige Würde, ihre unbedingte Positivität und eine widerspruchsfreie Erklärung der Bedingung ihrer Möglichkeit. Damit zeigt sich auch die Wahrheit der These von Niklaj A. Berdjajew: 'Keine einzige der Formen des konsequenten, abstrakten

will never be, the Son is *not* the Father and will never be, the Spirit is neither Father nor Son and neither Father nor Son are the Spirit, but the three are one single God. Despite its paradoxical formulation, the simultaneity of unity and diversity is a familiar experience in true love, when all those involved experience a personal growth, a fostering of their individual originality and at the same time an increased capacity of recognizing the originality of the others while feeling ever more united with them.

Trinitarian theology has given the technical name of "perichoresis" to the loving relationship that unites and constitutes the three divine persons.[22] The Greek prefix *peri-* means "around" and the root *choreo* can be translated as "to make place". Thus, love, according to trinitarian theology, implies "to make place around the loved one", to ease her way so that she can be in fullness, even when her fullness takes her away from me or runs contrary to my interests (see for example Jesus's prayer to his Father in the garden of Gethsemane).[23] According to the Gospel of John, the loving relationship of the three divine persons is not exclusive to them but (and this is one of the most daring aspects of Christianity), it is precisely according to perichoresis that human relationships are to be understood (John 17; Jesus prays four times that his disciples be "one" precisely in the same way that he and his Father are "one").

From a social and political perspective, the consequence of unity in diversity, and the respect for the irreducible originality of each individual is to foster plurality. Instead of tolerating plurality as a lesser good and hoping that it will progressively decrease to give rise to a shared unified view, plurality needs to be valued and fostered as a good in itself, as the most cherished good of all human groups and all authentically democratic societies. In this sense, those labeled "queer" and all people who do not fit in a given social or epistemic context fulfill a prophetic task: they remind us that the law (be it religious, social or epistemic) should be made for the people and not the people for the law (Mk 2:27).

Monismus ist imstande, innerlich auch nur den Ursprung der vielfältigen Welt zu erklären'." Gisbert Greshake, *Der dreieine Gott: Eine trinitarische Theologie* (Herder: Freiburg 1997), 224-225. Greshake refers here to Berdjajew, *Der Sinn der Geschichte* (Otto Reichl: Darmstadt 1925), 75.

[22] See George L. Prestige, *God in Patristic Thought* (SPCK: London 1964), 291. The first author who used the verb *perichoreo* was Gregorius of Nazianzen (4th century). The noun *perichoresis* can be found for the first time in the writings of Maximus the Confessor (7th century).

[23] Lk 22:39-46.

The Inseparability of Love and Freedom

Patriarchal society considers men more able than women to act freely and characterizes free action as the capacity to act against the opinions or expectations of significant others. Conversely, the patriarchal stereotype considers women more able than men to love and characterizes love as the capacity to sacrifice oneself, that is, to give priority to the needs and desires of the significant other, even when doing so goes against one's own interests or preferences.[24] I believe that these patriarchal stereotypes of masculinity and femininity are neither artificial nor essential. I believe that they reflect the persistence in the adult life of certain trans-historical childhood psychic structures and patterns of subjectivation.[25] I also believe that these internalized patterns are transcended in each act of free love and I thus believe that the patriarchal stereotypes can and should disappear. Understanding how gender identity arises should help us avoid essentializing it. Let us assume that the little girl is able to identify with her mother in a way that the little boy cannot, because the girl can think of herself as "a little mother" while the boy must accept that he will never be "a mother" (he will never conceive a child, be pregnant or give birth). Let us assume that it is with reference to the mother figure that the consciousness of "being a separate subject" arises in early childhood. For the girl, the consciousness of "being herself" would then be united to the experience of "having a personal identity in continuity with the beloved"; for the boy, the consciousness of "being himself" would on the contrary be united to the experience of "having a personal identity in discontinuity with that of the beloved". Both, the girl and the boy, are called to move beyond their initial personal identity as they grow up. Patriarchal society arises when a majority of subjects fail to do so and remain attached to a greater or lower degree to their initial childish sense of self. I believe that what patriarchal society calls men's "greater capacity for freedom" is rather a greater "fear of dependency", fear of being dominated by a female figure like they were in their early childhood. I believe that what patriarchal society calls women's "greater capacity for love" is actually a "greater fear of loneliness", the fear to conceive one's self independently of the maternal role, that is: the fear of having to account for one's life on its own terms, independently of what one's significant other

---

[24] See Carol Gilligan, *In a Different Voice* (Harvard University Press: Cambridge 1982).

[25] See Nancy Chodorow, *The Reproduction of Mothering: Psychoanalysis and the Sociology of Gender* (University of California Press: Berkeley 1978).

needs or desires.[26] If this be so, a revolutionary subject able to re-think social life without resorting to violence, needs to move beyond all gender stereotypes in her anthropological understanding, in order to experience subjectivity and inter-subjectivity as irreducible personal originality, in order to experience what is new and unique in each person.

The Christian proposal is essentially anti-patriarchal when it associates the fullness of humanity to a second birth that does not have the "mother figure" as a referent but the "water and the Spirit" (John 3:1-15). In Paul's words: "in Christ Jesus there is neither feminine nor masculine" (Gal 3:28).

The Christian notion of "personal freedom" needs to be conceived according to the image of the trinitarian perichoresis: each divine person enjoys a distinctive identity inseparable from her relationship to the other two persons. The practical consequences of such a relational notion of "personal freedom" are expressed in the Augustinian distinction between *libertas* and *liberum arbitrium*.[27] *Liberum arbitrium* is the capacity to choose. Without it, it would not be possible to speak of freedom. But the capacity to choose is not yet "freedom". I can use my capacity to choose in order to reaffirm my childish identity and thus refuse out of fear to experience something new. This is called "fear of freedom". I can choose "the already known" out of fear to make a mistake or to be punished. The gospel calls this refusing to die (or to deny oneself) in order to live a fuller life. Freedom is only present when I use my *capacity to choose* to choose what I really want and this, according to Christian anthropology, results always in an act of love. A truly free act is always an act of love, because only fear forces us to repress our loving nature, made in the image of God, and acting out of fear is incompatible with freedom. An act of love can be to separate from one's husband; an act of love can be an act of civil disobedience. The expulsion of the merchants from the temple in Jerusalem for instance (Mk 11:15-18 par) is theologically conceived as an act of love, an expression of Jesus's loving divine identity.

It is clear, then, that some acts of love can be quite vigorous, surprising or even violent. What characterizes an act of love is what inspires it, and this only God

---

[26] See Teresa Forcades i Vila, "Feminist Freedom: A Dialogue Between the Psychoanalytical Insights of J. Lacan and N. Chodorow and Classical Trinitarian Theology," in: *Journal of the European Society of Women in Theological Research* 16 (2008), 99-115. Cf. also Teresa Forcades i Vila, "Hacia una sociedad de iguales," in: *Iglesia Viva* 239 (July-September 2009), 31-48.

[27] See Joan Pegueroles, "'Libertas', fin del 'liberum arbitrium' según san Agustín," in: *Augustinus* 39 (1994), 365-72.

can judge. From the standpoint of Christian anthropology, it is decisive to expose as deluding those anthropologies that conceive freedom as something *previous* to love. Freedom and love are necessarily simultaneous. Love cannot be postponed because of freedom. Freedom cannot be postponed because of love. In the words of the anarchist tradition: "I will not be free until we all are free." Or, in the words of Saint Augustine: "Love and do what you will."[28] An act of love is always a loving act because human beings have been created from and for love and only decide to act contrary to love when dominated by fear, i.e., when we suspect that the loving act will have negative consequences for us. Against love, we can only act out of fear. This is why a non-loving act can never be a *free* act.

From a social perspective, the consequence of the inseparability of love and freedom is the discrediting of individualism (personal fulfillment to the exclusion of others) now taken as existentially inconsistent, without weakening the notion of personal responsibility. Anthropologically, the inseparability of love and freedom is contrary to the capitalist premise of the effort for maximal individual profit, and it is likewise contrary to so-called anthropologies of complementarity, because they essentialize gender identities. I believe that gender identities are cultural constructs with a trans-cultural core, but I do not consider this core an essential, positive feature of who I am. According to the Gospel, the only essential feature in us is our being God's children created in God's image and this – as I have argued in the previous section – is a *queer* identity, a dynamic identity that can be neither classified nor essentialized.

Metanoia

One last feature of the Christian vision of world and personhood relevant to social transformation is the notion of *homo viator*.[29] *Homo viator* describes the pilgrim character of human experience, its provisionality, the impossibility to conceive absolute realities in time and space. In the words of bishop, liberation theologian and poet Pere Casaldàliga: "There are only two absolutes: God and hunger".[30]

---

[28] St. Augustine, *Homilies on the Gospel of John; Homilies on the First Epistle of John; Soliloquies*, ed. Philip Schaff (Christian Literature Publishing Co.: New York 1886), 657. (http://www.ccel.org/ccel/schaff/npnf107.html [PL 34: 1977-2062], 26 March 2014).

[29] See Josef Pieper, *Unaustrinkbares Licht: Das negative Element in der Weltansicht des Thomas von Aquin* (Kosel-Verlag: München 1963), 129.

[30] Interview with Pere Casaldàliga, "Todo es relativo, menos Dios y el hambre", in: *Redes Cristianas*. 5 April 2007.
(http://www.redescristianas.net/2007/04/05/todo-es-relativo-menos-dios-y-el-hambre-entrevista-a-pedro-casaldaliga/, 25 March 2014).

Outside of these, all is relative, and it is not possible to reach paradise on earth. Despite this, the Christian notion of *homo viator* does not imply quietism or political passivity, quite the contrary. In liberation theology, the sobriety that comes from knowing that there is no lasting "ideal solution" transforms itself in the strength necessary for the long-term struggle, in the capacity to persevere in the pursuit of social justice without any illusion of easy fixes. The consciousness of being a *homo viator*, a pilgrim, allows one to assume the necessary critical distance from all concrete realizations of the ideal of living together, be it at the intimate level (couple, family, friendship), or at the social level. This critical distance does not preclude true commitment, but it does rule out the absolutization of one's achievements or convictions. It keeps one's eyes open to perceive when "more of the same" becomes a betrayal, to perceive the right moment for the necessary action, the moment to invite new people or new ideas into the dialogue.

From the idea of the *homo viator* emerges the theological notion of *metanoia*.[31] *Metanoia* or "conversion" relates to the notion of permanent revolution because both define reality as open and prescribe the need to reassess constantly one's position in relation to one's ideal. In Hebrew, the word "conversion" (*shuv*) indicates "movement, turn";[32] it gives witness to the dynamic and provisional character of everything human. In a revolutionary political context, it is not possible to think that a break with an unjust system will be achieved simply by the replacement of the present leaders by better ones. It is necessary to change the structures of power in order to make them truly participative; it is necessary to maximize the democratic quality of the checks and balances involved.

The very notion of democracy presupposes this openness and this dynamic balance, but the current western examples of democracy do not allow that the people take the political power into their hands. To vote every three, four or five years is not enough. We need democratic institutions that foster the true participation of the people and collective decision-making at the local level. The people of a democratic nation need to have effective means of power to terminate a political mandate when it is not proceeding according to expectations; the accountability of those in power needs to be real and controlled by the community of those affected by their decisions. The recent revolutionary experiences in some Latin American countries (Bolivia, Venezuela, Ecuador

---

[31] Cf. among others: Mt 18:21-35; Acts 26:20; Rev 2:5
[32] Cf. among others: Hos 6:1; Is 30:15; Dan 4:34; Jer 8:4; Ruth 1:7; 1:11; 1:22; 4:15.

etc.) show that it will not be easy. The crux of the matter is not to finally establish the "right structure" at the political, the social or the economic level, but to recognize that all revolution has the potential to betray itself, and to establish a system of checks and balances flexible enough to react to ever-changing circumstances. It seems obvious, in this sense, that smaller political units have a greater democratic potential than larger ones when operating within a constitution that guarantees the basic rights and precludes the concentration of power in the hands of a few.

In analyzing the theological notions of co-creation, unity in diversity, inseparability of love and freedom, and metanoia, I have emphasized their potential for grounding a notion of person able to carry on the political changes needed to achieve a greater social justice in what I have described as "fake democracies". To the notion of "co-creation" corresponds a subject (a person) able to assume political responsibility at the individual and at the collective level. To the notion of "unity in diversity" corresponds a subject (a person) able to foster plurality and queer identities. To the notion of "inseparability of love and freedom" corresponds a subject (a person) able to overcome gender stereotypes and false individualistic freedom. And finally, to the notion of metanoia corresponds a subject (a person) able to understand the need for a permanent revolution. This can be a Christian theological contribution to a necessary and urgent social change. A theological contribution inspired in the gospel that, far from being exclusivist, understands itself as being in dialogue with all other currents of thought that feel as their own the pleas for justice of the poor.

Las "falsas democracias" son sistemas de gobierno que permiten a sus ciudadanos votar, pero no tienen controles que eviten que los políticos electos legislen y gobiernen en contra de los intereses o incluso en contra de la voluntad explícita de la mayoría. Este es un fenómeno complejo propio de las sociedades capitalistas occidentales de principios del siglo XXI que debe ser cuidadosamente estudiado. En este artículo analizo las nociones teológicas de 1. co-creación, 2. unidad en la diversidad, 3. indisociabilidad del amor y la libertad y 4.metanoia, a fin de destacar su potencial para fundamentar una noción de persona capaz de llevar a cabo los cambios políticos necesarios para transformar las democracias falsas en verdaderas. A la noción de "co-creación" corresponde un sujeto (una persona) capaz de asumir responsabilidad política a nivel individual y colectivo. A la noción de "unidad en la diversidad" corresponde un sujeto (una persona) capaz de potenciar la pluralidad y las identidades queer. A la noción de "indisociabilidad del amor y la libertad" corresponde un sujeto (una persona) capaz de superar los estereotipos de género y la falsa libertad individualista. Y finalmente, a la noción de "metanoia" corresponde un sujeto (una persona) capaz de entender y de llevar a cabo una revolución permanente. Esta puede ser una contribución teológica cristiana a un cambio social urgente y necesario. Una contribución teológica basada en el evangelio que, lejos de ser exclusivista, se reconoce en diálogo con todas las corrientes de pensamiento que sienten como propias las exigencias de justicia de los pobres.

"Fake democracies" are systems of governance that allow their citizens to vote, but then lack effective controls to avoid that those elected legislate and rule against the interests or even against the explicit will of the majority. This is a complex phenomenon present in western capitalist societies at the turn of the 21st century that needs to be studied carefully. In this article, I analyze the theological notions of co-creation, unity in diversity, inseparability of love and freedom, and metanoia, in order to emphasize their potential for grounding a notion of person able to carry on the political changes needed to transform fake democracies into true ones. To the notion of "co-creation" corresponds a subject (a person) able to assume political responsibility at the individual and at the collective level. To the notion of "unity in diversity" corresponds a subject (a person) able to foster plurality and queer identities. To the notion of "inseparability of love and freedom" corresponds a subject (a person) able to overcome gender stereotypes and false individualistic freedom. And finally, to the notion of metanoia corresponds a subject (a person) able to understand and to carry on a permanent revolution. This can be a Christian theological contribution to a necessary and urgent social change. A theological contribution inspired in the gospel that, far from being exclusivist, understands itself as being in dialogue with all other currents of thought that feel as their own the pleas for justice of the poor.

"Scheindemokratien" sind Regierungssysteme, die zwar ihren Bürgern und Bürgerinnen das Wahlrecht zugestehen, aber dann nicht die Kontrollsysteme haben, um zu verhindern, dass die Gewählten gegen die Interessen oder sogar gegen den expliziten Willen der Mehrheit Gesetze erlassen und herrschen. Dieses komplexe Phänomen ist in westlichen kapitalistischen Gesellschaften an der Wende zum 21. Jahrhundert zu finden und muss sorgfältig untersucht werden. In diesem Beitrag analysiere ich die theologischen Begriffe der Teilhabe an der Schöpfung, der Einheit in Vielfalt, der Untrennbarkeit von Liebe und Freiheit und der Metanoia (Umkehr), um ihr Potential für die Begründung eines Konzepts von Person zu betonen, das die politischen Veränderungen tragen kann, die notwendig sind, um Scheindemokratien in wirkliche zu verwandeln. Dem Begriff der "Teilhabe an der Schöpfung" korrespondiert ein Subjekt (eine Person), das politische Verantwortung auf dem individuellen und kollektiven Niveau übernehmen kann. Dem Begriff "Einheit in Vielfalt" korrespondiert ein Subjekt (eine Person), das Pluralität und queere Identitäten fördern kann. Dem Begriff "Untrennbarkeit von Liebe und Freiheit" korrespondiert ein

Subjekt (eine Person), das Geschlechterstereotype und falsche individualistische Freiheit überwinden kann. Und dem Begriff Metanoia korrespondiert schließlich ein Subjekt (eine Person), das eine permanente Revolution verstehen und tragen kann. Dies kann ein christlich-theologischer Beitrag zu einer notwendigen und dringenden sozialen Veränderung sein. Ein theologischer Beitrag inspiriert vom Evangelium, das – weit davon entfernt, exklusivistisch zu sein – sich als im Dialog mit allen anderen Denkströmen versteht, die das Flehen der Armen um Gerechtigkeit als ihr eigenes empfinden.

Teresa Forcades i Vila is a specialist in Internal Medicine (SUNY 1995) and a theologian (Harvard 1997). She has a doctorate in Public Health (University of Barcelona 2004) and a doctorate in Fundamental Theology (FTC Barcelona 2008). Since 1997, she has been a Benedictine nun in the mountain monastery of Sant Benet de Montserrat (Spain).

Journal of the European Society of Women in Theological Research 22 (2014) 69-92.
doi: 10.2143/ESWTR.22.0.3040791

Janet R. Jakobsen[1]

Visions of Justice: New Economies and Solidarities

Movements for justice have been common in the first decades of the twenty-first century, including movements like "social justice feminism" or "environmental justice", that connect broad visions of justice to specific issues like feminism, environmentalism or anti-racism. But when movement actors or their academic counterparts invoke "justice", what precisely do they mean? What kinds of justice can currently be envisioned and how do such visions enable action? Several of the contributors to this volume advocate for a connection of feminist concerns, as expressed in the work of the ESWTR, to a vision of economic justice, and I whole-heartedly agree with this project.[2] The question that I take up in this essay is how do we give content to this vision, and how do we do so in a way that is realizable in action?

My hope to explore "visions of justice" in this essay comes out of my current book project entitled, "Why Sex?: A Queer Ethics of Possibility". The book takes up feminist and queer theory as a means of shifting the ethics and politics of gender and sexuality, and it also tackles broader sets of social relations, including those of political economy. The part of my book from which I draw this essay is based on four collaborative projects that have been done at the Barnard Center for Research on Women in recent years, projects on the relations among gender, sexuality and economic justice, on the politics

---

[1]   This article is based on a paper I presented at the conference of the European Society of Women in Theological Research in Dresden in 2013. I was quite honored to be invited to speak with the ESWTR and would like to thank the conference organizers, particularly Ulrike Auga and Cornelia Mugge, who responded to every contingency with aplomb. And I would also like to thank everyone who did the work of translation when I presented this paper at the ESWTR conference in Dresden, which is particularly demanding intellectual labor, and I appreciate the ways in which they have enabled us literally to speak with each other. It was a real pleasure to listen to the papers presented at the conference and to see the wonderful work that ESWTR is doing.

[2]   See, for example, the contributions by Kwok Pui-Lan and Joerg Rieger in this volume.

of domestic work and the context of neoliberalism.[3] All of these projects are available on the BCRW website.

These projects bring together activists and scholars, because our hope is always to create knowledge that can be of use to the realization of social justice feminism. Thus, they involve collaborations with activist organizations like Domestic Workers United (DWU) and Queers for Economic Justice (QEJ). Here, I am interested in how we might tie queer and feminist visions of justice to the economic justice that organizations like DWU and QEJ advocate. Different visions of justice are not always brought together, but gender justice and economic justice are intimately related. In fact, intimate relations represent one of the types of social relation that constitute political economy.

In the intimacy of my own life, the question of how domestic work gets done became particularly apparent when my lover, Christina, was injured in a bicycle accident that produced a spinal cord injury and resulting paralysis. Immediately after her accident – now more than ten years ago – I found myself utterly overwhelmed by questions of caring labor. In this moment of crisis I was sustained by a network of relations that might be called queer. To take just one example from that experience, over the five months that Christina was in the hospital, I was literally fed, and perhaps more importantly, our dog was regularly walked and fed, by a network of people who were certainly not my kin and who, as a group, met none of the usual definitions of a "community".

---

[3] The first, "Towards a Vision of Sexual and Economic Justice", was done in collaboration with Political Scientist Kate Bedford of the University of Kent as the lead researcher and involved an international team of about 30 scholars and activists, including Josephine Ho from the National Central University of Taiwan and Canadian journalist Naomi Klein (http://bcrw. barnard.edu/publications/towards-a-vision-of-sexual-and-economic-justice/, 25 March 2014). The next project was done with the local, community-based organization in New York, Queers for Economic Justice. The products of this project were a report by QEJ called, "Desiring Change", (http://bcrw.barnard.edu/publications/desiring-change/, 25 March 2014) and an issue of BCRW's webjournal, called "A New Queer Agenda" (http://sfonline.barnard.edu/a-new-queer-agenda/, 25 March 2014), which as the title suggests is a collection of essays considering what a queer agenda "beyond same-sex marriage" (which was the title of an earlier project by QEJ) might look like. The next was a project with Domestic Workers United, another community-based organization in New York and the U.S. national organization, the National Domestic Workers Association, called "Valuing Domestic Work", (http://bcrw.barnard.edu/publications/nfs-valuing-domestic-work/, 25 March 2014). The most recent is another scholarly collaboration with lead researcher Elizabeth Bernstein, on "Gender, Justice, and Neoliberal Transformations" that brings together another transnational research team to do some comparative and synthetic work on the meaning of neoliberalism (http://sfonline.barnard.edu/gender-justice-and-neoliberal-transformations/, 25 March 2014).

Many of these people I had never met, and some of them I still have not met. Because I was at the hospital all day through the fall and winter, they would simply drop food off on the back porch of the house, and I would eat it when I came home that night. Some of them were Christina's friends and colleagues, a work community and network with which we are familiar in academic circles. And some of them might be said to be members of the often-invoked "gay and lesbian community": the local lesbian ob-gyn, who I had once met, and the local crew coach, who I did not meet until much later, but who in the course of lesbian life in a relatively small city heard of our plight, and each pitched in. Some were members of Christian and Jewish congregations to which Christina's friends and colleagues belonged, but who did not know us personally. Some were simply friends of friends or people who had faced similar crises and knew what was needed or people with particular skills or a particular love of dogs. In other words, Babe the dog and I were sustained not by a community – a religious congregation or community defined by institutions of employment – but a network of people who came to their contributions and connections through various means. Since that moment of initial hospitalization, the network has expanded to include paid caregivers, my friends and colleagues and a range of disability support services and social movements. This queer network allowed Christina to recover to the point where she returned to work halftime and for us to build a life that is rich and sustaining in many ways. And while these relational networks may become most visible in extreme contexts, they may also form a crucial part of how people sustain each other in various circumstances.

Because these queer relations do not fit usual definitions of "family" and "community", they fall outside of traditional understandings of both politics and economics, despite their importance to life possibilities. Even when the various forms of care provided in such networks of relation are "economic" in the sense that they involve paid labor, that labor often takes place in grey economies, involving cash exchanges but few benefits, and often outside the realm of legal labor protections. Because these relations are intimate, they are rarely valued in the same way as publically meaningful work is valued – and this de-valuing remains true even when payment is involved. As the Filipina migrant workers organization, DAMAYAN, points out, domestic work is the labor "that makes all work possible", and yet it is valued at the level of an afterthought.[4] Moreover,

---

[4] DAMAYAN Migrant Workers Association & The Urban Justice Center with the assistance of Ninotchka Rosca, "Doing the Work that Makes All Work Possible: A Research Narrative of

the intimate and household relations that make all work possible are rarely taken up by progressive organizations in their visions of justice. Not only was Karl Marx unable to work out a full theoretical inclusion of these relations, creating what Heidi Hartmann diagnosed so long ago as the "unhappy marriage of Marxism and feminism", but labor unions have been slow to take up organizing with domestic workers, and radical movements for economic justice all too often ignore, or even denigrate, both household and queer relations, like those that sustained Christina and me.[5]

Just before Christina got hurt, I had been working with the American Academy of Religion's Committee on the Status of Women in the Profession (SWIP) on the issues surrounding what's frequently called "work-family balance". We set up childcare at the annual meeting and looked at other policies that might make it easier to participate fully in the profession and maintain a family life. I had always found it a little odd that these tasks had become part of my portfolio, since I have long participated in the feminist and queer critique of "family" as a category of social policy, but I also began to see that in fact this queer critique and the needs of those who valued, rather than criticized, the institution of the family were much more in line than one might have first guessed. As I noted in a short essay for SWIP on my experience with Christina, social supports for relations of caring and friendship are crucial whether or not one is married.[6] For those who are married such supports can relieve crucial and often crushing burdens on families and individuals within families, often particularly women. Yet, the failure to recognize these networks of relation has important consequences for social policy. As became all too clear in my own experience, these protections are vital when one lives in a formation that can be made to look like a family, and they are even more important when one does not. Healthcare policy in the United States presumes that care will be provided by families. If people with spinal cord injuries do not have families to care for them, they are often forced to live in institutional

---

Filipino Domestic Workers in the Tri-state Area," 23 October 2010. (http://www.cdp-ny.org/report/damayan_march11.pdf, 17 March 2014).

[5] See Heidi Hartmann, "The Unhappy Marriage of Marxism and Feminism: Towards a More Progressive Union," in: *Capital and Class* 3.2 (Summer 1979), 1-33. For an interesting reading of the masculinism of "old" social movements, see María Josefina Saldaña-Portillo, *The Revolutionary Imagination in the Americas and the Age of Development* (Duke University Press: Durham 2003).

[6] Janet R. Jakobsen, "Work is Not the Only Problem: How the Concept of Family Contributes to the Work-Family Dilemma," in: *Journal of Feminist Studies in Religion* 23.2 (2007), 127-48.

settings in the U.S., even though they could potentially live outside of institutionalized care.

Thus, my work in the context of BCRW with both Queers for Economic Justice and Domestic Workers United has taken on a specifically personal cast. Justice for domestic workers is central to any possibility for justice in my queer life, and I will argue here that queer justice is centrally important to any vision of justice.

How then can we make the connections between traditional feminist and queer concerns of gender, sexuality, and domestic work, on the one hand, and economic justice, on the other? One point at which to make the connections is the way in which assumptions about the material existence of human beings structure economic life. In fact, one of the contributions of the new disability studies is a renewed analytic focus on how dependence on caring relations is central to embodied life. The realities of vulnerability and dependence, rather than autonomy and independence, as central to the project of living, can be further connected to questions raised by the precarity movements against neoliberalism. These movements understand precarity as a central feature of our times and as something that intensifies human vulnerability. So, these movements provide a connecting point between an alternative vision of human being and broader questions of social justice.

Like the precarity movements, both DWU and QEJ are part of what might be called "new, new social movements" – movements like the Occupy movements that have arisen in the past 10-15 years specifically to address neoliberalism.[7] I would argue that they are also continuing the work of what used to be the new social movements – those movements of the 1960s and 1970s that were not explicitly class-based: feminism, civil rights, anti-colonial liberation movements, and gay liberation. Even in the 1960s and 1970s, there were debates over the relations between these "new social movements" and the "old" social movement organized around class. The promise of what were then seen as new movements was that they might realize visions of justice that included not just an end to the exploitation of capitalism, but also to the domination of racism, sexism, homophobia and colonialism. But, in the very naming of the movements as "new" in contrast to the "old", a split between the two was instantiated – between class-based liberation and feminist liberation,

---

[7]   See Occupy Wall Street Activists, *Occupy Wall Street Revolution Handbook* (Fixed Bay Publishing: New York 2011); Noam Chomsky, *Occupy* (Zucotti Park Press: New York 2012); and Kwok Pui-Lan / Joerg Rieger, *Occupy Religion: Theology of the Multitude* (Rowman & Littlefield: New York 2013).

for example. A correlative split was established between the injustices that these movements addressed, so that exploitation and domination became two separate issues. These divisions are imbricated with others – between rights and recognition, culture and the social, the personal and the political – all of which undercut possibilities for movements that can successfully create justice in terms of either political economy or intimate relations.

Movements: Their Histories and Possibilities

The project of rethinking how we conceptualize social movements has been taken on in a number of scholarly fields of late. For example, one of the recent innovations in the historiography of the civil rights movement in the United States has been to speak of the "long civil rights" movement. August 28, 2013 was an important day in the United States because it was the 50th Anniversary of the March on Washington for Jobs and Freedom at which Martin Luther King, Jr. gave the "I Have a Dream" speech. In rethinking the civil rights movement in the United States, scholars have been looking to precursors to the movement even before key moments like the March on Washington in 1963.

The usual way of telling the narrative of the civil rights movement is to begin in 1954 with the U.S. Supreme Court decision in *Brown v. Board of Education* that declared segregation in U.S. public schools to be unconstitutional, or with the 1955 Bus Boycott in Montgomery, Alabama, a boycott that famously began when Rosa Parks refused to give up her seat to a white person and move to the back of the bus.[8] This movement is generally seen to last through the 1963 March on Washington for Jobs, Peace and Justice, the passage of the Civil Rights Act in 1964 and the Voting Rights Act in 1965 (a Supreme Court decision this year overturned a major component of the Voting Rights Act and I will return to that point later), and until the assassination of Dr. Martin Luther King, Jr. in 1968.

The proponents of the "long civil rights" movements look to those people and actions that made the signal victories in Little Rock and Montgomery, the Civil Rights Act and the Voting Rights Act, possible.[9] They look to the labor activism of the 1930s as central to the possibilities for civil rights struggle in

---

[8] This is the version of the story told in the popular "Eyes on the Prize" series on the Public Broadcasting System (PBS). Juan Williams, *Eyes on the Prize: America's Civil Rights Years, 1954-1965* (Penguin Books: New York 1987).

[9] The Long Civil Rights Movement (LCRM) Project is based at the University of North Carolina and has sponsored archival work, as well as books and conferences in order to develop this

the 1950s and 1960s, and they look to the intertwining of civil rights and feminism. Feminist movements and anti-racist movements in the United States have been complexly intertwined since the nineteenth century, in ways that were both mutually supportive and deeply antagonistic. And these movements continued to develop together after 1968. Scholars like Roderick Ferguson have shown how thinking about the movements that proceed from 1968, including anti-colonial and queer movements, along with feminist and anti-racist movements is crucial to our understanding of social possibilities today.[10] For my purposes in this essay, the broader history of intertwined movements provides a way of linking visions of queer and economic justice that would simply not be visible if we began with the usual story of separate movements.

In other words, one of the reasons it is so hard to bring together different social movements is that we have told the story of these movements *as if* they are separate movements that *then* have to be put together. And in telling the story of separate movements, we have extracted from each the elements that might tie them together, thus removing the very foundation on which connections might be built. And, we also ignore the ways in which conflicts among movements have constituted those movements we now understand as "feminist" or "anti-racist". In other words, we fail to trace how racism within feminism and sexism within anti-racist movements helped to make the movements that may now seem difficult to connect. If, instead, we begin at the historical points of connection we have something on which to base a joint project.

For example, if we look at the Montgomery Bus Boycott through this new lens, what we find is that feminism, and specifically domestic workers, were absolutely central to the project of civil rights activism. It was no accident that Rosa Parks provided the spark for the boycott with her arrest. Specifically, as historian Danielle McGuire traces in her recent book, *At The Dark End of the Street: Black Women, Rape and Resistance: A New History of the Civil Rights Movement from Rosa Parks to the Rise of Black Power*, Parks had been involved in campaigns against sexual violence for years before the bus boycott.[11] In the

---

framework for the history of civil rights in the United States. See the LCRM Project website: https://lcrm.lib.unc.edu/voice/works/.

[10] See Roderick A. Ferguson, "The Historiographical Operations of Gay Rights," in: Robert Leckey (ed.), *After Legal Equality: Family, Sex, Kinship* (Routledge: New York forthcoming).

[11] See Danielle McGuire, *At The Dark End of the Street: Black Women, Rape and Resistance: A New History of the Civil Rights Movement from Rosa Parks to the Rise of Black Power* (Knopf: New York 2010).

mid-1940s, Parks was sent by the NAACP branch for which she worked to investigate a brutal rape in Abbeville, Alabama committed by seven white men who would have remained in the community with impunity had it not been for the actions of Parks and her fellow organizers. Campaigns to end violence against women were part of the necessary groundwork for the movement that followed and women organizers and feminist issues remained central as what is generally thought of as the civil rights movement got underway.

A significant proportion of the users of the Montgomery city buses were domestic workers, African American women who travelled from their homes in the segregated parts of the city to work in white homes and returned by bus at the end of each day. When these women stopped riding the buses in what was supposed to be a 24-hour boycott but turned into a year-long action, they literally broke the chokehold of not just the Montgomery bus company but of segregation in Montgomery. It is not wrong that we remember Martin Luther King Jr., who was a young pastor in Montgomery at the time and whose church organizing, preaching, and speeches, helped to maintain the boycott over the arduous year of action. But, if we forget about these women – the domestic workers – who were the ones carrying out the action, sometimes walking for miles both to and from work each day, while also carrying out the physical demands of domestic work and of caring for their own families, then we forget two things: 1) the women who were heroes of the civil rights movement; and 2) the ways in which women in an occupation that is specifically gendered as female – domestic work – and that is done in the United States predominantly by women of color, were the actors who propelled the boycott and much of the movement that followed to success.

If, however, we look at the long civil rights movement, the one stretching back to the anti-violence organizing of the 1940s and before that, then its relation to what we might call the long feminist movement also begins to look different. We can see that it is not just that women were central to the civil rights movement, although that is an important point in itself, but that feminist concerns – specifically gendered and racialized violence, as well as stratification in labor and segregation in housing – were very much a part of what civil rights was about. And, similarly, feminism does not just include women of color, but concerns about racism and its impact on women and on the gendered division of labor, are central to feminism as a movement. This alternative understanding of social movements has implications for how we understand possibilities for justice today.

For example, producing a full understanding of economic justice in the contemporary moment requires a connected analysis of sexism and racism, as well as of the ways in which a service economy enables contemporary neoliberal economic practices and policies. As Saskia Sassen has argued persuasively, the service economy – and the forms of life it enables in what has been termed the private sphere – is crucial to the possibility of the global city and its economic base in finance capitalism.[12] An analysis that centers not just on domestic life, but on domestic *work* can help us to understand the ways in which public and private spheres are intertwined and interdependent. Thus, a vision of justice that includes possibilities for both new economies and new solidarities can be built in part through overcoming divisions in both scholarly analysis and movement practice among gender, sexuality, race, and nation.

And as I noted at the beginning, one of the contributions made by specifically queer movements is a vision of possibilities for alternative relationality. LBGT people have often developed such networks out of a desire for a different, more just life – what QEJ focuses on as a "desire for change". And although these possibilities were developed in queer settings, they are not specific to gay and lesbian, bisexual and transgender people, but can make contributions to broader movements for social justice.

Connecting Movements, Assembling Justice

If, then, we hope for a feminist and queer vision of economic justice, we need an analysis that connects economics with gender, sexuality, race, and nation. One way to explore these relationships is through the concept of "assemblage", because it allows for a dynamic approach to how social relations work together. I have been influenced by Jasbir Puar's convincing use of a Deleuzian version of assemblage in her book, *Terrorist Assemblages*, and also by Annemarie Mol's version of assemblage as detailed in *The Body Multiple*.[13] Mol works within the Actor-Network-Theory school of thought to produce an ethnography of the disease atherosclerosis. By carefully documenting her observations of atherosclerosis in different settings, Mol shows that the disease is different if one is in the clinic listening to descriptions of symptoms, or if

---

[12] See Saskia Sassen, *The Global City: New York, London, Tokyo* (Princeton University Press: Princeton 2001), especially chapters 8-9.

[13] See Annemarie Mol, *The Body Multiple: Ontology in Medical Practice* (Duke University Press: Durham 2003); and Jasbir Puar, *Terrorist Assemblages: Homonationalism in Queer Times* (Duke University Press: Durham 2007).

one is in the operating room creating openings for the patient's veins, or if one is in the lab measuring the width of the veins. These differences create divergent versions of the disease – the symptoms might not be of the relative severity that would be indicated by lab results; or they may be more severe and not relieved by surgery; or the surgeon may well be surprised by what the lab reports from its tests. Mol then shows the various epistemological mechanisms by which these ontologically discontinuous versions of the disease are made to line up. Through each of these mechanisms, one indicator – symptoms, surgery, lab tests – becomes the leading indicator in relation to which others are brought into line. Mol suggests that a more accurate rendering of the disease would acknowledge the multiple realities of illness. It is true that the disease exists in the body of one person – but that body is multiple: it suffers pain, has blockages, might or might not be helped by surgery.

This view of how divergent realities are brought together in an assemblage that makes up the human body – in which these different realities can be divergent and yet also inter-related – is also helpful in thinking about the social body. The helpfulness of the concept of assemblage is that it gives a sense of dynamism to an analysis of social relations. In particular, the idea of assemblage allows for an analysis that tracks shifts among the different relations that make up an assemblage, and in so doing shows how this motion enables the assemblage as a whole to hold together.

There are two mechanisms that are important. One is the mechanism of lifting specific relations out of the assembled social fabric *as if* they are singular sets of relations – treating gender or race or sexuality or class *as if* they are not constituted in and through other social differences. The narrative of a singular civil rights movement that is not constituted in relation to labor organizing or women's issues would be an example of this mechanism at work.

The second mechanism is shifting amongst these relations in a way that strengthens the assemblage as a whole. Take, for example, the ways in which neoliberalism is enacted through interrelated binary oppositions: the rationalization for neoliberal privatization depends not only on the public/private opposition, but also on an opposition between the supposed benefits of efficiency offered by market forces and the presumed inefficiency of government bureaucracies. These oppositions are mobilized to enable the movement of resources from liberal to neoliberal institutions, to make it seem rational, and even natural, to move formerly public undertakings, such as schools and prisons, into corporate enterprises. For-profit schools are thought, for example, to be able to provide a better education for less money because market competition among providers allows parents to choose the better school for their children and the profit motive leads to containment of costs. This logic connects "privatization" to "marketization". The public/private dichotomy becomes intertwined with a divide between government and the market and is, then, further connected to the opposition between inefficient and efficient. "Private" is now made the equivalent of the market, which is presumed to be efficient, while "public" is governmental and inefficient. One can begin to see how effective the rhetoric enabled by these binary networks might be. If public is the same as governmental and inefficient, then it becomes all too easy for people to see government as also tyrannous and wasteful.

The assemblage formed by these relations allows for dynamic movement among the different oppositions so as to bolster the privatization logic at its weak points. When people question the idea of moving "public goods" into the "private sphere", the idea of the market as more efficient than government is brought in to provide the justification for the move. In fact, however, much of what is understood to be privatization is not a move toward market competition but is, instead, a use of public funds for private profit. And this profit is enabled precisely by the absence of market competition. Instead of a competitive marketplace, government contracts and funds may well go to those with connections to government officials, without the type of competition that is supposed to create efficiencies. (Whether competition does create efficiencies is another question.) The tight connections that make neoliberalism seem natural begin to unravel when the link is severed between the binaries like those of public/private and government/market.

This type of movement amongst sets of social relations, as described by the concept of assemblage, shows how hegemony is maintained *both* through the disjunction amongst relations *and* through the ways in which those relations are brought together. For example, the progress narrative that is so central to telling the story of U.S. social movements depends on the impression that issues are resolved one at a time and that this singular resolution is part of a long march of progress, an expansion of democracy within the United States. This becomes obvious in the recent series of Supreme Court rulings that came out in the week of June 24, 2013 on Affirmative Action, same-sex marriage and the Voting Rights Act. These cases are generally treated as a series of singular decisions, but I would like to suggest that they are actually about the interrelation among issues.

The first of these cases, on affirmative action at the University of Texas (*Fisher v. University of Texas, Austin*), focused on the constitutionality of taking race into account as part of a process of determining admission to the

University. In this case, a young white woman who had been denied admission sued the University, claiming that race-based admissions standards had unfairly denied her access.[14] In this case, the Court did not strike down any and all references to race in admissions policies, but argued if such policies are used, they should be subject to particularly "strict scrutiny" by the Courts. The result was that the Supreme Court sent the University of Texas program that was under consideration back to the lower court to be re-reviewed in relation to these stricter standards. This decision left open the possibility of affirmative action policies that would overcome the bar of strict scrutiny, but the decision also made it more difficult for university affirmative action programs to be acceptable in the eyes of the court system in the United States. Although this decision allowed affirmative action policies to continue for the moment to be part of university admissions policies, the decision had several effects beyond the immediate question of whether such policies had been "struck down".

As commentators both before and after the decision repeatedly pointed out, this decision provided a sense in which supposedly "race-neutral" means of ensuring fairness in university admissions could address diversity, but could do so through class-, rather than race-consciousness.[15] For example, policy institutes like the Washington think tank, The Century Fund, have recently advocated class-based approaches to university admissions, like "new admissions preferences to low-income and working-class students of all races", as better than those focused on race. My point here is not that class is not crucial in thinking about fairness and the university – the university is, after all, one of the fundamental institutions for class sorting in the United States. Rather, my point is that the way in which university admissions policies have worked in the United States is in and through the *intertwining* of class and race. The institution of the GI Bill after the Second World War, for example, was a major shift in class relations, allowing for massive class mobility as returning soldiers who could not have afforded college without government aid became

---

[14] We should note here that historically affirmative action in both college admissions and employment has focused on gender, as well as race, and that both access to college education and to professional employment have increased most for white women in the period since the institution of such policies. Sally Kohn, "Affirmative Action Has Helped White Women More Than Anyone," in: *Time*, 17 June 2013. (http://ideas.time.com/2013/06/17/affirmative-action-has-helped-white-women-more-than-anyone/, 25 February 2014).

[15] Richard D. Kahlenberg, "A Better Affirmative Action: State Universities that Created Alternatives to Racial Preferences," *The Century Foundation*. (http://tcf.org/assets/downloads/tcf-abaa.pdf, 25 February 2014).

students by the millions. But this was also a moment of affirmative action for white people: because the military had been racially segregated, the vast majority of beneficiaries of this policy were white people. In fact, it was a moment in which various Americans who had not previously understood themselves to be white – Italian Americans, Irish Americans, even my father and his Norwegian relatives – became white.[16] This intertwining of class-mobility, ethnic mobility and racial segregation is what solidified post-war white supremacy in the United States and made the civil rights movement – with its focus on ending legal segregation – necessary in the decades that followed.

In the current moment, the continuation of segregation in housing, combined with the policy of neighborhood school districts and the funding of schools through property taxes, means that schooling also continues to be one of the primary means of perpetuating *both* income inequality and white supremacy. Whites, even if not well-off, are more likely to be able to attend good primary schools and thus to have the credentials for good colleges and universities. They are more likely, for example, to live in highly segregated states in the middle of the country, with relatively well-funded public schools. In its decision on affirmative action, the Supreme Court not only bypassed the history of legal segregation, it utterly ignored the fact of continued segregation.

Those who argue that it is enough to focus on class in university admissions are also reinforcing the narrative that race is no longer relevant and all that matters is the distribution of goods. It sounds much more generous to offer something to "low-income and working-class students of all races", than to remain committed to racial "preferences". Why wouldn't this approach make sense? And yet, this commitment separates the history of denying rights to people of color from the effects of this history in the continuing unequal distribution of goods. White people of any class are simply more likely to see themselves as students than people of color, and once admitted to universities they are more likely to be treated as if they belong there. As Patricia Williams so eloquently said when discussing the possibility of this Supreme Court decision in *The New York Times*:

> The latest attestation to [wealth's] miraculous salutary power is the assertion that African-Americans who would but barricade themselves within a wall of middle-classness will be structurally exempted from racial resentments. According to this

---

[16] See Noel Ignatiev, *How the Irish Became White* (Taylor & Francis: New York 1996); and Ira Katznelson, *When Affirmative Action Was White: An Untold History of Racial Inequality in Twentieth-century America* (W.W. Norton & Company: New York 2006).

logic, when comfortably situated black people move into all-white areas, the neighbors will be delighted; property values will rise; police will not stop and frisk their children on their way to school; the neighborhood watch will not follow them about and demand to know their business [...] And of course a rich black person who gets good grades and becomes editor of the Harvard Law Review and is elected president of the United States will be regarded as the embodied American Dream. No one will ever say that Harvard isn't what it used to be, or that standards must have been lowered for him to rise so high [...] Yes, it is true that money can mitigate some of the effects of structural bias; it is a blessing to eat, to have shelter. At the same time, it is as silly to argue that prejudice against African-Americans doesn't exist beyond the wealth gap as it is to say that there is no glass ceiling for women, no backlash against Asians, no resentment of Jews, no harmful confusions about Islam. Our careful commitment to affirmative action – in law, in politics, in life – must be expanded not contracted. The world is too complex for our remediative aspirations to be limited by the crass metric of priced people.[17]

The switch from race to class advocated by commentators like those at the New Century Fund is the type of movement amongst elements in an assemblage that allows for the overall maintenance of hegemonic relations. It enables a narrative in which the march of progress in the United States has effectively brought racism to a close. Racism is over. Take, for example, the public reactions to President Obama's very personal statement of his own experiences of racism in response to the not-guilty verdict in the case of the shooting of Trayvon Martin, an unarmed African American teenager who was stalked and shot by a member of the Neighborhood Watch in the housing complex where his father lived. One public response as quoted in the newspaper *USA Today* was that even by speaking of racism in his own experience, Obama was "fanning the flames; it's time to move on."[18] Racism is so over that a public official, like the first Black President of the United States, should not even talk about it publically anymore.

---

[17] Patricia J. Williams, "Racism Remains Alive and Well," Room for Debate, in: *The New York Times*, 13 May 2013. (http://www.nytimes.com/roomfordebate/2013/05/13/can-diversity-survive-without-affirmative-action/we-need-race-based-affirmative-action, 25 February 2014).

[18] "A Post-racial America? Your Say," in: *USA Today*, 22 July 2013. (http://www.usatoday.com/story/opinion/2013/07/22/barack-obama-trayvon-martin-george-zimmerman-verdict-your-say/2576111/, 25 March 2014); and Catalina Camia, "GOP Rep on Zimmerman Verdict: Get Over It," in: *USA Today*, 17 July 2013. (http://www.usatoday.com/story/news/politics/2013/07/16/zimmerman-trial-trayvon-martin-andy-harris/2521823/, 25 March 2014).

My point here is twofold: 1) the idea that the elements of an assemblage, such as the structure of privilege in the United States, which is made up of race, class, rights and goods, are separable, helps to facilitate the maintenance of the injustice that their connection perpetuates. For example, because race is treated as separable from class, the continued, material effects of racism are harder to address, to describe or even to speak of in public; and 2) this kind of shifting among elements in an assemblage allows for an appearance of mobility – progress on race relations, for example – while the fundamental social relations of domination and oppression remain the same. A colleague of mine once asked, "why is the world self-correcting for patriarchy?". And the answer is: because social relations can change in constricted ways while remaining fundamentally the same. This type of change is effectively mobility for stasis.

Thus, it is not separability alone that reinforces domination. Race and class are not simply the same thing. As Williams points out, race has effects that extend beyond class, just as class has effects that extend beyond race. But the two are intertwined and they are intertwined in a dynamic fashion. An analysis that only understands interrelation in static terms will be insufficient to the workings of hegemony.

Importantly, because the Supreme Court of the United States has been such an important player in the narrative of historical progress, it can use this very narrative of progress as the basis on which to halt movements for rights. On Tuesday, June 25, 2013 the Court handed down a decision on the Voting Rights Act (*Shelby County v. Holder*) that was based on the idea that racism was over, and federal oversight of voting laws was no longer necessary. The federal government could choose to renew its oversight, but the Court knew perfectly well that a Congress that passed fewer pieces of legislation in its first year than any previous session of the U.S. Congress was hardly going to come together to act on this highly charged terrain.[19] Effectively, even if not technically, the Voting Rights Act has been gutted and the reasoning is that racism just doesn't matter anymore. The majority decision argued that because voting rights had been extended decades before, there was no longer any evidence for the contemporary existence of the type of racism that had led to the need for federal oversight of voting in those formerly confederate states that had

---

[19] Jonathan Weisman, "Underachieving Congress Appears in No Hurry to Change Things Now," in: *The New York Times*, 2 December 2013. (http://www.nytimes.com/2013/12/03/us/politics/least-productive-congress-on-record-appears-in-no-hurry-to-produce.html, 25 March 2014).

essentially denied voting rights to African Americans in the past. If the June 24 decision on affirmative action is part of a larger argument based on the idea that racism is over and we should instead focus on remedying the inequities of class, then the voting rights decision released on June 25 took this argument a step further to claim that remedies for racism that have been provided by the Court system in the U.S. may no longer be necessary at all.

And then, on Wednesday, June 26, 2013 came the decision on "same-sex marriage" striking down the Defense of Marriage Act (DOMA) (*U.S. v. Windsor*) and refusing to rule on California's Proposition 8 (*Hollingsworth v. Perry*), thus allowing the earlier Court ruling invalidating it to stand and marriage in California to return to legal standing. And, so we have the march of democracy in the United States: first the U.S. did away with racism and now it is doing away with discrimination against homosexuality.[20] In the narrative of the march of progress "gay rights" are connected to other civil rights, but only as separate steps on the path toward full democracy. If we fail to analyze them together, then the fight against gay rights can be the "civil rights" issue of the moment and it can replace the fight against racism. This is a problem on two counts: 1) gay rights is being used to enforce the idea that racism is, indeed, over, a thing of the past, not a living, breathing, gun-toting undertaking of the present; and 2) now that marriage has supposedly become legal – even though officially the battle was simply returned from the federal level to the states – gay rights will also be declared over. And anything else that might be associated with gay rights – protection against employment discrimination, for example – will be unnecessary: it's time to move on.

Taken together, this set of cases, released three days in a row, produces an overarching narrative: despite the direct hits that were taken by the cause of civil rights, we are to think that progress marches on. By shifting among class, race, and sexuality, the component parts of the assemblage come together to produce the hegemonic social fabric, and they do so precisely because of their discontinuities. Because race and class can be distinguished from and even opposed to each other, they become interdependent parts of a narrative that supports race *and* class dominance. Sexuality is brought into play in a way that effectively indicates that despite a major setback to the civil rights struggle,

---

[20] Ironically, both the DOMA at the federal level and California's Proposition 8 are relatively recently imposed forms of discrimination (passed in 1996 and 2008, respectively), but they are treated as if they simply represent an anachronistic, millennially old form of discrimination that is finally being removed by an enlightened court.

on which the gay rights movement is supposedly based, progress toward democracy continues. And, indeed, on Thursday and Friday of that week in June, all of the major news outlets were talking about the historic victory for gay rights, not the historic loss for racial rights – even as several states around the country moved to change their laws in a way that would make voting more difficult for people of color.[21]

Mol's conception of a "body multiple" introduced at the beginning of this article enables conceptualization of the distinct but inseparable social relations whose dynamic interactions make up the social body as a whole. If we simply connect different sets of relations, then we fail to see how movement among them welds together the edifice for overarching dominance. And if we treat them as simply distinct, then we fail to comprehend their mutual constitution. When we put them in motion we can come to understand how, together, they build a narrative in which the United States appears to be continually making progress toward equality, and yet inequality remains a perennial fact of life.

Assembling Neoliberalism
In other words, the social body is a "body multiple", but social analysis often works through various epistemological mechanisms to hide this fact. For example, much of social theory thinks of the social body as separate spheres that are tenuously and mechanistically interrelated such as public and private spheres that are also gendered as masculine and feminine. The alternative to this separate-spheres doctrine is to see caring labor as fundamental to – as constitutive of – both state and economy. There is plenty of historical evidence for this alternative view. In fact, there are books and books on this point, written by authors who are by no means marginal, like Theda Skocpol, historical sociologist at Harvard. Despite this extensive body of scholarship, gender and sexuality never seem to move to the center of analysis. The evidence for the constitutive nature of gender and sexuality is definitively there. Skocpol for example has developed a multi-causal understanding of the development of the welfare state in relation to multiple axes of social difference.[22] Meanwhile, the historian Maureen Fitzgerald demonstrated how the welfare state and its bureaucracy grew in part through ideas about the "welfare" of Catholic children

---

[21] Brennan Center for Social Justice, "Voting Laws Roundup 2013," 9 December 2013. (http://www.brennancenter.org/analysis/election-2013-voting-laws-roundup, 25 March 2014).

[22] See Theda Skocpol, *Protecting Soldiers and Mothers: The Political Origins of Social Policy in the United States* (Belknap Press: Cambridge 1992).

that supported the practice of removing them from their homes and placing them with Protestants. In Fitzgerald's case, both the "private" sphere and religious difference are central to state-formation.[23] And the historian Marisa Chappell has demonstrated how the idea of a particular organization of gender and sexuality in terms of the "family wage" undergirded arguments on behalf of building the welfare state. Domestic work is also part of this story.[24] As Eileen Boris and Jennifer Klein argue in their recent history of home healthcare in the twentieth-century U.S., it is possible to "rethink the history of the American welfare state from the perspective of care work."[25] As Boris and Klein show in great detail, state policies, including a "state-subsidized medical sector", have produced an economy in which caring labor in public and private, institutional and home settings is a major growth industry. In other words, even when caring labor actually takes place in "private" settings, it is still fundamentally intertwined with state and economic policy.

Now, as various countries have moved from welfare state formations to neoliberalism, we must ask what role this assemblage of relations across the public-private divide has played in the development of neoliberalism. In fact, as the National Domestic Workers Alliance has argued, instead of understanding caring labor as anomalous – as a special kind of labor in the private sphere – we could understand it as the model for precarious labor under neoliberalism.[26] If Sassen is right that service work is the material base for the new economy, then domestic workers are indeed at the center of this new social formation. Unlike the paradigmatic factory worker of the industrial economy, the domestic worker is a service worker who often finds work through transnational migration and labors under conditions of great vulnerability. As even professional jobs move toward consulting and freelancing done on a job-by-job basis and often across borders, the conditions of labor for domestic workers are extending to broader swaths of the economy as a whole. Moreover, caring labor – both in families and in the market – is central

---

[23] See Maureen Fitzgerald, *Habits of Compassion: Irish Catholic Nuns and the Origins of New York's Welfare System, 1830-1920* (University of Illinois Press: Champagne 2006).

[24] See Marisa Chappell, *The War on Welfare: Family, Politics and Poverty in Modern America* (University of Pennsylvania Press: Philadelphia 2011).

[25] Eileen Boris / Jennifer Klein, *Caring for America: Home Health Care Workers in the Shadow of the Welfare State* (Oxford University Press: New York 2012), 5.

[26] See Premilla Nadasen / Tiffany Williams, "Valuing Domestic Work," The Barnard Center for Research on Women, 2010. (http://bcrw.barnard.edu/wp-content/nfs/reports/NFS5-Valuing-Domestic-Work.pdf, 25 February 2013).

to the ways in which the contemporary, neoliberal state is organized. Efforts to cut the costs of care, whether those costs are borne by insurance companies or by the state, often depend on moving care from institutions like hospitals to private homes, a move that saves money in part by allowing caring labor to be done as an unpaid "labor of love" or when paid to take place in non-unionized settings with few protections for the workers. Thus, tracing the ways in which caring labor makes neoliberalism possible can help to illuminate not just how gender and sexuality are central to economic and state policy but also how a different, more just world might be created.

Importantly, an analysis that centers on domestic work and those who do it not only brings together public and private/economic and domestic spheres, but it also allows for new means of understanding the ethical values articulated by movements for social change, values like those of recognition and redistri-bution of rights and goods. Like public and private, the split between recogni-tion through civil rights and redistribution of material goods separates types of moral goods that are so valuable precisely because of the way that they are assembled together. As Patricia Williams details in the quotation above, civil rights remain important even as there is an urgent need to address material inequalities – racism has historically been powerful in the United States pre-cisely because of the combination through which it has denied recognition of fundamental personhood to people of African descent *and also* equal distribu-tion of material goods. One of the ways that racism works through the simul-taneous denial of rights and goods is by pretending that all that matters is *either* rights *or* goods. In other words, it is the discontinuities as well as the connections among gender, sexuality, race, and class, and among recognition and redistribution, rights and goods that make dominating and hegemonic social relations.

Caring labor is another site at which rights and goods are deeply tied together; not just civil rights related to race and ethnicity, but the rights of migrants to move freely across national boundaries are connected to the polit-ical economic relations that make for the goods of caring labor. Moreover, caring labor is also one of the connecting points between the increased precar-ity of individuals and families under neoliberalism and neoliberal shifts in economic and state policy. For example, in the United States, health care that was once provided in hospital settings – often in public hospitals, but sometimes also in for-profit settings – has been pushed toward private provi-sion or "at home" care. The expected hospital stay after women give birth has been reduced from nearly a week to as short a time as conceivably possible –

sometimes less than 24 hours. Hospital recovery times for serious injuries have been reduced from a matter of months to a matter of weeks. The expectation that people will now be cared for by the private individuals in their lives during relatively intense periods of recovery has been fully incorporated into the "healthcare system", as healthcare "customers" do more of the needed labor, just as customers in other industries scan and bag groceries, manage commodity orders online, and otherwise do the work of corporations. The burden on families of these increased expectations for care can be extreme. People often have to quit their jobs in order to care for family members who are ill or injured. These burdens and attendant vulnerabilities are only increased for those who – for whatever reason – do not have a "family" to fall back on. Even if one has lived in a traditional family and remained married for a lifetime, the loss of a spouse may produce intense vulnerability, unless one's children can take on new responsibilities of care or one can afford to pay wages for such help.

New Economies and Solidarities

Here we see the intersection between neoliberal political economy and the personal desires and relations that are (thought to be) appropriate to new social movements like the feminist movement. In particular, the labor done within the context of families is crucial to the neoliberal economic system as a whole. In the United States, this work is structured so that it is bound to be exploitative in some form, either as unpaid housework or as paid employment that is subject to both the race and gender segregation of the U.S. labor market and to the forces of transnational migration.[27]

In other words, domestic labor is actually not domestic. It is not domestic in either sense of the word in English – it is not contained within the private sphere of the home, and neither is it contained within the boundaries of the nation. Instead, it is part of (it is *constitutive* of) the international division of labor. If we put domestic work at the center of analysis, justice requires something more than the march of liberal progress; it requires transnational solidarity.

In order to illustrate some of the possibilities for such solidarity, I would like to return in conclusion to the projects recently co-sponsored by community-based organizations and the Barnard Center for Research on Women

---

[27] See Boris / Klein, *Caring for America*, 7.

(BCRW). In particular, the project with Domestic Workers United and the National Domestic Workers Alliance showed how the traditional organizing framework of civil rights in the United States was crucially important to contemporary domestic worker organizing, but also needed to be expanded. The report produced by this project provides an analysis of domestic workers' status as part of a group of workers excluded from the protections of labor law in the United States and much of the world. Through histories that deny the personhood of some workers in the United States, workers in fields like domestic work, farm work, and various forms of piecework, which are associated with slavery and immigration, have also been excluded from basic labor protections, including the right to time off and basic compensation for severance of employment. The movement shows that the effects of chattel slavery are not over, given that labor associated with slavery is not as "free" as other forms of work. Nor is the free market actually free. It does not allow for the free movement of individuals to sell their labor, but rather uses national boundaries to devalue and coerce the labor of immigrants. Even more profoundly, however, the work undertaken by domestic workers challenges the liberal humanist concept of the autonomous individual at its core.

DAMYAN's analysis of "Doing the Work that Makes All Work Possible" clarifies that the people usually recognized as autonomous individuals are not, in fact, autonomous.[28] Rather, those who historically have been able to sell their labor through protected freedoms are dependent upon forms of domestic labor provided by others, including family members and paid domestic laborers. Those who are most dependent on the service economy tend to be the very wealthy individuals who understand themselves to be both "free" and "autonomous" actors in the world. DAMAYAN's report goes on to detail the working conditions experienced by members of DAMAYAN and the ways in which the free market and the liberal myth of autonomy enforce global labor migration and exploitation.[29]

In other words, taking seriously the claims of those who do "the work that makes all work possible" requires more than an expansion of the liberal humanist social contract. It requires alternative means of providing the caring labor that all persons need. These creative responses provide a means of building all kinds of relationships that meet both needs and desires. Such creativity also provides a means of building connections across issues, as, for example,

---

[28] See DAMAYAN, "Doing the Work that Makes All Work Possible".
[29] See DAMAYAN, "Doing the Work that Makes All Work Possible", 9-11.

when healthcare, economics, and sexuality all come together at the nexus of caring labor and so-called "private life". This is also a point of potential assemblage among social movements, between feminist and queer movements – both of which consider alternatives to the privatized family life that leaves people vulnerable in the face of neoliberalism – and among feminist movements, queer movements, worker rights movements, migrant movements, precarity movements and anti-racist movements. Clearly articulating the relational basis for social justice can help us to build a scaffolding of connection and to resist divisions among those whose interests and values might be actively aligned. If I have suggested anything in this essay, I hope it is that today's world demands a vision of justice that is not universal in the liberal sense, but that is connected and engaged through a broad sense of solidarity.

"Visiones de Justicia: nuevas economías y solidaridades" considera las interpretaciones feministas y queer de la justicia en relación con la justicia económica. El ensayo se sitúa en un análisis del trabajo doméstico, teniendo en cuenta un marco de relaciones sociales que son al mismo tiempo discontinuas e interconectadas. Al colocar el trabajo doméstico en el centro de este análisis complejo, el ensayo pretende describir las relaciones entre género, sexo, raza, la nación y la economía en el contexto íntimo de las relaciones de cuidado. Con el fin de explicar la utilidad de este ensamblaje como categoría analítica, el ensayo explora tres casos resueltos por la Corte Suprema de los Estados Unidos en junio de 2013, relativo a la acción afirmativa, la protección de los derechos de voto basado en la raza, y el matrimonio entre personas del mismo sexo. Estos casos se presentaron en los medios nacionales como un ejemplo de cómo hacer frente a cuestiones diversas en una línea de progreso liberal de derechos civiles contra el racismo a los derechos civiles de los gays. La lectura de estos casos a través del concepto de ensamblaje, sin embargo, muestra las formas en que estos casos no marcan etapas separadas en el camino hacia la continua expansión de los derechos civiles, sino la ida y venida de temas relacionados que crea una sensación de movilidad, que en realidad está promoviendo el status quo hegemónico. Para contrarrestar los efectos dominantes de esas relaciones hegemónicas se requiere la creación de una solidaridad a través de estos movimientos. El activismo a favor de los derechos de los trabajadores domésticos puede ser una manera de crear esta solidaridad. El trabajo doméstico agrupa cuestiones sobre la migración transnacional, los efectos históricos de la esclavitud, el género y la sexualidad, y la economía neoliberal. Abordar estos problemas juntos es una manera de construir dos nuevas economías y nuevas solidaridades.

"Visions of Justice: New Economies and Solidarities" considers feminist and queer understandings of justice in relation to economic justice. The essay places an analysis of domestic work in the framework of an assemblage of social relations that are simultaneously discontinuous and interconnected. By placing domestic work at the center of this complex analysis, the essay describes relationships among gender, sex, race, nation, and economics in the intimate context of caring relations. In order to explain the usefulness of assemblage as an analytic category, the essay explores three cases decided by the United States Supreme Court in June of 2013, dealing with affirmative action, race-based voting rights protections, and same-sex marriage. These cases were presented in the national media as dealing with separate issues in a line of liberal progress from anti-racist civil rights to the civil rights of gay people. Reading these cases through the concept of assemblage, however, shows the ways in which these cases do not mark separate steps along a path toward ever-expanding civil rights, but rather a back and forth between related issues that creates an appearance of mobility but actually promotes the hegemonic status quo. To counter the dominating effects of these hegemonic relations requires the creation of solidarity across movements, and activism on behalf of domestic workers' rights can be a way of creating this solidarity. Domestic work brings together issues of transnational migration, the historical effects of slavery, gender and sexuality, and neoliberal economics. Addressing these issues together is one way of building both new economies and new solidarities.

"Visions of Justice: New Economies and Solidarities" denkt über das feministische und queere Verständnis von Gerechtigkeit in Bezug auf Wirtschaftsgerechtigkeit nach. Der Beitrag situiert die Analyse von Hausarbeit im Rahmen der Assemblage von sozialen Beziehungen, die gleichzeitig diskontinuierlich und verbunden sind. Indem Hausarbeit ins Zentrum dieser komplexen Untersuchung gestellt wird, beschreibt der Artikel Beziehungen zwischen Geschlecht, Sex, "Rasse", Nation und Wirtschaft im intimen Kontext von Fürsorgebeziehungen. Um den Nutzen von Assemblage als Analysekategorie zu erklären, untersucht der Beitrag drei Fälle, die im Juni 2013 vom US Supreme Court entschieden wurden und mit der Förderung von Minderheiten, Wahlrechtsschutz auf der Basis von "Rasse" und gleichge-schlechtlicher Ehe zu tun haben. Diese Fälle wurden in den US-Medien präsentiert, als ginge es um getrennte Themen in einer Linie des liberalen Fortschritts von anti-rassistischen Bürgerrechten zu den Bürgerrechten von Homosexuellen. Wenn man diese Fälle mit dem Konzept der Assemblage liest, zeigt sich dagegen, dass sie nicht einzelne Schritte auf einem Weg hin zu immer ausgedehnteren Bürgerrechten sind, sondern vielmehr ein Hin und Her zwischen zusammenhängenden Themen, das den Anschein von Mobilität schafft, aber in Wirklichkeit einen hegemonischen Status Quo fördert. Um den bestimmenden Folgen dieser hegemonischen Beziehungen entgegenzuwirken, ist die Schaffung von Solidarität quer durch Bewegungen notwen-dig, und Aktivismus zu Gunsten von Hausangestellten kann ein Weg sein, solche Solidarität zu schaffen. Hausarbeit verbindet Fragen von transnationaler Migration, den historischen Folgen von Sklaverei, Geschlecht und Sexualität mit neoliberaler

Ökonomie. Diese Fragen gemeinsam zu behandeln, ist ein Weg, um sowohl neue Ökonomien als auch neue Solidaritäten zu entwickeln.

Janet R. Jakobsen is Ann Whitney Olin Professor of Women's Gender and Sexuality Studies and Director of the Center for Research on Women at Barnard College, Columbia University. She is the author of *Working Alliances and the Politics of Difference: Diversity and Feminist Ethics* and co-author with Ann Pellegrini of *Love the Sin: Sexual Regulation and the Limits of Religious Tolerance.*

Journal of the European Society of Women in Theological Research 22 (2014) 93-104.
doi: 10.2143/ESWTR.22.0.3040792

Kwok Pui-lan

Occupy Heaven and Jesus's Movement

A Year in Revolt – 1989

In 1989, the people of East Germany rose up against the Communist regime, and held mass demonstrations that led to the fall of the Berlin Wall, a symbol of the Cold War. The disintegration of the former Soviet Union and the transformation of the Eastern Bloc drastically changed the geopolitics of the world. The collapse of the so-called Second World meant that global capital could reach further into societies that had formerly not been easily accessible. As a result of the reunification, East Germany's economy has improved, partly due to the infusion of capital from the two Solidarity Pacts offered by the German federal government. But the economic gap between eastern and western Germany is still considerable. Economic development also brought in new social issues, such as an aging population, as many young people have left East Germany for the West.

The year 1989 was a year of protest and demonstration. In China, the student-led peaceful demonstration occupied Tiananmen Square for several weeks to demand democracy, government accountability, freedom of speech, and freedom of the press. The Chinese government responded with a military crackdown, resulting in bloodshed with thousands of unarmed citizens among the casualties. In response to the student demonstration and the changes happening in the Eastern Bloc, the Chinese government hastened the liberalization process and the implementation of economic reforms. Today China is the world's second largest economy, but the gulf between prosperous cities and poor rural areas has grown considerably since the 1990s. Social inequality and government corruption are major sources of social unrest and protests.

Economic globalization has improved the livelihood of some people, but has also created a transnational capitalist class that wields enormous power in the economic, political, and cultural realms.[1] Wealth is increasingly controlled

---

[1] See Leslie Sklair, *The Transnational Capitalist Class* (Blackwell: Malden 2001).

by the international elite, while many people live below subsistence level. In China, for example, there are many millionaires and billionaires, but 13 percent of its population live on less than US$1.25 per day, according to United Nations data.[2] In the United States, the top one percent of households owned 35.4 percent of all privately held wealth in 2010, while the bottom 80 percent shared only eleven percent.[3] Such gross economic disparity and wealth concentration has been characterized as the one percent versus the 99 percent.

Following protests in northern Africa, the Middle East, and Europe, the Occupy movement started in New York in the fall of 2011 and quickly spread to more than 900 cities. "We are the 99 percent" became the rallying cry of people demanding radical changes in a global economic system dictated by Wall Street big banks and massive corporations.

Occupy Heaven and Religion

Can religion, and in particular Christianity, play a meaningful role in the promotion of social justice in solidarity with the 99 percent? Or is the Christian religion beyond rescue? There are reasons to be suspicious of religion and to have reservations. Karl Marx has famously said that religion is a false consciousness and the opium of the people. The promise of rewards in heaven can be used to justify suffering and inequality in this world. In popular belief, "heaven" connotes an otherworldly place, where God and other spiritual beings reside. But the phrase "occupy heaven" means something quite different. As used in the Occupy movement, the term "occupy" connotes "taking back what is supposed to belong to the public, so that power and wealth will be shared more equitably and not concentrated in the hands of the few."[4] Occupy heaven signals that heaven belongs to all, and cannot be dominated by a few. It challenges religious hierarchy and institutions that have domesticated the sacred and monopolized religious goods. The Lord's Prayer says, "thy kingdom come, thy will be done, on earth as in heaven." God's reign of peace and justice is intended to exist here on earth and not

---

[2]   See Sim Chi Yin, "In China, a Vast Chasm between the Rich and the Rest," in: *The New York Times*, 9 February 2013. (http://opinionator.blogs.nytimes.com/2013/02/09/in-china-a-vast-chasm-between-the-rich-and-the-rest/?_r=0, 23 September 2013).

[3]   See G. William Domhoff, "Wealth, Income, and Power," in: *Who Rules America?* (http://www2.ucsc.edu/whorulesamerica/power/wealth.html, 23 September 2013).

[4]   Joerg Rieger / Kwok Pui-lan, *Occupy Religion: Theology of the Multitude* (Rowman and Littlefield: Lanham 2012), 5.

in some faraway place. Occupy heaven means creating the social conditions and imaginary spaces so that an alternative world can be imagined and experienced.

Occupy heaven invites us to reimagine the relationship of God and politics in new ways. There are dramatic changes taking place in our world and in global Christianity: the shift of the center of gravity of Christianity to the Global South and the shift of geopolitics from the North Atlantic to the Asia-Pacific region. Christianity can no longer be viewed as the climax or the culmination of all other religions. Facing challenges and uncertainties, some Christian leaders operate in a defensive mode, reaffirming what they believe to be traditional orthodox beliefs. Christian fundamentalists of all kinds have sprung up, preaching a very conservative brand of God and politics. Many, especially in secular Europe, have left the church, dismissing religion as a relic of the past. But there are others who are developing postcolonial interpretations of the Bible and theology. The prefix "post-" does not simply mean the temporal period after colonialism, it also refers to a reading strategy and discursive practice that challenge a Eurocentric and imperialistic mindset, epistemological framework, and stereotypical representations. Postcolonial studies of religion have stimulated some of the liveliest debates in the field today.

Postcolonial theologians have pointed out that Christianity has been used to condone colonialism, slavery, racism, the subordination of women, and discrimination against lesbian, gay, bisexual, and transgender people. But the problems go much deeper in that most theology has been conceived in dominant cultures, laden with imperializing motives and structures. For example, God is often depicted as king, ruler, and lord, who can command, order, and even annihilate God's enemies. In the book *Occupy Religion*, Joerg Rieger and I write, "The deepest problem of our common images of God, supported by conservatives and liberals alike, is that images of the divine as omnipotent, impassible, and immutable tend to mirror the dominant powers that be, from ancient emperors to modern CEOs."[5] Such a God also determines who gets to go to heaven and who is condemned to hell. It is little wonder that progressive, feminist, and postcolonial theologians have all criticized this top-down understanding of God. During the Second World War, Dietrich Bonhoeffer, in his letters and papers from prison, spoke about "man come of age" and about a

---

[5] Rieger / Kwok, *Occupy Religion*, 88.

"religionless Christianity", because as mature Christians we can no longer conceive of God as either a metaphysical hypothesis or an existential stopgap.[6]

Occupy heaven means resistance against a top-down theism that is often aligned with the interests of the powerful one percent. The questions that Dorothee Soelle asked some fifty years ago are still valid today: "Why do people worship a God whose supreme quality is power, not justice; whose interest lies in subjection, not mutuality; who fears equality?"[7] For Soelle, God is not beyond and above our embodied existence, but is living and active among and between us. She critiqued thoroughly the cherished Christian notion of obedience, which she saw as the main virtue of an authoritarian religion. Instead, she argued that in the face of evil, injustice, and suffering, Christians must choose resistance and solidarity with others.[8]

The Multitude and Jesus's Movement

Occupy heaven invites us to reimagine God from the bottom up, and in the process expand our vocabularies and imagination about God and God's relation to us in the contemporary world. This requires us to look at power and politics not from the center and from the perspective of the so-called winners, but from the margin and the periphery. It is often from the margin that we can grasp most clearly the meaning and significance of the Jesus movement. When we look at Jesus's life and ministry in the Gospels, we tend to focus on Jesus's words and actions and his relationship with the disciples. Korean *minjung* theology subverts this paradigm by focusing on the *ochlos* – the crowd who followed Jesus from place to place. The term *minjung* comes from two Chinese characters, meaning the masses or the multitude. According to Korean New Testament scholar Ahn Byung Mu (1922-1996), the *ochlos* in Mark's Gospel gathered around Jesus and formed the background of his activities (Mark 2:4; 2:13; 3:9; 3:20; 3:32; 4:1; 5:21; 5:24; 5:31; 8:1; 10:1). In contrast to the ruling class from Jerusalem, the *ochlos* frequently sided with Jesus and were against the ruling class.[9] The diverse groups of Galilean *ochlos*,

---

6 Dietrich Bonhoeffer, *Letters and Papers from Prison*, ed. Eberhard Bethge (Macmillan: New York 1967, rev. ed.), 179, 196.

7 Dorothee Soelle, *Beyond Mere Obedience* (Pilgrim Press: New York 1982), xiv.

8 See Soelle, *Beyond Mere Obedience*.

9 See Ahn Byung Mu, "Jesus and the Minjung in the Gospel of Mark," in: Kim Yong Bock (ed.), *Minjung Theology: People as Subjects of History* (Commission of Theological Concerns, Christian Conference of Asia: Singapore 1981), 136-150, here 140-141.

coming from the lower class, were the audience whom Jesus's message addressed. *Minjung* theologians argue that Jesus was part of the *minjung*, and his teaching must be interpreted in the context of the social aspirations of the people.[10] The recovery of the importance of the *ochlos* in the Bible does not mean that we are trying to romanticize the multitude. After all, the crowd was stirred by the high priests to demand the release of Barabbas and to crucify Jesus (Mark 15:11-13). The consciousness of the multitude needs to be raised so that the diverse groups of people can unify to become political agents to change society and develop a broader and deeper form of solidarity.

How do we look at Jesus and his movement from the perspective of the *minjung*, the multitude of people? Since the 1960s, there has been a strong theological current called liberation theology. The Peruvian theologian Gustavo Gutiérrez offers the image of Jesus as the liberator in his classic work *A Theology of Liberation*.[11] He emphasizes that Jesus has come to bring political liberation, the liberation of human beings throughout history, the liberation from sin and communion with God. Other versions of Christ as liberator can be seen in various black theologies and feminist theologies. This conceptualization of Christ dispels the myth of a gentle and meek Jesus often preached in middle-class churches. But postcolonial theory has led me to question this masculinist portrayal of the savior who intervenes in human history, because very often a concomitant critique of such a patriarchal and heterosexist image of Christ is missing.

I have also begun to see history and politics as more than black and white and have recognized the limitations of a binary construction of oppressors and oppressed. In *The Colonizer and the Colonized*, Albert Memmi proposes that colonization is not possible without the collaboration of the colonized.[12] Today in our globalized and interlocking world, it is difficult to say where the empire begins and where it ends. We are all implicated, in one way or another, though to different degrees. There is the further question of what happens as long as the oppressed are not liberated yet? How does one live in the in-between space between the now and the not-yet?

---

[10] Kim Yong-bok, *Messiah and Minjung: Christ's Solidarity with the People for New Life* (Christian Conference of Asia: Hong Kong 1992).

[11] Gustavo Gutiérrez, *A Theology of Liberation: History, Politics, and Salvation*, trans. Caridad Inda and John Eagleson (Orbis Books: Maryknoll 1988, rev. ed.), 102-105.

[12] Albert Memmi, *The Colonizer and the Colonized*, trans. Howard Greenfeld (Orion Press: New York 1965).

Here I benefit from postcolonial theorist Homi Bhabha's discussion of the political and moral agency of the subaltern in a time of social and political transition in his lecture "The Global Measure: Writing, Rights and Responsibilities."[13] The word "subaltern" was first used in the work of Antonio Gramsci. The subalterns are the "low rank" people in a particular society who suffer under the domination of a ruling elite class, and who are socially, culturally, and politically outside the hegemonic political structure.[14] Bhabha said, "The subaltern strategy of counter-hegemonic power is replete with the nuance of the partial and the incipient. Indeed, its efficacy lies in knowing how to work with the moment of transition, how to turn the condition of historical incubation into a form of interrogation and insurgency."[15]

In the Gospels, Jesus's movement attracts a broad spectrum of people from different classes, including peasants, fishermen, tax-collectors, artisans, and women. His disciples are often portrayed as misunderstanding his mission and even obstructing what he was doing. Bhabha's description of the partial and incipient nature of subalternity offers a valuable portrayal of the Jesus movement described in the Gospels. Gramsci's subalternity recognizes the political and ethical agency below the radar of the state. Unlike movements that champion social contradictions, whose target is a nation state, subaltern movements take many forms and work to change the status quo without hegemonizing the state. Bhabha's characterization allows us to see the political and ethical agency of a wide variety of people in the Gospels, including women's agency. The Syro-Phoenician woman who came to ask Jesus to heal her daughter (Mark 7:25-30), the Samaritan woman at the well (John 4), Mary and Martha who received Jesus (Luke 10:38-42), and the woman who bled for twelve years (Mark: 5:25-34) were not members of a self-conscious movement resisting Rome. It is important to see the Jesus movement as heterogeneous and polymorphous, and not one-dimensional, to do justice to the Gospel account.

A parallel can be seen in the Occupy movement, which has attracted people from diverse backgrounds and various social strata: college students, the homeless, activists, artists, religious people, and professionals. The movement

---

[13] See Homi Bhabha, "A Global Measure: Writing, Rights, and Responsibilities," Lecture at University of California, Santa Barbara, 4 October 2004. (http://www.uctv.tv/search-details. aspx?showID=8903, 6 March 2014).

[14] See Antonio Gramsci, *Selections from the Prison Notebooks of Antonio Gramsci*, ed. and trans. Quintin Hoare and Geoffrey Nowell Smith (Lawrence and Wishart: London 1971).

[15] Bhabha, "A Global Measure."

is often called a leaderless movement, since it refused to label a few people as the designated spokespersons. It does not want to narrow its focus to a few identifiable sets of demands and goals, and there are no fixed strategies or tactics to achieve them. Instead, the Occupy movement provides a space and a forum for people of diverse interests and agendas to gather and to work together through a process of direct democracy. Similarly, the Jesus movement cannot be summarized as having only a few identifiable political goals.

But we seldom hear about the Jesus movement as a subaltern, insurgent, and incipient movement that challenges the status quo. The Christian message that we are more familiar with is an individualistic Gospel that concerns the salvation of our souls. Such a Gospel has little relevance to our daily life and to the gross inequity that plagues so much of humanity. So, are God, religion, and politics beyond rescue? This depends on why they have to be rescued in the first place. If the goal were simply to restore the cultural significance of Christianity from a bygone era, or the prestige of the church, then such a rescue would certainly have its limits. However, if the aim is to reconstruct an understanding of God and politics that promotes the subaltern's political agency, then the outcome would prove a worthwhile project. Let us not forget, religion continues to play a significant role in our world, especially in the Global South. Furthermore, with a Christian population estimated to be about 80-100 million, China is becoming a country with a significant number of Christians. Spirituality still means a lot to many people. Even in secular Europe and in many places in North America, many people say that they are spiritual, but not religious.

Occupy heaven means we reclaim the religious and spiritual resources that belong to the people in order to inspire and sustain them in the struggle for justice. For a long time, theology has been reserved for the church or the academy, and thus has become a specialized knowledge for those educated in the field. The Occupy movement challenges the boundaries between the sacred and profane, and demands that we do theology in the public square. Jesus's teaching that "it will be hard for a rich person to enter the kingdom of heaven" (Mt 19:23) and his turning the tables of the money changers at the temple (Mt 21:12) have particular relevance in a social movement against corporate greed. The Lord's Supper, as a covenantal meal, took on new meanings when shared in the Occupy campsites among the homeless, the activists, and the young people who risked civil disobedience for nonviolent social change. Doing theology in the public square means changing religious jargon and rituals to become living symbols of hope and solidarity among the people.

Many religious people who have participated in the Occupy movement said that their involvement has helped them understand that worshiping God and seeking justice are inseparable.

The belief that only Christians can go to heaven has justified cultural imperialism and narrow-minded evangelism. Occupy heaven means that Christians have no monopoly over heaven or salvation. Religious blessings, goodwill among people, and spiritually satisfying lives should be available to all. I went to see the spirituality tent at Occupy Boston and saw that religious symbols from Christian, Buddhist and other traditions were present in the tent. The tent was used for prayers, studies, and meditation led by people from different traditions. Priests, rabbis, imams, rabbinic students, and seminarians led religious rituals and provided counseling in the campsites. I interviewed Getzel Davis, a rabbinic student who helped organize and preached the sermon at the Kol Nidre service held at Yom Kippur in 2011 across Occupy Wall Street in New York. Citing the words of prophet Isaiah, he reminded the Jewish people not to confuse gold and God, citing the golden calf as an example. At Occupy Oakland in California, Jewish, Christian, and pagan religious leaders worked together to plan for the Occupy Faith National Gathering in 2012. Through these interfaith efforts, I saw the possibilities for religious people sharing their resources and working together for the common good across religious difference.

Reimagining the Church
Occupy heaven requires the development of an astute class analysis for the church. In *The Protestant Ethic and the Spirit of Capitalism*, Max Weber notes that Calvinistic ethics, with its emphasis on hard work, saving, and vocation, contributed to the rise of early capitalism.[16] Many mainline Protestant churches in western Europe and North America inherit a church model with close ties to the rising bourgeoisie. It is little wonder that many churches today function more like a middle-class club, rather than a prophetic and insurgent movement. Christian churches serve as a stabilizing force in society, helping people to cope with society rather than changing it. This is very far from the Jesus movement described in the Gospels. In order to recover its prophetic potential, the church needs to disassociate itself from this Christendom mentality, which places the church at the center rather than at the margin and aligns the church's

---

[16] See Max Weber, *The Protestant Ethic and the Spirit of Capitalism*, trans. Talcott Parsons (Scribner: New York 1958).

interest with that of the rich and the powerful.[17] The church cannot ask people to believe in the promise of heaven without creating conditions where people can have a moment to experience and have a foretaste of it.

As a leaderless movement, the Occupy movement provides an interesting example of organizing and challenges the institutional structure of the church. Very often, sacred space is associated with houses of worship, such as churches, synagogues, temples, and mosques. But the Occupy movement claimed creative use of public spaces and developed new cultural forms, including posters, slogans, songs, blogs, websites, videos, lifestreams, public lectures, street theater, and social networks. This movement challenges us to think about the church as beyond the confines of the "brick-and-mortar" and to reclaim the meaning of church as an assembly of people of God. The virtual environment also complicates the simple demarcation of the "sacred" and the "profane". When the churches turn inward to care about their survival and maintenance, God's presence is not felt even in these so-called "sacred spaces". In contrast, the presence of the divine is keenly felt in the public square when people stand shoulder to shoulder to work for justice.

Traditional religious institutions usually have a two-tier structure – the clergy or religious professionals and the people. There is a class of professionals who produce and control religious goods and services and a class of people who consume these goods. The Occupy movement's principles of direct democracy and self-organizing call into question this model of leadership. Instead of a top-down hierarchal model, it has a decentralized network that values people's participation. Some social scientists have called this a starfish organizational model.[18] The starfish does not have a brain and has no central command. For the starfish to move, one of the arms must convince the other arms that it is good to do so. In starfish-like organization, power is spread throughout and there is no central command, as members are all equal. Examples of starfish organization include the music-sharing site Napster and Wikipedia. The early church movement was more like a starfish organization. Jesus and his disciples met in people's houses, on the mountain, near the Sea of Galilee. People shared the food they brought and took care of the sick and brought them to Jesus. The Jesus movement did not have its center in one

---

[17] See Stuart Murray, *Post-Christendom: Church and Mission in a Strange Land* (Paternoster Press: Carlisle 2003).

[18] See Ori Brafman / Rod A. Beckstrom, *The Starfish and the Spider: The Unstoppable Power of Leaderless Organizations* (Portfolio: New York 2006).

location, as Jesus and his followers traveled from place to place. In the first century, women were leaders of house churches, teachers, and missionaries working along with Paul. Paul and the other leaders traveled and formed different communities and visited the small groups from time to time. When the church became more institutionalized, a top-down hierarchy replaced the loose structure of the early period, modeled more and more after the Roman bureaucracy.

If we are to imagine a church of the multitude that will embody a new relationship between God and politics, the organizational structure of the Occupy movement may have something important to offer. If the church continues to treat women as second-class citizens, discriminate against gay people and lesbians, and look down upon the lower class and people of color, it will have little credibility left to proclaim the good news.

Working with other social movements, such as the women's movement, the labor movement, and the environmental movement, the church is called to witness and bring about God's shalom. Shalom is not just the absence of war or conflict, but is concerned with justice, equity, and integrity.[19] There will be no peace if our economic system condemns so many people as "disposable" – people who are left to scramble for survival and do not benefit from the globalization process. The work of the Occupy movement is not finished, and mass uprisings continue to take place in Syria, Egypt, and Taiwan. The multitude continues to demand that their voices be heard. The church cannot work for shalom without challenging state terrorism and class warfare targeting the 99 percent. It cannot work only with people who share its values and class background, but must build coalitions with people working for other causes.

People sometimes lose heart and wonder if grassroots movements can change anything because the power of the one percent seems to be overwhelming. In Jesus's time, many people also wondered whether God's kingdom would ever arrive. The Pharisees once asked Jesus when the kingdom of God was coming. The Pharisees had in mind a kingdom bringing material benefits. Jesus gave them a surprising answer: "The kingdom of God is not coming with things that can be observed; nor will they say, 'Look, here it is!' Or 'There it is!' For in fact, the kingdom of God is among you" (Luke 17:20-21).

---

[19] See Bruce Ellis / Malinda Elizabeth Berry / Peter Goodwin Helzel, "The Just and Peaceful Kingdom," in: Bruce Ellis / Malinda Elizabeth Berry / Peter Goodwin Helzel (eds.), *Prophetic Evangelicals: Envisioning a Just and Peaceful Kingdom* (Eerdmans: Grand Rapids 2012), 8-30, here 9.

The reality of God's kingdom or heaven is always present and available. It is a moment of transition, a turning point of history; the incubator of something new and possible. If we are to practice occupy heaven in our time, we must work with others as global citizens to seek justice and use our privilege and power to care for others. The Chinese have a saying that says, "The people regard having something to eat as heaven." Occupy heaven means working to ensure that everyone will have something to eat and have their basic needs met.

En este artículo se argumenta que la creciente disparidad entre los ricos y los pobres – el uno por ciento frente al 99 por ciento – nos obliga a repensar la relación entre Dios y la política. "Ocupar el cielo" significa que algunas instituciones religiosas desafiantes han domesticado lo sagrado y acaparado los bienes religiosos, y la creación de las condiciones sociales y los espacios imaginarios para que un mundo alternativo puede ser imaginado y experimentado. El centro de este nuevo imaginario religioso es el redescubrimiento de las importantes funciones de las multitudes en el movimiento de Jesús. A partir de las ideas de la teología coreana minjung y la teoría poscolonial, el artículo expone la limitación de una interpretación machista y heterosexista del Cristo libertador. Sobre la base de la discusión de Homi Bhabha de la agencia política y moral de subalterno, el artículo interpreta el movimiento de Jesús como un movimiento heterogéneo y polimorfo contra los poderes dominantes. Como tal, los paralelos se pueden identificar con el movimiento Occupy, que también atrajo a gente de diversos estratos sociales. El movimiento Ocupar sin líder y su estructura organizativa horizontal puede tener algo importante que enseñar a la iglesia, como un modelo de liderazgo igualitario y descentralizado.

This article argues that the growing disparity between the rich and the poor – the one percent versus the 99 percent – requires us to rethink the relation between God and politics. "Occupy heaven" means challenging religious institutions that have domesticated the sacred and monopolized religious goods, and creating the social conditions and imaginary spaces so that an alternative world can be imagined and experienced. Central to the new religious imaginary is the rediscovery of the important roles of the multitude in the Jesus movement. Drawing from the insights of Korean *minjung* theology and postcolonial theory, the article exposes the limitation of a masculinist and heterosexist portrayal of the liberator Christ. Building on Homi Bhabha's discussion of the political and moral agency of the subaltern person, the article interprets the Jesus movement as a heterogeneous and polymorphous movement against dominant powers. As such, parallels can be identified with the Occupy movement, which also drew people from various social strata. The leaderless Occupy movement and its horizontal organizational structure may have something important to teach the church, such as an egalitarian and decentralized leadership model.

Dieser Beitrag vertritt die These, dass die zunehmende Disparität zwischen Reich und Arm – dem einen vs. den 99 Prozent – es notwendig macht, die Beziehung zwischen Gott und Politik neu zu bedenken. "Occupy heaven" bedeutet, religiöse Institutionen, die das Heilige domestiziert und religiöse Güter monopolisiert haben, in Frage zu stellen und soziale Bedingungen und Räume der Vorstellungskraft zu schaffen, damit eine alternative Welt vorgestellt und erfahren werden kann. Zentral für das neue religiöse Imaginäre ist die Wiederentdeckung der wichtigen Rolle der Menge (*multitude*) in der Jesus-Bewegung. Unter Bezug auf die koreanische *Minjung*-Theologie und postkoloniale Theorie zeigt der Beitrag die Grenzen des maskulinistischen und heterosexistischen Bildes eines befreienden Christus auf. Aufbauend auf Homi Bhabhas Diskussion der politischen und moralischen Wirkung der subalternen Person, interpretiert der Artikel die Jesus-Bewegung als eine heterogene, polymorphe Bewegung gegen herrschende Mächte. Als eine solche gibt es Parallelen mit der Occupy-Bewegung, die ebenfalls Menschen aus einem breiten sozialen Spektrum anzog. Die führungslose Occupy-Bewegung und ihre horizontale Organisationsstruktur könnten ein Vorbild für die Kirche sein, zum Beispiel im Hinblick auf egalitäre und dezentralisierte Führungsmodelle.

Kwok Pui-lan is the William F. Cole Professor of Christian Theology and Spirituality at the Episcopal Divinity School in Cambridge (MA), USA, and the 2011 President of the American Academy of Religion. Her recent books include *Occupy Religion: Theology of the Multitude*, co-authored with Joerg Rieger (Rowman and Littlefield: Lanham 2012) and the edited volume *Anglican Women on Church and Mission* (Church Publishing: New York 2013).

Journal of the European Society of Women in Theological Research 22 (2014) 105-117.
doi: 10.2143/ESWTR.22.0.3040793

Joerg Rieger[1]

Occupy Heaven: Are God, Religion, and Politics beyond Rescue?

Religion as a Conservative Phenomenon

When Americans look toward Europe, it may seem to them as if religion on the continent has sunk into oblivion, particularly since religion continues to play such an important role in the United States. Statistics show that more than 80 percent of all Americans still believe in God and almost half of them state that they participate in religious services on a regular basis.[2] In the United States, religion shapes not only the private sphere but also politics and economics. Even in the board rooms of large corporations meetings are frequently begun with prayer.

Unfortunately, for progressives this religiosity provides little reason for hope, because religion manifests itself in public mostly as a conservative phenomenon. In the United States this is no accident, as religion has been intentionally and successfully utilized by conservative interest groups. This dynamic has been at work since the 1960s and has contributed to the conservative reputation of religion.

Even in Europe, the remainder of religious fervor appears to be located in the conservative camps. American religiosity has often contributed to this trend, for instance through its missionary zest and charitable support after World War II, especially in Germany. Ideological factors play a role here as well, for instance the theological sanctioning of patriarchy and the bourgeois nuclear family, which is promoted by conservative movements on both sides of the Atlantic.

Not surprisingly, it seems to progressives as if God, religion, and politics are beyond rescue. Too often in history religion puts itself on the side of the

---

[1]   This text was first presented as a public lecture in occasion of the ESWTR conference 2013 in Dresden, together with Kwok Pui-lan, whose contribution is also published in this volume.

[2]   See the latest report of the Pew Forum on Religion and Public Life. (http://religions.pewforum. org, 25 February 2014).

status quo. Too often religion supported the side of the dominant powers: even today God is still envisioned in the role of monarchs, authoritarian father and leader figures, and captains of industry. Both literature and art are full of examples.[3]

In our presentation tonight we want to introduce counter models. However, our concern is not to develop yet another idealist model, which may sound attractive, but which has no foundation in reality. It is our concern not to lose sight of alternatives in a context where conservative religiosity dominates. We will do that by displaying and further developing progressive forms of religion. Alternative images of God, church, and politics are couched in active resistance and in progressive ways of life. Unlike in idealist ways of thinking, theory and praxis are not separated here but mutually determine each other.

Religion in Progressive Form

Though today religion in the United States presents itself mostly in conservative forms, historically, in the United States, there is also a common thread of progressive religion. Moreover, progressive forms of religion were part of the most significant transformations in U.S. history. The abolition of slavery in the nineteenth century, for instance, was supported by progressive religious traditions, which were fed from several sources: not only did the opponents of slavery refer to Christian values, the slaves also developed unique forms of Christianity. The latter are still vibrant today in Spirituals, Gospel Hymns, and witness to the spirit of liberation: "Go down, Moses, tell old Pharaoh to let my people go."

Women's suffrage,[4] not even a hundred years old, had many religious opponents but there was also support from progressive religious figures. Elizabeth Cady Stanton, a representative of the American women's movement in the nineteenth century, together with twenty-six other women wrote the so-called "Woman's Bible". Sojourner Truth, an emancipated slave who was actively involved in the liberation of slaves and advocacy of women in the nineteenth century, was closely related to Christian communities (Methodists and Adventists).

The religious overtones of the American Civil Rights movement are better known in Europe. Dr. Martin Luther King, Jr. was an ordained Baptist minister, and Malcolm X practiced various forms of Islam. But only few people

---

[3]   One example is the book by Laurie Beth Jones, *Jesus, CEO: Using Ancient Wisdom for Visionary Leadership* (Hyperion Books: New York 1996).

[4]   In the United States women won the right to vote in 1920, in Germany in 1918.

know about the relationship between religion and the labor movement. Nevertheless, in contradistinction to Germany, in the United States the established churches have at times sided with workers. The so-called Social Creed, which was first adopted in 1908 by the Methodist Church, and later by other national church bodies, linked religion and the concerns of workers and called for shorter hours, the introduction of a day without work, more adequate salaries, pension plans, and health insurance.[5] After several interruptions, the connection of religion and the labor movement is now once again gathering steam. My own academic work has received important impulses from these developments. We must not forget that the concerns of workers are not the special interests of a particular group but closely connected to the well-being of all.

The Occupy Wall Street movement (short: the Occupy movement) embodies this current trend, as it manifests many progressive ideals, particularly in the interrelating of progressive politics, economics, and religion. Its critique is not merely directed at dominant power forces, expressed today in politics and economics, but also at conservative religious voices. It is important to bear in mind, however, that the goal is not merely critique. The Occupy movement is concerned about lived alternatives in which power does not flow from the top down but from the bottom up. This changes everything, including our relation to the reality of God.

Religion and Power
The Occupy movement has reminded us once again of the role of power. Talking about the 1 percent and the 99 percent draws our attention to the question of social class. In the United States, the contrast is obvious and growing, especially in regard to the 0.1 percent: the top 10 percent earn $100,000 or more a year, the top 1 percent earn $368,000, the top 0.1 percent earn about $1 million or more, and this group holds 7.7 percent of the national income.[6] The point, however, is not primarily money: money symbolizes power.

While this insight might go without saying, it is new in the thinking of many Americans, who have tended to assume for the most part that class is not particularly significant in the United States. For many, the Occupy movement has helped them understand for the first time, at least to some degree,

---

5   See http://www.ncccusa.org/pdfs/1908-Social-Creed.pdf, 13 February 2014.
6   See Timothy Noah, "The United States of Inequality," slate.com, 13 September 2010. (http://www.slate.com/articles/news_and_politics/the_great_divergence/features/2010/the_united_states_of_inequality/introducing_the_great_divergence.html, 25 February 2014).

the importance of the question of class, although much is yet to be examined and deepened. In the meantime, more and more Americans sense that the "rags-to-riches" American Dream remains merely a dream. After all, class boundaries in the United States are less permeable than in almost all other industrialized countries. Class mobility in the United States is only one third of class mobility in Denmark and only one half of class mobility in Canada, Finland, and Norway.[7]

Obviously, power plays a crucial role in the realms of politics and economics. Unfortunately, it is too often overlooked that power also calls the shots in religion. Religious groups and churches embody the power of the status quo in different ways, and our images of God often reflect dominant visions of power as well. It is not surprising, therefore, that in the past God was envisioned as a feudal ruler and a monarch.

One consequence of this hidden power is that it is commonly assumed that church and God can only exist in specific hierarchical configurations of power. Those who reject these configurations of power seem to have no choice but to reject church, God, and ultimately religion.

In the Roman Empire, the elites came to this exact conclusion regarding the early Christians: Christians were denounced as atheists, because they did not believe in a God aligned with the hierarchical power of the gods of Antiquity. Jesus Christ, the manifestation of the Christian God, had rebelled publicly against the hierarchical power of the Roman occupiers and their Jewish vassals, and he identified with the oppressed against the oppressors. His mother, Mary, expressed this forcefully when she noted that God pushes the powerful from their thrones and lifts up the lowly (Luke 1:52). At the same time, the Romans could be tolerant of other religions: they incorporated other Gods in their religion, like the Egyptian Gods Isis and Osiris, as long as their adherents conformed to the power of the empire. In addition, the Romans had little difficulty exalting humans to the role of god, and revered their emperors as divine rulers. The difficulty was, therefore, not with the divinity of Jesus as such, but with the form that this divinity took. This particular God did not fit in with the theism of the powerful.

As a result, Christians often find themselves in closer proximity to atheists than to those kinds of theists who believe in the hierarchical power of God.

---

[7]   See Isabel V. Sawhill and John E. Morgen, "Economic Mobility: Is the American Dream Alive and Well?". (http://www.brookings.edu/~/media/research/files/papers/2007/5/useconomics%20morton/05useconomics_morton, 25 February 2014).

The rejection of hierarchical power brings together Christians and atheists, especially in situations where religion shores up the hierarchical dominance of the status quo. This is not only true for the Roman Empire, it is also true for situations in the contemporary United States and even in Europe, where shrinking churches tend to cling to the status quo.

Religion and Alternative Power

Based on these observations, some conclude that alternative approaches must reject power as a matter of principle. If the dominant status quo claims power, it is often assumed, all others should choose powerlessness. Nevertheless, the Jewish and the Christian traditions demonstrate early on that there are alternatives, which embody power in a totally different way. Powerlessness is not the only alternative to dominant power. Not only could the Jewish and Christian traditions never be controlled completely by the prevailing empires, they also produced alternative dynamics of power, connected to alternative images of God.[8]

The Occupy movement has once again brought to the fore some of these alternative dynamics of power. "Dangerous memories" (Johann Baptist Metz) of the life and work of Jesus reemerged in new forms. People remembered once more that Jesus did not align himself with the elites of his time, but practiced solidarity with the common people – the so-called multitude. He sided with those who experienced oppression and marginalization, like the sick, the socially despised, women, children, and the working population like fishermen and peasants. It is also not unimportant that Jesus himself was raised as a construction worker with little formal education, which also means that he must have been in close touch with many of the unemployed of his time.[9] It is likely that he experienced unemployment himself, since construction work at that time was strongly determined by the fluctuating demand of the Roman Empire and its vassals.

The power which is lived out in Jesus's relationships is not hierarchical and elitist. It is not oligarchic, aristocratic, or plutocratic, that is, it is not the rule of the few, the elites, or the wealthy. It is not even democratic in the strict sense of the word, because in the Greek world democracy signified the rule of

---

[8] The considerable list of studies of religion and empire continues to grow and includes authors such as John Dominic Crossan, Neil Elliott, Richard Horsley, Brigitte Kahl, and many others.

[9] The Greek term *tektoon* does not connote the well-structured world of a German carpenter and his guild, although the term is often misunderstood in this way.

a privileged strata of citizens, which excluded the lower classes. Jesus – this should be noted especially in Germany – does not represent the power of the well-heeled bourgeoisie, not even the educated middle-class.

Inspired by the New Testament terms of *laos* and *ochlos*, translated as "people" and "crowd" or "multitude", we are therefore talking about "laocracy" and "ochlocracy". The notion of laocracy, shaped in collaboration with Euro American and Latin American liberation theologians, connotes the alternative power of the common people, as it finds expression in the Jesus movement.[10] What is at stake here is solidarity and cooperation rather than competition and one-upmanship.[11]

Likewise, the term ochlocracy, which was initially conceptualized in Korean Minjung theology, connotes the power of the so-called multitude, which must not be misunderstood as a rabble or mob. In an ochlocracy,[12] the multitude becomes the acting subject that, in opposition to the elites, does not usurp the place of a hierarchical God, and does not exercise power from the top down. If communal life is not understood in terms of hierarchy and competition, the various members of society tend to give each other strength in a positive fashion.[13]

It is important to note that these alternatives to the hierarchical paradigm of power provide not only an alternative political model but also an alternative theology. Instead of assuming the place of God, the multitude does the will of God and embodies therefore not only alternative images and imaginations of God but also an alternative reality of God. The masses are fed not necessarily because of a one-time supernatural spectacle, which is not relevant for anyone else, but because the distribution of the loaves of bread and fish encourages the crowd to do the same (Mark 6:30-44).

These alternative images and imaginations of God bring us closer to the reality of the natural world and of the cosmos than any of the more traditional images of God. This implies a fundamental shift in perception in other areas

---

[10] See Néstor Míguez / Joerg Rieger / Jung Mo Sung, *Beyond the Spirit of Empire: Theology and Politics in a New Key* (SCM Press: London 2009).

[11] The often overlooked theme of solidarity is reflected in Jesus's parable of the unforgiving servant in Matthew 18:21-35.

[12] See Ahn Byung Mu, "Jesus and the Minjung in the Gospel of Mark," in: Kim Yong Bock (ed.), *Minjung Theology: People as the Subjects of History* (Commission of Theological Concerns, Christian Conference of Asia: Singapore 1981), 138-152.

[13] Kwok Pui-lan and I, in our book *Occupy Religion: Theology of the Multitude* (Rowman and Littlefield: Lanham 2012), deal with the work of Antonio Negri and Michael Hardt. See, for instance, their book *Multitude: War and Democracy in the Age of Empire* (Penguin: New York 2004).

as well, as the focus is still on the achievements of the elites rather than on the achievements of the multitude. This is true not only for achievements in the social sphere, but also for technical, economic, and intellectual ones. Re-examining the power and success of the multitude unlocks the potential of the future.

This alternative power is, therefore, not only at work on the political stage. All levels of society are constantly more or less connected, and in the classical context distinctions between politics and religion, in the sense of the distinguishing between the public and private, did not yet exist. Feminist thinkers have reminded us for many years that the personal is the political.

Consequently, laocracy and ochlocracy can be enacted in all realms of life including the life of community and in families. Jesus opposed narrow and conservative visions of families, which are still supported by conservative representatives of religion and politics. True relationships are not rooted in biology but in collaboration: "Whoever does the will of God," says Jesus, "is my brother and sister and mother" (Mark 3:35). Furthermore, Jesus decisively rejects the subordination of women and children. Children have a special place in the eyes of God, which reflects the principles of laocracy and ochlocracy: "It is to such as these that the kingdom of God belongs" (Mark 10:14b). The only regulation concerning the relation of the genders, which Jesus denounces and toughens, is divorce,[14] because in patriarchal society it placed an enormous economic and social burden on the backs of women and children. It is interesting that conservative politics and religion have long made peace with divorce and denounce other problems, which were of no concern to Jesus, such as committed homosexual relationships.

What is reversed here, as the Occupy movement emphasizes, is the relation of the 99 percent and the 1 percent: "So the last will be first, and the first will be last" (Matthew 20:16). While the normative flow in politics and religion is from the top down, in this new paradigm the direction is from the bottom up. This does not mean that the 1 percent is automatically excluded: it is free to take the side of the 99 percent, which actually happens every now and then.[15]

Deep Solidarity
One of the most important insights, which follows from what has been said so far, has to do with a new understanding of solidarity. In the past, even progressives understood solidarity often in terms of *noblesse oblige*. Solidarity tended

---

[14] Matthew 19:7-9 is a better example of the patriarchal context than Mark 10:1-11.
[15] See http://westandwiththe99percent.tumblr.com/, 25 February 2014.

to be a well-meaning declaration of solidarity by the privileged for the under-privileged, rooted in the willpower of the privileged.

The principle that we are calling *deep* solidarity, by contrast, is based on the assumption that most of us are in the same boat, without being aware of it. The global economic crisis, which began in 2007 and which is not over yet for many people, has served as a wake-up call for many, especially in the United States. The American Dream has turned into a nightmare, not only for the mass of the underprivileged, but also for the so-called middle-class. Half of the jobs that have been lost are never going to return. More and more full-time jobs are being replaced by part-time jobs, casual jobs, or temporary jobs without social benefits, as well as those which require only the most minimal of commitments from employers. Whereas the older generation is concerned about its future and retirement – decline of one's social status in retirement is the sad norm in the United States – the younger generation has little hope for socio-economic advancement. In the United Sates, youth unemployment was at 13 percent in 2007, by 2010 it rose to 21 percent. The duration of unemploy-ment has risen as well.[16]

Deep solidarity implies that more than 99 percent of the population are no longer benefiting from the capitalist system, if they ever did. As a result, new relations emerge between different sectors of societies and groups which have so far never really understood themselves to be in solidarity. This means that those ethnic and racial majorities who belong to the 99 percent are more closely related to those ethnic and racial minorities who also belong to the 99 percent rather than to representatives of the 1 percent. For example, men who belong to the 99 percent are more closely related to the women of the 99 percent than to other men who belong to the 1 percent.

This does not mean, however, that differences no longer play a role and should be erased. On the contrary: differences are as real as ever and need to be reflected upon. The new idea is that these differences need no longer be used against the 99 percent, as was historically the case. In the United States, for instance, black and white workers were often pitted against one another, so that white workers identified with white bosses even without benefiting a whole lot in the end. In Europe, too, we need to ask ourselves who really benefited when working men, for instance, were played off against working women. Whenever working men identify with men who are employers, as is

---

[16] See http://en.wikipedia.org/wiki/Youth_unemployment, 25 February 2014.

customary in a patriarchy, the latter have the advantage. Working men and women could achieve considerably greater improvements if they would work with, instead of against, one another. This is what we mean by deep solidarity. When working men become conscious of their deep solidarity with women, they can use their institutionally derived advantages for the benefit of all while severing the false ties on which a patriarchal society is based.

Deep solidarity enables us to employ our differences in a constructive fashion. Now relative advantages – like for instance certain remaining economic and political advantages of the middle class – can be used for the benefit of all. This kind of deep solidarity presupposes that we clarify for ourselves the boundary between the 99 percent and the 1 percent. This boundary is so commonly overlooked that the middle class often considers itself to be aligned with the 1 percent, even though that is not the case.

The bigger goal that we envision is the interrelation of the streams of various liberation movements. Even though there are tensions between these movements that must be addressed, it is now more apparent than ever that we have a lot more in common than previously understood.

Let us not forget that the status quo has always benefited from playing these various movements against each other, and from cleverly using the tension for its own purposes. For instance, when some talk about the question of class or put themselves in solidarity with workers, others who work on issues of gender or race quickly suspect that they are about to be excluded. But the issues of gender or of race are often closely tied to the question of class. After all, we are not just concerned about abstract prejudices but about the question of power, which in our societies is most clearly expressed in economic terms: women earn less than men and are less often to be found at the top of the corporate ladder; racial minorities are more likely to be unemployed and are often discriminated against at work, and so on. When we talk about class, we also need to consider questions of gender, race, as well as the questions of ethnic and sexual minorities. Vice versa, when we talk about questions of gender, race, ethnicity, and sexuality, we need to keep in mind the question of class and the distinction between the 99 percent and the 1 percent. Of course, the question of class will need to be examined at greater depth, but we cannot deal with this question here.[17]

---

[17] On the topic of class and religion see Joerg Rieger (ed.), *Religion, Theology, and Class: Fresh Engagements after Long Silence* (Palgrave Macmillan: New York 2013).

Immanence and Transcendence

In conclusion I want to return to the theological implications. For many years we understood theology and religion in terms of the tension between immanence and transcendence. Unfortunately, however, a misunderstanding becomes apparent as immanence is defined as natural reality and transcendence as supernatural reality. Things get worse when the task of theology and religion is mainly understood as dealing with this kind of transcendence.

An alternative understanding of immanence and transcendence reaches back all the way to the roots of the Jewish and Christian traditions. In the Old Testament the work of God and salvation are not at all oriented towards supernatural things but towards life in the world. Here we are not dealing with a kind of immanence that is in opposition to transcendence but with a completely different understanding of transcendence: transcendence is the work of God in the world.

In the New Testament the incarnation of Jesus illuminates this understanding of transcendence. God is at work in the world and for the world through the life and work of Jesus. The realm of God is not only in heaven but also on earth; the will of God is supposed to be done on earth as it is in heaven, as Jesus taught. Transcendence refers here not first of all to the supernatural but to an alternative reality in the world, i.e., an alternative immanence, where we receive our daily bread, where real debts are forgiven, and where the liberation from evil is experienced. It is also noteworthy that there is a shorter version of the Lord's Prayer in the Gospel of Luke, which does not even mention heaven.[18]

The transcendence that characterizes this kind of religious outlook is, therefore, essentially related to this world. Even Karl Barth has understood this, although few Barthians followed him in this direction. The contrast possibly has do to with the fact that Barth was aware of the question of class.[19] Transcendence is, speaking in terms of early Christian symbols, the Christ child in the manger, in poverty, at the margins of society. Transcendence is found not above the world but in the midst of the world, in an alternative immanence in which the multitude can live truly free lives. Alternative immanence and transcendence take sides: they stand on the side of the lowly. They are not to be found on the side of the powerful. According to Barth, "God always takes

---

[18] See Matthew 6:9-13; Luke 11:2-4.

[19] See Joerg Rieger, "Klassenkampf und Religion: Karl Barth, Sabine Plonz und aktuelle Alternativen zur bürgerlichen Theologie," in: *Das Argument* 299.5 (2012), 699-707.

His stand unconditionally and passionately on this side and on this side alone: against the lofty and on behalf of the lowly; against those who already enjoy right and privilege and on behalf of those who are denied it and deprived of it."[20] The Abrahamic religions support each other in this case. In the Quran (4.75) the following question is raised: "And what is [the matter] with you that you fight not in the cause of Allah and [for] the oppressed among men, women, and children?"

Whether God, religion, and politics are not beyond rescue depends on this matter. Here, religion has to lay its cards on the table. Is it on the side of the oppressed and does it find God there, or is it on the side of the status quo? There is no third option. In a situation shaped by dramatic differentials of power, there is no middle road. Even the so-called middle class needs to choose a side.

La religión actualmente se presenta frecuentemente como un fenómeno conservador. Con demasiada frecuencia en la historia de la religión, ésta se ha posicionado del lado del statu quo. Por consiguiente, puede parecer que Dios, la religión y la política están más allá de la Salvación. Este ensayo tiene por objeto introducir modelos alternativos, comenzando con la constatación de que las formas progresistas de la religión son parte de las transformaciones importantes en la historia. Las experiencias recientes con el movimiento Occupy Wall Street reflejan muchas de estas características progresistas, sobre todo la relación de la política progresista, la economía y la religión. Las críticas que surgen de estas experiencias no son sólo críticas dirigidas a la potencia dominante, expresadas, hoy, en la política y la economía, sino también críticas al poder dominante que se materializa en la religión. Tales críticas apuntan a las alternativas vividas en las que el poder no fluye de arriba hacia abajo, sino de abajo hacia arriba.

Estas experiencias alternativas de la religión y el poder arrojan nueva luz sobre muchas de las tradiciones judía y cristiana, que encarnan el poder de una manera diferente. No sólo pueden estas tradiciones controlar completamente por los imperios dominantes, sino que también pueden generar alternativas de poder, ligados a las imágenes alternativas de Dios. El resultado es una nueva comprensión de la solidaridad, que tiene el potencial para reunir a las corrientes de los diversos movimientos de liberación sin dejar de lado las diferencias y tensiones. Basándose en esta nueva solidaridad, imágenes arraigadas de inmanencia y trascendencia se pueden reconstruir, produciendo nuevas visiones de Dios, de la religión y de la política.

---

[20] Karl Barth, *Church Dogmatics*, trans. T.H.L. Parker et al. (Charles Scribner's Sons: New York 1957), vol. II.1: *The Doctrine of God*, 386.

Religion today presents itself mostly as a conservative phenomenon. Too often in history religion put itself on the side of the status quo. As a result, it may seem as if God, religion, and politics are indeed beyond rescue. This essay seeks to introduce alternative models, beginning with the realization that progressive forms of religion were part of significant transformations in history. Recent experiences with the Occupy Wall Street movement reflect many of these progressive characteristics, particularly the relation of progressive politics, economics, and religion. The critique that emerges from these experiences is not merely directed at dominant power, expressed today in politics and economics, but also at dominant power as it is embodied by religion. Such critique points to lived alternatives in which power does not flow from the top down but from the bottom up.

These alternative experiences of religion and power throw new light on many Jewish and Christian traditions, which embody power in a different way. Not only could these traditions never be controlled completely by the prevailing empires, they also produced alternative embodiments of power, linked to alternative images of God. The result is a new understanding of solidarity, which has the potential to bring together the streams of the various liberation movements without neglecting differences and tensions. Based on this new solidarity, entrenched images of immanence and transcendence can be reconstructed, producing new visions of God, religion, and politics.

Religion zeigt sich heute meist als ein konservatives Phänomen. Allzu oft hat sich Religion in der Geschichte auf die Seite des Status quo geschlagen. Und so scheint es, als ob Gott, Religion und Politik tatsächlich rettungslos verloren wären. Dieser Artikel will alternative Modelle einführen, angefangen mit der Wahrnehmung, dass progressive religiöse Formen an wichtigen Veränderungen in der Geschichte beteiligt waren. Die Erfahrungen mit der Occupy Wall Street Bewegung reflektieren viele dieser progressiven Merkmale, vor allem die Beziehung zwischen progressiver Politik, Wirtschaft und Religion. Die Kritik, die aus diesen Erfahrungen hervorgeht, richtet sich nicht nur gegen die herrschende Macht, wie sie heute in Politik und Wirtschaft realisiert wird, sondern auch gegen die herrschende Macht, wie sie die Religion verkörpert. Diese Kritik verweist auf gelebte Alternativen, in denen Macht nicht von oben nach unten fließt, sondern von unten nach oben.

Diese alternative Erfahrungen von Religion und Macht werfen ein neues Licht auf viele jüdische und christliche Traditionen, die Macht anders verkörpern. Diese Traditionen konnten nie völlig von den herrschenden Mächten kontrolliert werden und mehr noch, sie produzierten alternative Verkörperungen von Macht, verknüpft mit alternativen Gottesbildern. Das Ergebnis ist ein neues Verständnis von Solidarität mit dem Potential, die Ströme der verschiedenen Befreiungsbewegungen zusammenzuführen, ohne Unterschiede und Spannungen zu vernachlässigen. Auf der Basis dieser neuen Solidarität können fest verwurzelte Bilder von Immanenz und Transzendenz rekonstruiert werden und neue Visionen von Gott, Religion und Politik entstehen.

Joerg Rieger, Prof. Dr., is Wendland-Cook Professor of Constructive Theology at Perkins School of Theology, SMU. Among his most recent books are his edited volume *Religion, Theology, and Class: Fresh Engagements after Long Silence* (2013), *Occupy Religion: Theology of the Multitude* (with Kwok Pui-lan 2012), *No Rising Tide: Theology, Economics, and the Future* (2009), and *Christ and Empire: From Paul to Postcolonial Times* (2007, German and Portuguese translations).

Journal of the European Society of Women in Theological Research 22 (2014) 119-137.
doi: 10.2143/ESWTR.22.0.3040794

Julia Enxing

Guerilla Gardening – Grüner Protest: Seine Bedeutung für Visionen und Widerstände in der Kirche

Es ist Mitternacht. Sie gehen auf die Straße, mal alleine, mal in Gruppen, haben Setzlinge oder bereits blühende Pflanzen im Gepäck. Sie bezeichnen sich als "Guerillas", als "kleine Kriegerinnen und Krieger", und wie ihre spanischen Vorbilder[1] ist ihr Kampf gegen die Betonwüsten der Erde indirekt und überraschend. Meist sind es junge Leute. Manchmal sieht man sie auch am helllichten Tag. Dann tragen sie kleine Samenkugeln in ihren Taschen, sogenannte *Seed Bombs*, die sie im Vorbeigehen fallen lassen, aus dem Auto werfen oder beim Inline-Skaten "auswerfen" – meist in den grauen Großstädten auf unbeliebten, aber oft passierten Plätzen. In den folgenden Wochen werden die Samen oder kleinen Pflänzchen gehegt und gepflegt, gegossen und von Schädlingen befreit, meistens nachts, um nicht gesehen zu werden. Es dauert nicht lange, dann sprießen bunte Blumen, häufig Wildblumen, die man sonst eher am Rande von Kornfeldern erwarten würde, aus dem grauen und harten Asphalt. Sie bahnen sich ihre Wege zwischen Pflastersteinen, durch Risse in Hausmauern und Kübeln, um Straßenlaternen und in Verkehrsinseln. Offiziell ist das *Guerilla Gardening* verboten, es ist definiert als "die unerlaubte

---

[1] Spanische Schreibweise "guerrilla/guerrilleros/guerrilleras", englisch "guerilla", vgl. Barbara Uhlig, "Guerilla Gardening: Zwischen Street Art und der Rückkehr zur Natur". (http://www.edoc. hu-berlin.de/kunsttexte/2012-4/uhlig-barbara--5/PDF/uhlig.pdf, 26. August 2013); Patrick Huhn, *Mit Spaten, Pflanzen und Visionen: Guerilla Gardening als Nutzung von Brachflächen* (Der Andere Verlag: Uelvesbüll 2011), 8. Ich verwende im Folgenden die englische Schreibweise. Für zahlreiche weitere Informationen, Fotos und Videos siehe auch: Richard Reynolds, "The Guerilla Gardening Homepage". (http://www.guerrillagardening.org/, 24. Juli 2013) "Das G-Wort [Guerilla] selbst wurde 1808 zum ersten Mal verwendet und zwar für die militärische Antwort der Spanier auf Napoleon Bonapartes Invasion. Sechs Jahre lang zermürbten lose Banden spanischer Kämpfer die übermächtige französische Besatzungsmacht, indem sie sie aus dem Hinterhalt angriffen und die Zivilbevölkerung aufwiegelten. Ganz gewöhnliche Männer, keine ausgebildeten Soldaten, griffen mutig zu den Waffen, um ihr Land gegen die Eindringlinge zu verteidigen, und sie bezeichneten sich selbst als Guerilleros." Richard Reynolds, *Guerilla Gardening: Ein botanisches Manifest* (Orange Press: Freiburg im Breisgau ²2012), 13, vgl. auch 12-13.

Kultivierung von Land, das jemand anderem gehört."[2] Die Gestaltung der öffentlichen Plätze obliegt in der Regel den städtisch angestellten Gärtner_innen, und es geht dabei im Allgemeinen um ein Anpflanzen von pflegeleichten, nett aussehenden und aufeinander sowie auf die Umgebung abgestimmten, mehrheitlich in Gewächshäusern herangezogenen Pflanzen.

Was motiviert die Guerilla-Gärtner_innen? Wozu der ganze Aufwand – so drängt sich die Frage auf? Zugegeben, zumindest in Deutschland sind bisher keine harten Sanktionsmaßnahmen bekannt, dennoch, es ist nicht erlaubt, Feld zu bestellen, das einem nicht gehört,[3] und es ist in der Regel anstrengend, mühsam, und weder mit Anerkennung noch mit Dank zu rechnen. Die Frustration muss hoch sein, angesichts der unachtsamen Passant_innen, die auf den frisch gesetzten oder gesäten kleinen, zarten Pflänzchen herum trampeln.[4] Ganz zu schweigen von "Pflanzendiebstählen", die immer wieder vorkommen.[5] Was also ist die Motivation und was das Ziel dieses sozialpolitisch-ökologischen Protests, wie ihn seit geraumer Zeit zahlreiche Großstädte – weltweit – erleben? Was wollen die Krieger_innen? Ihre Waffen sind bekannt, doch wer ist ihr Feind? Was soll hier – symbolisch – angezeigt werden, was soll durch das vitale Pflanzengrün im grauen Asphalt aufblühen? Was soll aufbrechen und unterbrochen werden?

Im Folgenden werde ich zunächst näher auf Geschichte und Selbstverständnis, die Motivation, die Ziele und auf die verwendete Terminologie der Protestbewegung eingehen, bevor ich in einer anschließenden Reflexion die

---

[2] Reynolds, *Guerilla Gardening*, 12 (im Original in Kapitälchen); vgl. Uhlig "Guerilla Gardening," 4; Julia Jahnke, *Guerilla Gardening anhand von Beispielen in New York, London und Berlin* (Der Andere Verlag: Tönning/Lübeck/Marburg 2010), Berliner ökophysiologische und phytomedizinische Schriften 11, 26. "Vor einer Verwechslung solltest du dich allerdings in Acht nehmen: Gärtnerische Aktivitäten, für die du eine offizielle Erlaubnis hast, sind kein Guerilla Gardening. Etwas anderes so zu bezeichnen als die unerlaubte Gestaltung von Land, das dir nicht selber gehört, wäre eine Herabwürdigung von Courage und Kreativität der echten Guerillas." Reynolds, *Guerilla Gardening*, 18. Um eine unrechtmäßige Selbstbezeichnung als "Guerilla Gardener/Gardening" zu vermeiden, schlägt Huhn – als man sich unsicher sein – als Alternative "Garden Pioneers/Pioneering" vor. Huhn, *Mit Spaten, Pflanzen und Visionen*, 77-78. Zur Begriffsanalyse und zum Selbstverständnis vgl. auch Jahnke, *Guerilla Gardening anhand von Beispielen in New York, London und Berlin*, 73-77, 103.

[3] Mögliche Straftatbestände: "Vandalismus"/"Sachbeschädigung", siehe Reynolds, *Guerilla Gardening*, 136-143; zu Legalisierungsprozessen vgl. 243-252. Zur Rechtslage in Deutschland siehe Huhns gute Übersicht in: Huhn, *Mit Spaten, Pflanzen und Visionen*, 45-46.

[4] Vgl. Reynolds, *Guerilla Gardening*, 143-149.

[5] Reynolds hierzu: "Wir tragen diese Diebstähle mit Fassung. Sie sind enttäuschend, aber akzeptable Verluste in dieser Schlacht." Reynolds, *Guerilla Gardening*, 145; vgl. Huhn, *Mit Spaten, Pflanzen und Visionen*, 57-58.

Verbindungen zwischen dem sozialpolitisch-ökologischen Protest der Guerillas und dem kirchlicher Protestgruppen aufzeige. Aufgrund der Kürze des Artikels wird auf eine ausführliche kritische Beurteilung der *Guerilla Gardening*-Bewegung verzichtet. Da der Beitrag eine für die theologische Forschung eher extravagante Verbindung herstellt, soll er einführenden und diskussionseröffnenden Charakter haben.

Ich werde mich in diesem Artikel ausschließlich auf den politischen Widerstand des *Guerilla Gardenings* beziehen und nicht auf seine weiterentwickelte Form, das *Urban Gardening* oder auch *Urban Farming*,[6] das heißt die zunehmende Nutzbarmachung urbaner Flächen zum Anbau von Obst und Gemüse oder schlicht zur ästhetischen Aufwertung des städtischen Grau.[7] Auch Uhlig weist in ihrer Einführung zum *Guerilla Gardening* darauf hin, dass "Guerrilla Gardening von einem stark ökologischen Gedanken getragen [wird]. Hier ist das bewusste Bepflanzen von Stadtraum von einem zufälligen Begrünen, wie etwa durch die Methode der Seed Bombs, zu trennen."[8]

Geschichte und Selbstverständnis

Das Bemühen, Grünflächen und Naturgärten auch in Großstädten am Leben zu erhalten, ist keinesfalls ein neues Phänomen. Solange es Städte gibt, solange gibt es Menschen, die die Verbindung zur Natur auch in der Großstadt erhalten wollen.

Der "Begriff" des *Guerilla Gardenings* bzw. der *Green Guerillas* tauchte erstmals 1970 in New York auf. Damals war der Protest

---

[6] Uhlig bezeichnet *Guerilla Gardening* als eine "Unterart der urbanen Gartenbewegung". Weiterhin diskutiert sie in ihrem Beitrag, inwieweit *Guerilla Gardening* als "Street Art" zu verstehen ist, vgl. hierzu den Abschnitt "Ist Guerrilla Gardening Kunst?," in: Uhlig, *Guerilla Gardening*, 1, vgl. besonders ab Seite 5; vgl. Martin Rasper, *Vom Gärtnern in der Stadt: Die neue Lust zwischen Beton und Asphalt* (Oekom Verlag: München 2012); Christa Müller, *Urban Gardening: Über die Rückkehr der Gärten in die Stadt* (Oekom Verlag: München 2011); Thomas J. Fox, *Urban Farming: Sustainable City Living in Your Backyard, in Your Community, and in the World* (Hobby Farm Press/BowTie Press: Irvine 2011); Huhn, *Mit Spaten, Pflanzen und Visionen*, 37-38; Jahnke, *Guerilla Gardening anhand von Beispielen in New York, London und Berlin*, 46-49, 67-69, 101, 103.

[7] Dass ihnen Letzteres aber auch zum Verhängnis werden kann, zeigt Jahnke auf: "In New York hat sich bereits drastisch gezeigt, wie *Guerilla Gardening* ein 'Opfer des eigenen Erfolges' werden kann: Die positiven Auswirkungen der Gärten auf die soziale Struktur der Nachbarschaften haben zur Wertsteigerung und Gentrifizierung dieser Gegenden mit beigetragen, in deren Folge viele der Gartengrundstücke an Immobilieninvestoren verkauft wurden und die Gärten zerstört wurden." Jahnke, *Guerilla Gardening anhand von Beispielen in New York, London und Berlin*, 103.

[8] Uhlig, *Guerilla Gardening*, 4.

an die Besetzung eines brachliegenden Grundstücks zwischen East Houston und
Bowery (Manhatten) geknüpft, das eine Gruppe von Aktivisten [Green Guerillas]
um die Künstlerin Liz Christy innerhalb eines Jahres in mühevoller Arbeit von
Schutt und Müll säuberte [...] und [...] es in einen öffentlich zugänglichen Garten
[verwandelte]. [...] Die illegal gestaltete Initiative fand so seine [sic!] legale Fortsetzung und es entstand der erste Gemeindegarten in der Stadt New York, der seitdem
für 1$ im Jahr von der Stadt gemietet und von Freiwilligen gepflegt wird.[9]

Während Reynolds in seiner einschlägigen Monografie *Guerilla Gardening:
Ein botanisches Manifest* darauf insistiert, dass es statt des "einen" festen
Startpunkts des *Guerilla Gardenings* viele verschiedene Inspirationen gab,
die bis heute anhalten,[10] nennt Uhlig eine "Geburtsstunde des Guerilla Gardenings": Vor 13 Jahren, genauer gesagt am 1. Mai 2000, bewaffneten sich im
Zuge der "Reclaim the Streets"-Demonstrationen dieses Tages "Kämpfer für
'globale und lokale sozialökologische Revolution(en), [...die das Ziel hatten,]
die hierarchische und autoritäre Gesellschaft zu transzendieren'",[11] mit Spaten
und Samen, um eine Fläche des Parliament Square umzugraben, mit Mutter-
erde aufzustocken und zu bepflanzen.[12] Reynolds selbst empfindet die Aktion
des 1. Mai 2000 als "irritierend" und bescheinigt ihr nur wenige Gemeinsamkeiten mit echtem Guerilla-Gärtnern.[13] Reynolds geht zwar nicht näher darauf

---

9   Uhlig, *Guerilla Gardening*, 2; vgl. Reynolds, *Guerilla Gardening*, 14-15; Liz Christy, "Liz
    Christy Garden". (http://www.lizchristygarden.us/, 25. Juli 2013); Huhn, *Mit Spaten, Pflanzen
    und Visionen*, 9, 13-14.
10 Vgl. Reynolds, *Guerilla Gardening*, 71. Zu Geschichte und Entwicklung des Guerilla Gardenings
    vgl. auch Huhn, *Mit Spaten, Pflanzen und Visionen*, 13-21.
11 Reynolds, *Guerilla Gardening*, 84.
12 Vgl. Reynolds, *Guerilla Gardening*, 83-84; Uhlig, *Guerilla Gardening*, 4; Jahnke, *Guerilla
    Gardening anhand von Beispielen in New York, London und Berlin*, 70-81.
13 "Was hat das [die Aktion am 1. Mai 2000] dem Guerilla Gardening gebracht? Das Foto
    Churchills als Öko-Punk und eine fette Schlagzeile zum Thema fegten kurz durch den Blätter-
    wald, halfen aber überhaupt nicht der Bewegung. Die Straßen waren zwar immerhin einen
    lustigen Nachmittag lang vom Autoverkehr befreit, aber die Matschlandschaft, die die Demons-
    tranten hinterließen, war nicht halb so fruchtbar, wie die geistreichen Transparente verkündet
    hatten. [...] Langfristig bewirkte die Aktion, dass gemäßigtere Teile der Gesellschaft auf
    Distanz zur Guerilla-Gardening-Bewegung gingen. Noch heute fragen mich Guerilla-Gärtner,
    die gerade ganz neu anfangen, nach jenem 1. Mai. Schließlich war das die bis dahin größte
    Publicity, die Guerilla Gardening je bekommen hatte. Eigentlich sind mir die Aktionsformen
    der verschiedenen Guerilla-Gärtner-Abteilungen alle recht, aber diese eine Geschichte, sozu-
    sagen vor meiner Haustür, irritiert mich immer noch. Denn auch wenn zweifelsohne so etwas
    wie Guerilla-Spirit darin zu erkennen war: Mit Liebe zum Gärtnern hatte das bestimmt nichts
    zu tun. Ich würde es höchstens als 'nachwachsendes Graffiti' bezeichnen – echtes Guerilla

ein, erwähnt jedoch bereits eine gewisse biblische Analogie zum *Guerilla Gardening* im Matthäusevangelium (13,24-30). Nach Reynolds handelt es sich beim "Gleichnis vom Unkraut unter dem Weizen" "um eine düstere biblische Parabel über das Aussäen von Unkraut auf dem Feld eines anderen".[14] Reynolds verweist auf weitere Beispiele für *Guerilla Gardening* quer durch die Geschichte, von St. George's Hill in England (1649), über Pennsylvania, Ohio (1801), Berkeley, Kalifornien (1969) und andere.[15]

Mag ihre Authentizität als Ursprungsgeschichte auch strittig sein, so mobilisierte die Aktion am 1. Mai 2000 dennoch urbane Gartenaktivist_innen weltweit,[16] die in den kommenden Jahren für manch blühende Ecke verantwortlich zeichneten. *Guerilla Gardening* beschränkt sich allerdings nicht nur auf bunte Wegmarkierungen in Großstädten, sondern wird als politischer Protest ebenfalls durch ein Anpflanzen von Nutz- und Nahrungspflanzen (wie beispielsweise Kartoffeln) auf öffentlichen Grünflächen und Parkanlagen sichtbar. Es geht um eine Unterbrechung, um eine Störung der profitgesteuerten "Monokulturen des Spießbürgertums".[17] Durch ein Anpflanzen von Blumen, Sträuchern oder anderen Gewächsen in ungewöhnlichen Gegenden, in denen diese Form von Natürlichkeit dem Selbstbild ihrer Bewohner_innen widerspricht, wird Unmut und Protest zum Ausdruck gebracht. Die Provokation drückt sich in Dornbüschen aus, die auf dem schicken, zartgrünen Rasen eines Golfplatzes eingesetzt werden, oder in der Störung von Gentechnikversuchen durch das Zwischensäen von "hinderlichen" Pflanzen, die die Proben bis zur Unbrauchbarkeit verändern.

Neben Liz Christy gilt es zwei weitere Aktivisten, "Gartenguerillas", besonders hervorzuheben, deren Gärtnern weit über die nationalen Grenzen hinweg Aufmerksamkeit erfährt: Zum einen den bereits erwähnten Londoner Richard Reynolds,[18] zum anderen den Münsteraner Aktionskünstler Wilm Weppelmann,[19] der erst kürzlich auf dem Münsteraner Aasee eine "Aa-Farm" zu Wasser

---

Gardening hingegen ist 'lebendiges Graffiti'." Reynolds, *Guerilla Gardening*, 84-85; vgl. Jahnke, *Guerilla Gardening anhand von Beispielen in New York, London und Berlin*, 70.

[14] Reynolds, *Guerilla Gardening*, 71.
[15] Vgl. Reynolds, *Guerilla Gardening*, 71-88.
[16] Vgl. Reynolds, *Guerilla Gardening*, 17.
[17] "Leitfaden für den revolutionären Weisheitskampf". (http://weltenschule.de/Ratiokraten/Weisheitskampf.html, 15. August 2013); Guerilla-Gärtnern wird auch als "Zivilisationskritik" verstanden, so in Uhlig, *Guerilla Gardening*, 10.
[18] Vgl. Reynolds, *Guerilla Gardening*; Uhlig, *Guerilla Gardening*, 2. Zu Reynolds eigenen ersten "Undercover-Gartenzwerg"-Aktionen (86), siehe: Reynolds, *Guerilla Gardening*, 85-88.
[19] Nach oben genannter Definition ist Weppelmann streng genommen kein Guerilla-Gärtner.

gelassen hat, einen 24 Quadratmeter großen schwimmenden Garten, auf dem sich neben einem Apfelbaum auch ein Gemüse- und Kräuterbeet befinden.[20] Reynolds bezeichnet die Aqua-Guerillas als die "Marinedivision"[21] der Gärtner_innen-Bewegung. Auf seiner Website[22] informiert Reynolds über weltweite Aktionen, vermittelt Interessierte, erstattet Bericht und bietet ein ausführliches Informationsforum sowie eine Plattform zur Unterstützung und gegenseitigen Vernetzung.[23]

Motivation

In ihrem Aufsatz unterscheidet Uhlig vier Motivationsgründe für *Guerilla Gardening*: einen pragmatischen, einen ökologischen, einen politischen sowie einen ästhetischen. Die ästhetische Ebene bewertet Uhlig als eine der gewichtigsten.[24] Reynolds weist allerdings darauf hin, dass die Motivationen so vielfältig sind wie das Gärtnern selbst und in der Regel am meisten durch die eigene Umgebung der Guerillas bestimmt sind.[25] Als mögliche Beweggründe für *Guerilla Gardening* nennt er – wie Uhlig – den Drang zur Verschönerung (hierzu gehört auch die wirtschaftliche Aufwertung einer Region durch die Steigerung der Attraktivität des Wohnraums), das Bedürfnis nach Nahrung, den Wunsch nach Gemeinschaft, das Achten auf die eigene Gesundheit sowie den Willen, den eigenen (politischen, ökologischen, sozialen) Ideen Ausdruck zu verleihen.[26] Die Motivation des "politischen" Widerstands artikuliert Reynolds wie folgt:

> Indem sie Regeln brechen, stellen Guerilla-Gärtner die gesellschaftlichen Konventionen in Frage. Dies im öffentlichen Raum zu tun, ist eine klare Absage an das politische Umfeld. Die meisten von uns kämpfen als Guerilla-Gärtner in einem demokratischen System, wo es möglich sein sollte, seine Meinung frei zu äußern

---

[20] Vgl. Wilm Weppelmann. (http://www.weppelmann.de/, 25. Juli 2013); Münstersche Zeitung, "Der schwimmende Garten". (http://www.muensterschezeitung.de/lokales/muenster/bilder/cme140369,3999768, 29. August 2013). Siehe auch die Abbildungen des schwimmenden Gartens unter Münstersche Zeitung, "Der schwimmende Garten". (http://www.muenstersche zeitung.de/lokales/muenster/bilder/cme140369,3999768, 29. August 2013).

[21] Reynolds, *Guerilla Gardening*, 121.

[22] Richard Reynolds. (http://www.guerrillagardening.org/, 24. Juli 2013); vgl. Huhn, *Mit Spaten, Pflanzen und Visionen*, 22-23.

[23] Vgl. Reynolds, *Guerilla Gardening*, 85-88; Uhlig, *Guerilla Gardening*, 2.

[24] Vgl. Uhlig, *Guerilla Gardening*, 5.

[25] Vgl. Reynolds, *Guerilla Gardening*, 19. Jahnke nennt ebenfalls eine Vielfalt von Motiven, die sie aus ihren Interviews (siehe 115-121) zusammengestellt und systematisiert hat. Vgl. Jahnke, *Guerilla Gardening anhand von Beispielen in New York, London und Berlin*, 79-97.

[26] Vgl. Reynolds, *Guerilla Gardening*, 19-44.

und auch gehört zu werden. Die meisten von uns sind auch Teil des kapitalistischen Systems, wo alles einen Preis hat und mit Ressourcen gehandelt wird.[27]

Dennoch betont er, dass Guerilla-Gärtner_innen nicht einer einzigen "typischen" politischen Gruppierung zuzuordnen sind.[28]

Ziele

Visualisierung – so scheint es – ist eines der Hauptanliegen der Guerilla-Gärtner_innen. Es geht ihnen darum, das Verschwinden der Natur aus dem städtischen Raum sichtbar zu machen. Die Bevölkerung soll auf ökologische Probleme – auch vor ihrer eigenen Haustür – aufmerksam gemacht werden. Die Massivität, mit der sich manch ein Lavendelstrauch aus dem beinharten Asphalt herauskämpft und allem Smog, allen Passant_innen und dem hektischen Leben der Stadt zum Trotz beständig blüht, ist dabei beeindruckend. Sensibilisierung und Wachheit für die Verdrängung der natürlichen Lebensressourcen und der natürlichen Lebensenergien aus hoch- und überbevölkerten Ballungsgebieten sind es, wofür die Gärtner_innen sich einsetzen.[29] Ihre politischen Forderungen verlangen nach mehr Mitbestimmungsrecht hinsichtlich der Nutzung und Gestaltung öffentlicher Flächen.[30] Es ist längst kein Geheimnis mehr, dass es zur Sicherung der Ernährung bereits gestern und nicht erst morgen klug (gewesen) wäre, Grünflächen des urbanen Raumes als Ackerflächen mitzunutzen. Ron Finley, ein Guerilla-Gärtner aus dem Süden von Los Angeles, verdeutlicht diesen Gedanken in einem seiner TV-Auftritte: Auf den freien Flächen von Los Angeles – insgesamt circa 26 Quadratmeilen (67,34 km^2), das ist ungefähr 20 mal die Fläche des Central Parks – ließen sich 724.838.400 Tomatenpflanzen anbauen.[31] Zukunftsweisende Projekte mit einem hohen positiven pädagogischen Nebeneffekt sind auch in Deutschland anzutreffen, beispielsweise in Berlin Tempelhof.[32]

---

[27] Reynolds, *Guerilla Gardening*, 260.

[28] Vgl. Reynolds, *Guerilla Gardening*, 260.

[29] Vgl. Uhlig, *Guerilla Gardening*, 1.

[30] Das Bedürfnis nach Gestaltung des öffentlichen Raumes findet aktuell auch im "Guerilla Knitting" Ausdruck. Vgl. hierzu z.B. Huhn, *Mit Spaten, Pflanzen und Visionen*, 98.

[31] Vgl. Ron Finley. (http://ronfinley.com/, 24. Juli 2013); David Hochman, "Urban Gardening: An Appleseed with Attitude". (http://www.nytimes.com/2013/05/05/fashion/urban-gardening-an-appleseed-with-attitude.html?pagewanted=all&_r=0, 29. Juli 2013).

[32] Vgl. Christoph Cadenbach, "Es grünt so grün," in: *Süddeutsche Zeitung Magazin* 14 (2012). (http://sz-magazin.sueddeutsche.de/texte/anzeigen/37255, 25. Juli 2013); Reynolds, *Guerilla Gardening*, 39; Rasper, *Vom Gärtnern in der Stadt*, 20-22, 25. Für weitere Fallbeispiele siehe

In einem weiten Sinn geht es also um eine langfristige, ökologisch vertretbare und nachhaltige Steigerung des Gemeinwohls und der städtischen Lebensqualität.[33] Uhlig hebt hervor, dass so auch der "Anspruch auf Gestaltung des eignen Umfelds zum Ausdruck [gebracht werden soll]."[34] Der politische Protest ist ein Aufruf gegen "die zunehmende Privatisierung [...] von öffentlichem Raum".[35] Es ist auch ein Kampf gegen Verteilungsungerechtigkeit, wie Reynolds verdeutlicht: Unter Verweis auf Kevin Cahills Werk *Who Owns the World* macht er darauf aufmerksam, dass "gerade einmal 15 Prozent aller Menschen Besitz- oder Pachtrechte an der insgesamt 13,58 Millionen Hektar großen Landmasse der Erde habe. Der Rest von uns braucht eine Nutzungserlaubnis".[36] Die grünen Guerillas bringen mit den symbolischen Pflanzungen ihre Themen (Ökologie, Naturschutz, Bürgerpolitik) in die Diskussion.[37] Methodisch gehen sie dabei äußerst geschickt vor, indem sie ihre Anliegen in Metaphern oder Symbolen ausdrücken und gezielt dort platzieren, wo keiner sie erwartet, und somit schon mittels dieser Dekontextualisierung Aufmerksamkeit erreicht wird.

---

auch Huhn, *Mit Spaten, Pflanzen und Visionen*, 38-43; Jahnke, *Guerilla Gardening anhand von Beispielen in New York, London und Berlin*, 71-73; "Garten Rosa Rose: Ein Nachbarschaftsgarten in Berlin Friedrichshain". (http://www.rosarose-garten.net/de/start, 1. August 2013; vgl. auch http://rosarose.twoday.net/, 1. August 2013). Vgl. auch die spektakuläre Gemüsefarm "Gotham Greens" auf dem Flachdach eines New Yorker Gebäudes: Christian Mattauch, "Salatköpfe in luftiger Höhe," in: *Süddeutsche Zeitung Magazin* 135 (2013), 26.

[33] Vgl. Uhlig, *Guerilla Gardening*, 4.

[34] Uhlig, *Guerilla Gardening*, 4; vgl. Reynolds, *Guerilla Gardening*, 38.

[35] Uhlig, *Guerilla Gardening*, 4.

[36] Reynolds, *Guerilla Gardening*, 46, vgl. 46-50; vgl. Marita Wiggerthale, "Reiche essen Erde auf," in: Oekom e.V. – Verein für ökologische Kommunikation (Hg.), *Welternährung: Global denken – lokal säen* (Oekom Verlag: München 2012), Politische Ökologie 128, 24-29; Kerstin Lanje, "Europa muss sein Feld gerechter bestellen," in: Oekom e.V. – Verein für ökologische Kommunikation (Hg.), *Welternährung: Global denken – lokal säen* (Oekom Verlag: München 2012), Politische Ökologie 128, 53-59. Zum Thema "Verteilungsungerechtigkeit und Geschlecht" siehe auch: Anne C. Bellows / Maria Daniela de Nunez Burbano Lara / Stefanie Lemke / Roseana do Socorro Goncalves Viana, "Hunger hat ein Geschlecht: Frauen und Ernährungssouveränität," in: Oekom e.V. – Verein für ökologische Kommunikation (Hg.), *Welternährung: Global denken – lokal säen* (Oekom Verlag: München 2012), Politische Ökologie 128, 98-104. "Doch auch diejenigen unter den Guerilla-Gärtnern, die sich nicht als politisch betrachten, reagieren durch ihre Aktionen auf politische Missstände, auf verfehlte Stadtpolitik, die zunehmende Einebnung von Grünflächen innerhalb der Stadt, auf zu viel Privatisierung und zu wenig Mitspracherecht." Uhlig, *Guerilla Gardening*, 5.

[37] Vgl. Uhlig, *Guerilla Gardening*, 5.

Terminologie

Besonders auffällig ist an der doch weitestgehend friedlichen Protestbewegung[38] ihre Kriegsmetaphorik. Guerillas, so ihr bereits erläuterter Name, wecken sofort eine Assoziation mit ihren Vorbildern im spanischen Unabhängigkeitskrieg. Darüber hinaus propagieren gerade Christy und Reynolds, die Gründungsaktivist_innen, weitere Slogans, die an paramilitärische Parolen erinnern, so etwa "Fight the Filth" oder "Resistance is fertile".[39]

Einerseits mag die militärische Sprache der Gärtner_innen auf pazifistische Christ_innen abschreckend oder geradezu beängstigend wirken; bei einigen weckt sie womöglich Assoziationen an christlich(-fundamentalistische) Kontexte – beispielsweise die Legionäre Christi.[40] Andererseits kann hiermit der Vehemenz und Kreativität der Bewegung Ausdruck verliehen werden: Während die einen meinen, nur mit herkömmlichen Waffen kämpfen zu können und damit jegliches Leben vernichten (nicht nur menschliches!), zeigen die Guerilla-Gärtner_innen, wie die *Schwerter zu Pflugscharen*[41] geschmiedet werden können, die im besten Fall sogar neues Leben bewirken.

Wie die Guerillas im Unabhängigkeitskrieg des 19. Jahrhunderts "ganz gewöhnliche Männer"[42] und nicht etwa "ausgebildete Soldaten" waren, ist ein Expert_innenwissen in Sachen Gärtnern keine Voraussetzung, um Guerilla-Gärtner_in zu werden. Ebenso wenig gibt es eine Alterseinschränkung. "Die

---

[38] Reynolds spricht von "ökologischer Bewegung" (Reynolds, *Guerilla Gardening*, 17), Huhn von einer "Graswurzelbewegung" (Huhn, *Mit Spaten, Pflanzen und Visionen*, 8, 21); vgl. Jahnke, *Guerilla Gardening anhand von Beispielen in New York, London und Berlin*, 101.

[39] Siehe Reynolds. (http://www.guerrillagardening.org/, 24. Juli 2013); Reynolds, *Guerilla Gardening*, 51. An dieser Stelle möchte ich an den bekannten feministischen Programmspruch "Seid furchtbar und wehret euch" erinnern.

[40] "Gute Manieren und seriöses Auftreten gehören zum Markenzeichen der Legionäre [...]. Beginnen wir lieber bei ihrem selbst gewählten Namen, der für sich schon Programm ist: 'Legionäre Christi'! Der Ausdruck als solcher müsste bereits für einen normalen denkenden Christen ein Skandal sein. Militanz klingt an, der Gedanke an Kreuzzug und Schwert ist unvermeidlich. Und die Assoziation trügt nicht: Auch und gerade nach ihrem eigenen Verständnis sind die Legionäre keine friedfertigen Verkünder des Glaubens, sondern kämpferische Soldaten des Papstes." Hanspeter Oschwald, *Im Namen des Heligen Vaters: Wie fundamentalistische Mächte den Vatikan steuern* (Heyne: München 2010), 215.

[41] Vgl. Micha 4,3; Joel 4,10.

[42] Reynolds, *Guerilla Gardening*, 13; vgl. Fußnote 1 dieses Aufsatzes. "Jeder und jede kann Guerilla-Gärtner werden – am wenigsten brauchst du dafür militärische Erfahrung." Reynolds, *Guerilla Gardening*, 127. Für die weniger Erfahrenen gibt es in einigen Städten "Gärtner-Workshops" oder "Trainingseinheiten" für "Rekruten". Reynolds, *Guerilla Gardening*, 164; vgl. Huhn, *Mit Spaten, Pflanzen und Visionen*, 82.

jüngste Guerillera, an deren Seite ich gekämpft habe, war die vierjährige Bea-
trice 2930 aus Plymouth, und die älteste ist meine 91 Jahre alte Großmutter
Margot 623",[43] schreibt Reynolds.

Der Abschnitt "Das Handbuch" in Reynolds Werk beginnt mit dem Kapitel
"Waffenarsenal",[44] in welchem diverse Pflanzen beschrieben werden. In die-
sem Kapitel fällt die Rubrik "Angriffspflanzen" besonders auf. Im Wortlaut:
"Um den Kampf mit möglichst wenig Aufwand zu gewinnen, empfehlen sich
Waffen, die lange nachwirken. Ohne deine abermalige Intervention sollten sie
sich idealerweise doch weit über ihren ersten Einsatzort hinaus ausbreiten."[45]
Unter dem Abschnitt "Pflanzen beschaffen" heißt es:

> Ein neuer Guerillero wird deshalb eher vorsichtig sein und nicht gleich viel Geld
> in Pflanzen investieren wollen, die anschließend allen möglichen Feinden ausge-
> setzt sind. Ist die Wahrscheinlichkeit hoch, dass du Verluste erleiden wirst, schick
> nicht deine kostbarsten Truppen an die Front. […] Wie jeder Kämpfer brauchst du
> möglichst direkten Zugriff auf deine Pflanzen.[46]

Uhlig zeigt weiterhin auf, dass auch das Vorgehen der Guerilla-Gärtner_innen
ihren spanischen Vorgänger_innen im Unabhängigkeitskrieg ähnelt. Es handelt
sich um "kleine, selbstständig operierende Kampfeinheiten[, die] 'nadelstich-
artige' militärische Operationen durchführen."[47] Bekannt wurde diese Kriegs-
technik unter anderem durch politische Führer wie Mao Tse Tung (1937),
Che Guevara (1960) und Emiliano Zapata (1911); besonders Maos "Kämpfer-
weisheiten" werden von Reynolds häufig zitiert.[48] In Anlehnung an ihre Forderungen nach "Land und Freiheit" kämpfen auch die Guerilla-Gärtner_innen
für eine gerechtere Aufteilung von Flächen. Weiterhin setzen sie sich besonders in den Großstädten für eine Verbesserung der Lebensqualität ein, was

---

[43] Reynolds, *Guerilla Gardening*, 127. Die im Zitat erwähnten Nummern dienen der Identifikation der Gärtner_innen.

[44] Reynolds, *Guerilla Gardening*, 91.

[45] Reynolds, *Guerilla Gardening*, 100.

[46] Reynolds, *Guerilla Gardening*, 106.

[47] Uhlig, *Guerilla Gardening*, 3.

[48] Vgl. Reynolds, *Guerilla Gardening*, 13-16; Uhlig, *Guerilla Gardening*, 3. Beispiele für Reynolds
Mao-Zitate: "'Guerilla-Einheiten müssen mit Mitteln ausgestattet sein, die zügige Kommuni-
kation erlauben'" (117); "Eine Guerilla 'muss sich flüssig wie das Wasser und leicht wie der
Wind bewegen'" (119); "'Wir dürfen nicht angreifen, wenn wir nicht sicher sind, dass wir
gewinnen. Wir müssen unsere Operationen auf kleine Gebiete begrenzen und die Feinde und
Verräter dort zerstören'." Reynolds, *Guerilla Gardening*, 123. Als Beispiel für ein Che Guevara-
Zitat, siehe Seite 137.

auch ein Ringen um mehr Möglichkeiten, öffentlichen Raum nahe der eigenen Wohnung selbstbestimmt bewirtschaften zu dürfen, einschließt.[49]

Mit einer gezielten Kriegsmetaphorik operiert Reynolds auch auf seiner bereits erwähnten Website. Hier können Mitglieder lokale Gruppen bilden, die "Zellen" genannt werden, ihnen werden "Truppennamen" gegeben. Jedes Mitglied erhält eine Nummer zur Identifikation, der eigene Name bleibt bis zum Tod des Mitglieds unsichtbar, um eine Strafverfolgung zu erschweren.[50]

Interessant ist auch der Abschnitt auf Reynolds Website über die empfohlene Gärtner_innenkluft, hier "Kampfanzug[…]"[51] genannt, wobei explizit vom "Soldatenlook"[52] abgeraten wird. Guerillas lassen sich nicht anhand eines Einheitsoutfits erkennen, Vielfalt und Praktikabilität stehen an oberster Stelle, wobei es Truppen gibt, die ihre eigenen "Uniformen"[53] tragen.

Die "Waffen" der Guerillas, oben bereits mit ihrem heute üblichen Terminus *Seed Ball* oder *Seed Bomb* – Saatbomben – eingeführt, trugen ursprünglich die Bezeichnung "Seed Grenades";[54] es gibt sie sogar in Form von Neun-Millimeter-Pistolen.[55]

Zu Beginn wurde eine Mischung aus Samen, Dünger und Wasser in Ballons oder Kondome gefüllt, die dann aus Autos geschleudert, über Zäune hinweg geworfen oder schlicht im Vorbeigehen fallen gelassen wurden.[56] Heute, über vierzig Jahre später, werden *Seed Balls* nach einem ausgetüftelten Konzept hergestellt und bestehen aus einer 1:3:5 Mischung aus Samen, Kompost und Lehm. Kompost und Lehm fungieren als Bodenersatz, da dieser gerade in den Großstädten kaum anzutreffen ist. "Aus Tod bringenden Bomben und Granaten werden [so] lebensspendende Objekte."[57]

---

[49]   Vgl. Uhlig, *Guerilla Gardening*, 3.

[50]   Vgl. Reynolds. (http://www.guerrillagardening.org/, 24. Juli 2013); Felicitas Rhan, "Pflanzen statt Tanzen," in: art – Das Kunstmagazin (11/04/2008). (http://www.art-magazin.de/szene/5486/?p=1, 29. Juli 2013).

[51]   Reynolds, *Guerilla Gardening*, 114.

[52]   Reynolds, *Guerilla Gardening*, 113.

[53]   Reynolds, *Guerilla Gardening*, 116.

[54]   Uhlig, *Guerilla Gardening*, 3.

[55]   Siehe den Farbabdruck in: Reynolds, *Guerilla Gardening*, 206 sowie in: Danny Kriengel, "Guerilla Gardening: Blumenkinder im Großstadtdschungel," in: *Spiegel online*. (http://einestages.spiegel.de/static/entry/blumenkrieger_im_grossstadtdschungel/93136/explosive_saat.html, 17. Februar 2014).

[56]   Vgl. Uhlig, *Guerilla Gardening*, 3.

[57]   Uhlig, *Guerilla Gardening*, 3. "Guerilla Gardening ist eine Schlacht, in der Blumen die Munition sind (meistens jedenfalls)" (Reynolds, *Guerilla Gardening*, 12, vgl. 108-109 u.ö.); vgl. Rasper, *Vom Gärtnern in der Stadt*, 104-105.

Weiterhin empfiehlt Reynolds – ganz in Anlehnung an Mao –, stets auf eine gute Kommunikation zu den "Reservetruppen"[58] zu achten, um schnell Hilfe vom "Basislager"[59] holen zu können oder Warnungen abzugeben.[60]

Hinsichtlich der Terminologie der Guerillas, wie sie im "Botanischen Manifest" vorgestellt wird, möchte ich einen weiteren – gerade für diesen Beitrag besonders interessanten – Hinweis aufgreifen. Im "Botanischen Manifest" gibt es ein Unterkapitel mit dem Titel "Propaganda".[61] In diesem beschreibt Reynolds verschiedene Werbe- und Wettbewerbsstrategien. In einer Fußnote erläutert der Autor den Gebrauch des Terminus "Propaganda" wie folgt:

> Propaganda ist ein Wort, das man sofort mit Kommunikation assoziiert, während "propagation" im Englischen Ausbreitung bedeutet, also mit Gartenbau assoziiert werden kann. Die beiden Begriffe sind eng miteinander verwandt. Unser Verständnis des Wortes Propaganda geht auf den lateinischen Ausdruck *propaganda fidei* zurück, was so viel wie "den Glauben verbreiten" bedeutet.[62]

Eine Brücke zur Theologie ist damit bereits geschlagen. Im Folgenden werde ich auf die Bedeutung des *Guerilla Gardenings* für den innerkirchlichen Protest eingehen.

Bedeutung für den innerkirchlichen Protest

Es ließen sich zahlreiche Anknüpfungspunkte zwischen Theologie und dem Ausdruck zivilen Ungehorsams, wie es das Guerilla-Gärtnern darstellt, finden: Ich denke beispielsweise an eine Diskussion um die *creatio continua*, die kontinuierliche Schöpfung und Neuschöpfung in unserem Leben, und die Frage, warum wir uns nicht mit Leblosem abgeben möchten. Es wäre ein religionssoziologischer Diskurs denkbar, in dem die Religion der Großstadt und die Frage nach Möglichkeiten, kleine aber feine Hoffnungszeichen zu setzen, in einem Metadiskurs erörtert würden. Weiterhin stellt sich die Frage nach einer Öko-Theologie immer dringlicher: Die Theologie kann und darf sich nicht auf einen Binnendiskurs der Gottes- und Glaubenskrise beschränken, sondern muss sich auch der ökologischen Krise stellen, in die Debatten und Forschung

---

[58] Reynolds, *Guerilla Gardening*, 117.

[59] Reynolds, *Guerilla Gardening*, 119.

[60] Wobei Reynolds betont, dass Passanten zunächst einmal nicht gefürchtet werden sollten, denn "jeder einzelne von ihnen ist ein potenzieller Rekrut." Reynolds, *Guerilla Gardening*, 156.

[61] Vgl. Reynolds, *Guerilla Gardening*, 153-175.

[62] Reynolds, *Guerilla Gardening*, 175, FN 1.

zur Nachhaltigkeit einsteigen und ihren Beitrag dazu leisten. Wenn die Welt Teil Gottes ist, dann bedeutet die Zerstörung dieser Welt weit mehr als ein Raub von Lebensraum.[63]

In diesem Beitrag möchte ich jedoch ein Schlaglicht auf einen anderen Aspekt des politischen Ungehorsams werfen. Ich möchte eine Verbindung vom stillen Protest der Guerilla-Gärtner_innen zu Protestformen innerhalb der Kirchen – in erster Linie der Katholischen Kirche – ziehen und nach dem Potential des grünen Protests für den innerkirchlichen Widerstand fragen. Am *Guerilla Gardening* fasziniert mich die meist leise, lebendige, bunte und oftmals erst auf den zweiten Blick – dann aber umso eindringlichere – Art und Weise, in der Guerilla-Gärtner_innen vorgehen und auf ihre Anliegen aufmerksam machen. Zunächst geht es doch um nichts anderes als darum, die eigenen Anliegen zum Ausdruck zu bringen und auf Missstände aufmerksam zu machen. Hierbei verzichten Guerilla-Gärtner_innen auf *ad personam* Angriffe; die Verantwortlichen werden weder benannt, noch explizit aufgesucht. Der Kontakt zu ihnen wird über ein florales Medium hergestellt. Dadurch werden die Anliegen der Guerilla-Gärtner_innen, ihre Protestinhalte und ihre Kritik weder banalisiert noch verniedlicht, sondern sehr deutlich zum Ausdruck gebracht.

Wo sind die inhaltlichen Gemeinsamkeiten der Proteste und wie unterschiedlich ist ihre Gestalt? Im Folgenden sollen stichpunktartig einige Anregungen zum Weiterdenken gegeben werden:

• Wie die Guerilla-Gärtner_innen, so fordern auch kirchliche Protestgruppen mehr Partizipationsmöglichkeit und -gerechtigkeit. Lai_innen werden oft nicht oder nicht ausreichend an innerkirchlichen Entscheidungsprozessen beteiligt, selbst dann nicht, wenn sie – wie in der aktuellen Situation der Zusammenlegung von Pastoralräumen – diejenigen sind, die unter den Auswirkungen der an der Kirchenspitze getroffenen Entscheidungen maßgeblich mitleiden. Jedoch ist selbst innerhalb des Klerus keine ausreichende Kommunikation und Mitbestimmungsmöglichkeit gegeben. Die hierarchischen Strukturen führen – zumindest in einigen Bistümern – dazu, dass die Entscheidenden mit den Ausführenden selten bis nie gesprochen haben. Zu erinnern sei an dieser Stelle

---

[63] Vgl. Julia Enxing, *Gott im Werden: Die Prozesstheologie Charles Hartshornes* (Pustet: Regensburg 2013), ratio fidei 50, 139-190. Julia Enxing, "God's World – God's Body," in: Peter Jonkers / Marcel Sarot (Hg.), *Embodied Religion* (Utrecht Publishing: Utrecht 2013), Ars Disputandi 6, 229-240. In letztgenannter Referenz werden ökofeministische Überlegungen explizit aufgegriffen.

auch an die Forderungen des Memorandums "Kirche 2011: Ein notwendiger Aufbruch",[64] in dem die Autor_innen und Unterzeichner_innen eine größere Transparenz und Beteiligung aller Gläubigen in Entscheidungsfragen fordern. Sie rufen auf zu synodale(re)n Strukturen innerhalb der Katholischen Kirche und verweisen auf das "alte Rechtsprinzip 'Was alle angeht, soll von allen entschieden werden'".[65] Auch "Wir sind Kirche" fordert in ihrem Kirchen-VolksBegehren "Mitsprache und Mitentscheidung der Ortskirchen bei Bischofsernennungen – *Bischof soll werden, wer das Vertrauen des Volkes genießt.*"[66] Der Freckenhorster Kreis setzt sich ebenfalls für eine konsequente Umsetzung des Subsidiaritätsprinzips in den Lokalkirchen und Gemeinden vor Ort ein, das heißt, dass Anliegen, die die Gläubigen vor Ort betreffen, nicht von Rom aus gesteuert und kontrolliert werden, sondern die Gläubigen auf lokaler Ebene sowohl primäres Mitsprache- als auch Entscheidungsrecht erhalten. Sie sollen – entsprechend der unterschiedlichen Charismen – je eigenverantwortlich ihre Aufgaben wahrnehmen und ausüben dürfen, ohne hierbei von einer kirchlichen Kontrollinstanz observiert oder gar gegängelt zu werden. Die hiermit verbundenen Anliegen bezeichnet der Freckenhorster Kreis als notwendigen "Strukturwandel" in der Katholischen Kirche. Begründet wird die Forderung mit dem Leben und Wirken Jesu Christi, wie es in der Bibel tradiert wird. Wenn Jesu Vorbild und seine Weisungen auch für die Kirche von heute handlungsbestimmend sein sollen, dann muss, ebenso wie für Jesus allein der Glaube Kriterium für die Berufung und Bevollmächtigung seiner Jünger war, ein wahrer Glaube an Jesus Christus und das Evangelium das Kriterium sein, nach dem entschieden wird. Zusätzliche, sekundär und teilweise erst Jahrtausende später eingeführte Kriterien, wie etwa Lebensstand oder sexuelle Orientierung, gelten als von Jesus nicht legitimierte und mit der Botschaft Jesu deshalb nicht zu vereinbarende, nachträglich hinzugefügte machtpolitische Kriterien, von denen die Amtskirche Abstand nehmen sollte.[67]

---

[64] "Memorandum Kirche 2011: Ein notwendiger Aufbruch." (http://www.memorandum-freiheit.de/, 25. Juli 2013).

[65] Abdruck des Memorandums in: Judith Könemann / Thomas Schüller (Hg.), *Das Memorandum: Die Positionen für und wider* (Herder: Freiburg im Breisgau 2011), 14-18, hier 16.

[66] Abdruck des KirchenVolksBegehren in: Herder Verlag (Hg.), *"Wir sind Kirche": Das Kirchenvolksbegehren in der Diskussion* (Herder: Freiburg im Breisgau 2013), 12-14, hier 13 (Hervorhebung im Original).

[67] Vgl. Thomas Großbölting, *"Wie ist Christsein heute möglich?": Suchbewegungen des nachkonziliaren Katholizismus im Spiegel des Freckenhorster Kreises* (Oros Verlag: Altenberge 1997), Münsteraner Theologische Abhandlungen 49, 149-169.

- Von einem "Aufruf gegen Unterdrückung" kann in vielen Fragen, die die Rolle der Frau – primär im katholischen Kirchenmilieu – betreffen, gesprochen werden. Viele kirchliche Protestgruppierungen fordern explizit, vehement und bereits seit langem eine volle Gleichberechtigung von Mann und Frau, die sich in einer paritätischen Besetzung von Kirchenämtern verwirklichen soll und Frauen explizit in Entscheidungsgremien einsetzt.[68] Hiervon ist die Diskussion um die Frage nach einer Diakoninnen- und/oder Priesterinnenweihe nochmals zu unterscheiden. In letzterer führen Skeptiker_innen und viele Vertreter der Kirchenleitung Gründe an, die den Charakter der Weihe an sich betreffen, das heißt, hier wird mit dem Mangel einer notwendigen ontologischen Voraussetzung des anderen Geschlechts argumentiert, ein Argument, das vielen Gläubigen in erster Linie Glaubensgehorsam abverlangt. Nicht sakramental begründen lässt sich jedoch die massive Ungleichheit der Besetzung von Kommissionen, Lehrstühlen oder Direktionsaufgaben, bei denen die Anzahl der Frauen bisher lediglich als ein *Appetizer* auf volle Gleichberechtigung bewertet werden kann.[69]
- Eine weitere Forderung der Guerillas, die man ebenso im Memorandum "Kirche 2011: Ein notwendiger Aufbruch" findet, lautet: Den "Anspruch auf Gestaltung des eignen Umfelds zum Ausdruck zu bringen".[70] Die Einmischung der Kirche in Fragen des persönlichen Lebens, besonders in moralischen oder ethischen Konfliktsituationen, empfinden viele Gläubige als Bevormundung und Eingriff in die Privatsphäre. So wird im Punkt "4. Gewissensfreiheit" des Memorandums Folgendes gefordert:

> Der Respekt vor dem individuellen Gewissen bedeutet, Vertrauen in die Entscheidungs- und Verantwortungsfähigkeit der Menschen zu setzen. Diese Fähigkeit zu unterstützen, ist auch Aufgabe der Kirche; sie darf aber nicht in Bevormundung umschlagen. Damit ernst zu machen, betrifft besonders den Bereich persönlicher Lebensentscheidungen und individueller Lebensformen.[71]

---

[68] Vgl. Günter Endruweit, "Bewegung, soziale," in: Günter Endruweit / Gisela Trommsdorff (Hg.), *Wörterbuch der Soziologie* (Lucius & Lucius: Stuttgart 2002, 2. völlig neubearb. und erw. Aufl.), 65-66; Großbölting, *"Wie ist Christsein heute möglich?"*, 247.

[69] Vgl. Gabriele Rüttiger, "Frauen in kirchlichen Leitungspositionen – Erfahrungen und Perspektiven," Vortrag beim Studientag "Das Zusammenwirken von Frauen und Männern im Dienst und Leben der Kirche", 20. Februar 2013. (http://www.dbk.de/fileadmin/redaktion/diverse_downloads/presse_2012/2013-036g-Studientag-FVV-Trier_Vortrag-Ruettiger.pdf, 15. März 2013).

[70] Uhlig, *Guerilla Gardening*, 4; vgl. Abdruck des Memorandums in: Könemann / Schüller (Hg.), *Das Memorandum*, 14-18, hier 17-18.

[71] Abdruck des Memorandums in: Könemann / Schüller (Hg.), *Das Memorandum*, 14-18, hier 17-18.

Was Guerillas als zunehmende Privatisierung anprangern, ließe sich hier als zunehmende Entprivatisierung bezeichnen. Auch das KirchenVolks-Begehren bezieht sich auf dieses Anliegen, wenn es eine "Anerkennung der verantworteten Gewissensentscheidung" – hier in Bezug auf sexualethische und sexualmoralische Fragen – fordert.[72]

• Im KirchenVolksBegehren wird weiterhin "Mitsprache und Mitentscheidung in allen kirchlichen Gremien"[73] gefordert. Es geht um ein Interesse für ein gegenseitiges Hören und Diskutieren, *contra* Bevormundung und Entscheidungsmonarchie,[74] ein Anliegen, das einem weiteren Ziel der Guerillas ähnelt. Auch sie sind angetreten, "einen Dialog zu eröffnen".[75]

In einem abschließenden Gedanken möchte ich noch auf ein weiteres Merkmal des grünen Protests eingehen: Uhlig beschreibt "Begrenzungsstreifen zwischen Fahrbahn und Gehsteig" als "beliebte Objekte für Gartenguerillas, da sie zwar ausgesprochen funktional sind, ästhetisch gesehen jedoch meist weit hinter ihren Möglichkeiten zurückbleiben."[76] Grenzstreifen, symbolisch

---

[72] Abdruck des KirchenVolksBegehren in: "Wir sind Kirche", 12-14, hier 13.

[73] Abdruck des KirchenVolksBegehren in: "Wir sind Kirche", 12-14, hier 13.

[74] Vgl. auch die Formulierung im Memorandum: "Der begonnene kirchliche Dialogprozess kann zu Befreiung und Aufbruch führen, wenn alle Beteiligten bereit sind, die drängenden Fragen anzugehen. Es gilt, im freien und fairen Austausch von Argumenten nach Lösungen zu suchen". Abdruck des Memorandums in: Könemann / Schüller (Hg.), *Das Memorandum*, 14-18, hier 18. Vgl. auch die Kritik des Freckenhorster Kreises: Großbölting zitiert aus dem FK-Archiv: Gründungserklärung des Freckenhorster Kreises, 2: "In vielen für die Kirche entscheidenden Fragen wird die innerkirchliche Diskussion nach Möglichkeit zu verhindern versucht (z.B. Reform des Eherechts, Problem des Zölibats, Verhältnis von kirchlichem Lehramt und theologischer Wissenschaft, Reform der päpstlichen und bischöflichen Kurien); manche als notwendig erkannten [sic!] Reformen und dazu notwendige Experimente werden unterbunden. In lehramtlichen Stellungnahmen, im Führungsstil und in den Verwaltungsmaßnahmen zeigt sich, in welchem Ausmaß noch heute vorkonziliare Denk- und Verhaltensweisen wirksam sind (vgl. die Entscheidung der Kardinalskommission zum holländischen Katechismus, das Lehrschreiben der deutschen Bischöfe vom Dezember 1968 u.a.). Das deutlichste Zeichen dieser Situation war die Enzyklika 'Humanae vitae' in ihrer Theologie, ihrer Sprache und in der Art ihres Zustandekommens. Die weltweite Reaktion auf diese Enzyklika hat die Krise in der Kirche vollends offengelegt." Großbölting, *"Wie ist Christsein heute möglich?"*, 79.

[75] Uhlig, *Guerilla Gardening*, 5.

[76] Uhlig, *Guerilla Gardening*, 5. Reynolds schreibt *"Straßenränder, Kreisverkehre und Mittelstreifen* sind von strategischer Priorität." Reynolds, *Guerilla Gardening*, 125 (Hervorhebung im Original). Huhn hat ein eigenes Kapitel "Aktionsräume", in dem es heißt: "Guerilla Gardening ist aber vor allem ein Phänomen, das auf Flächen auftritt, die am Rande der konventionellen Raumwahrnehmung liegen. Solche Phänomene gibt es vor allem an Orten, die nicht zum

verstanden, verraten viel über das Ansinnen der Protestler_innen: Es geht darum, Grenzen auszuloten, Grenzen zu ziehen, Grenzen abzustecken, Grenzgänger_innen zu sein. Und es geht darum, diese Grenzen zu nutzen, sie nicht einfach hinzunehmen, sondern immer wieder zu bepflanzen, zu prüfen, ob sie noch nötig sind, sie zu modifizieren, wenn sie nicht mehr gebraucht, aber trotzdem noch ge- oder benutzt werden. Es ist an der Zeit, auf ihnen Neues entstehen zu lassen, nicht nur, sie von ihrem Staub zu befreien, sondern das Alte – womöglich ehemals sinnvoll und notwendig – zu nutzen und daraus Neues zu machen, neue Ideen, Fruchtbares ergrünen zu lassen. Ein Stück Eden eben.

Grenzbepflanzer_innen sind auch Grenzgänger_innen, sie bewegen sich auf der Grenze zwischen legal und illegal, manchmal geduldet, selten geschätzt und oftmals verflucht. Doch eines wird in beiden Kontexten des Protestes deutlich: Grenzen schlicht zu dulden, hat noch wenig Fortschritt gebracht.

So unterschiedlich der Kontext, und dennoch können auch kirchliche Protestler_innen etwas von den blühenden Zeichensetzer_innen lernen, und zwar: eine sensible Kommunikation, die Grenzen nicht einfach überspringt, ignoriert oder ausradiert, sondern diese bewusst wahrnimmt, respektiert und pflegt, indem sie sie farbig gestaltet. Solch ein sensibel-kreativer Umgang könnte beiden gut tun: denjenigen, die die Grenzen ziehen, und denen, die sie diskutieren möchten.

Guerilla Gardening es un movimiento de protesta actual, en la que los activistas en su mayoría jóvenes en secreto siembran o "esparcen" semillas de plantas – las llamadas "bombas de semillas" – en las plazas públicas de las ciudades como un signo de protesta política y la desobediencia civil. Como consecuencia las plantas, flores, hierba, musgo, frutas y verduras crecen en ambientes inusuales, donde no pocas veces causan al transeúnte inocente, en la hora punta de la ciudad, el detenerse y asombrarse de la situación. ¿Por qué aquí? ¿Por qué un ramo de flores silvestres crece en esta esquina fea, gris y descuidada? ¿Las flores y plantas pueden ser un símbolo de resistencia política o una representación de los deseos y visiones? Ya sea como una "denuncia de la opresión", o como una expresión de "el derecho a dar forma al propio entorno", esta forma de resistencia botánica articula las preocupaciones, deseos y demandas que tienen numerosos paralelismos con la resistencia y los movimientos de protesta dentro de las iglesias, como realiza la Freckenhorster

---

Modellbild der Stadt gehören. Diese Orte sind Möglichkeitsräume. Möglichkeitsraum ist hierbei nur eine Bezeichnung für diese Räume. Andere Begriffe in diesem Zusammenhang sind *Heterotopie, Nicht-Orte* oder *Thirdspace*." Huhn, *Mit Spaten, Pflanzen und Visionen*, 27-34, hier 27, vgl. auch 47-48 (Hervorhebung im Original).

Kreis, Somos Iglesia o el memorándum "Iglesia 2011: la necesidad de un nuevo comienzo". De esta manera, los grupos de protesta en las iglesias expresan su afán por ampliar su derecho a tener voz y voto en los procesos de toma de decisiones, así como su derecho a la participación activa en determinados procesos en la iglesia. Además, se resisten a cualquier forma de opresión, como el trato injusto de las mujeres y los hombres dentro de la iglesia .

Guerilla Gardening utilizan una forma sensible de comunicación que no sólo traspasa, hace caso omiso o borra las fronteras, sino que conscientemente reconoce, respeta y cultiva estas plantas de una manera colorida. Un manejo tan sensible y creativo de las fronteras podría ser un modelo a seguir en la protesta dentro de la iglesia y que podría enriquecer a ambas partes: los que construyen las fronteras y los que desean hablar de ellas.

Guerilla Gardening is a modern protest movement, in which mostly young activists secretly sow or "drop" plant seeds – so called "seed bombs" – in the public squares of cities as a sign of political protest and civil disobedience. As a consequence, flowers, grass, moss, fruit and vegetable plants grow in unusual environments, where they not seldom cause the innocent passerby, the rush hour (wo)man of the city, to stop and wonder. Why here? Why does a bunch of wild flowers grow at this ugly, grey and disregarded corner? Flowers and plants as a symbol for political resistance or as a representation of desires and visions? Whether as a "call against oppression", or as an expression of "the right to shape one's own environment", this form of botanical resistance articulates concerns, desires and demands that have numerous parallels with resistance and protest movements within the churches, such as the Freckenhorster Kreis, We Are Church or the Memorandum "Church 2011: The Need for a New Beginning". In this manner, protest groups in the churches express their quest to expand their right to have a say in decision-making processes, as well as their right to actively co-determine the processes in the church. In addition, they resist any form of oppression, such as the unjust treatment of women and men within the church.

Guerilla gardeners use a sensitive form of communication which does not just skip, ignore or erase borders, but consciously recognizes, respects and cultivates them in a colorful way. Such a sensitive and creative handling of boundaries could be a role model for protest within the church and it could enrich both parties: those who draw boundaries and those who wish to discuss them.

Guerilla Gardening bezeichnet eine moderne Protestbewegung, in der meist junge Aktivist_innen heimlich Pflanzensamen – sogenannte "Samenbomben" – an öffentlichen Plätzen der Großstädte aussäen beziehungsweise "fallen lassen" als Zeichen politischen Protests und zivilen Ungehorsams. Blumen, Gras, Moos, Obst- und Gemüsepflanzen entstehen so in ungewohnter Umgebung und versetzen die ahnungslosen Passant_innen, die Rushhour-Menschen der Großstädte, nicht selten ins Grübeln und lassen sie stocken. Warum hier? Wieso wächst gerade an dieser hässlichen, grauen, vernachlässigten Ecke ein ganzer Strauß wilder Blumen? Blumen und Gräser als Symbole politischen Widerstands oder als Verkörperung von Sehnsüchten und Visionen? Ob als "Aufruf gegen Unterdrückung" oder als Ausdruck des "Anspruchs auf Gestaltung des eigenen Umfelds" – der botanische Widerstand artikuliert Anliegen, Sehnsüchte und Forderungen, die zahlreiche Parallelen zu innerkirchlichen Widerständen und Protesten aufweisen, wie sie beispielsweise der Freckenhorster Kreis, Wir sind Kirche oder das Memomerandum "Kirche 2011: Ein notwendiger Aufbruch" benennen. So wollen auch innerkirchliche Protestgruppen ihr Mitsprache- und Mitentscheidungsrecht ausbauen und den innerkirchlichen Prozess aktiv mitgestalten. Weiterhin wehren sie sich gegen jede Form von Unterdrückung, wie beispielsweise die ungleiche Behandlung von Frauen und Männern in der Kirche.

Guerilla-Gärtner_innen bedienen sich dabei einer sensiblen Kommunikation, die Grenzen nicht einfach überspringt, ignoriert oder ausradiert, sondern diese bewusst wahrnimmt, respektiert und pflegt, indem sie sie farbig gestaltet. Solch ein sensibel-kreativer Umgang könnte auch für den innerkirchlichen Protest Vorbild sein und beide Parteien bereichern: diejenigen, die die Grenzen ziehen, und diejenigen, die sie diskutieren möchten.

Julia Enxing, Dr. theol., studierte Katholische Theologie an der Johannes Gutenberg-Universität Mainz und an der Westfälischen Wilhelms-Universität Münster. Visiting Scholar am Center for Process Studies (Claremont, USA); derzeit wissenschaftliche Mitarbeiterin am Exzellenzcluster "Religion und Politik in den Kulturen der Vormoderne und der Moderne" der Westfälischen Wilhelms-Universität Münster; Mitglied des Vorstands der ESWTR/BRD.

Journal of the European Society of Women in Theological Research 22 (2014) 139-156.
doi: 10.2143/ESWTR.22.0.3040795

Musa W. Dube

Boundaries and Bridges: Journeys of a Postcolonial Feminist in Biblical Studies

As a young girl, one of the derisive comments I frequently heard at our family retail shop was: "Dilo ke lona le tsile le tlola melolwane le melolwane; dinoka le dinokana, le tsile go bapala kwano." That is, "you came crossing one boundary after another, one river after another to trade in our country." The subtext in the statement was that we were foreigners who did not deserve, or had merely been favored to access economic resources in Botswana. My parents and five of my eldest siblings were born in Zimbabwe, and the last five of us were born in Botswana. Before we migrated to Botswana, it had happened that the village where my parents lived was declared a white man's ranch. Indigenous people in the area were given two choices: to remain in their homes and assume the status of servants to the owner of the ranch, or to move to the reserves. The reserves were arid and crowded places, where black indigenous people of Zimbabwe were moved from their villages and resettled. My parents chose to remain. And so their status was redefined to servanthood. After a while they were restricted to ploughing only an acre and to owning a maximum of five cows. That was when my parents decided to move to Botswana, a semi-desert country that did not attract white colonial settlers due to its harsh temperatures.

I was thus born in Botswana due to this colonial experience. Yet even those of us who were born in Botswana bore Zimbabwean names and spoke Ndebele in our family, which immediately marked us as those who do not have roots among the indigenous ethnic groups of Botswana. As many diaspora narratives attest,[1] people living in diaspora contexts often permanently bear the stamp of

---

[1] See Psalm 137:1-6, which reads, "By the rivers of Babylon, there we sat down and there we wept, when we remembered Zion, On the willows there we hung our harps [...] How could we sing the Lord's song in a foreign land? If I forget you, O Jerusalem, let my right hand wither!". This text does not only express the exiled and diasporic Jewish communities' yearning for home, but has also provided a popular language for many other contemporary diaspora

being foreigners even when they have long settled in their host country, because their very existence is an unending process of crossing boundaries, living in between spaces and of continuous negotiation with the larger cultural, economic and political community. One remains unsettled. And so recently a friend of mine told me that some people have remarked that I behave and carry myself as if I am a foreigner in Botswana, even though I was born and bred in Botswana. Indeed I have no other country to call my own, save Botswana. If I were to return to Zimbabwe, as we occasionally do with my family, I would find myself even at a stranger place there. Describing this diasporic experience, Fernando Segovia, a Cuban American New Testament scholar, says it is tantamount to "having two places and no place on which to stand."[2] Edward Said, in his now classical book, *Culture and Imperialism*, points out that modern imperialism covered three quarters of our world. He holds that "the great imperial experience of the past two hundred years was global and universal [and] it has implicated every corner of the globe, the colonizer and the colonized together."[3] He also notes that it is a unique characteristic of this age "to have produced more refugees, migrants, displaced persons, and exiles than ever before in history."[4] I am part of this history.

In the past four centuries, most colonial travelers came from the western hemisphere in the form of traders, explorers, colonizers, and missionaries, or through forced migration in the form of enslavement, indentured labor or resettlements of indigenous people. However, in the contemporary era of the global economy,[5] the picture has become much more complex: the Empire does not only write back,[6]

---

communities expressing their unsettled identities. A good example is its use in Reggae music. See also Fernando F. Segovia, "Towards a Hermeneutic of the Diaspora: Hermeneutics of Otherness and Engagement," in: Fernando F. Segovia / Mary A. Tolbert (eds.), *Reading from the Place: Social Location and Biblical Interpretation in the United States* (Fortress Press: Minneapolis 1995), 57-78.

[2] Segovia, "Towards a Hermeneutic of the Diaspora," 68.

[3] Edward Said, *Culture and Imperialism* (Alfred Knopf: New York 1993), 259.

[4] Said, *Culture and Imperialism,* 332.

[5] Cf. Sankaran Krishna, *Globalisation and Postcolonialism: Hegemony and Resistance in the Twenty-first Century* (Rowman & Littlefield Publishers: New York 2009) explores the link between modern colonialism and contemporary globalization and some postcolonial forms of resistance that characterize this period.

[6] The statement evokes the book by Bill Aschroft / Gareth Griffiths / Hellen Tiffin (eds.), *The Empire Writes Back: Theory and Practice in Postcolonial Literatures* (Routledge: New York 1989), which was one of earliest literary expositions on postcolonial analysis, highlighting the centrality of the empire in commonwealth literary writers.

it also travels back to the colonial mother countries – seeking a share in the commonwealth.[7] According to Avtar Brah,

> There has been a rapid increase in migrations across the globe since the 1980s. These mass movements are taking place in all directions. The volume of migration has increased to Australia, North America and Western Europe. Similarly, large-scale population movements have taken place within and between countries of the "South". Events in Eastern Europe and the former Soviet Union have provided impetus for mass movements of people [...]. People on the move may be labor immigrants (both documented and undocumented), highly-qualified specialists, entrepreneurs, students, refugees and asylum seekers or the household members of the previous migrants.[8]

The intensity of movements across the borders has become a major feature among contemporary philosophers who have begun to theorize border-crossing, exile and the diaspora as a framework of being, seeing, thinking, living, and doing scholarly work. Said, a Palestinian scholar who lived and died in the USA, holds that "exile, far from being the fate of the nearly forgotten unfortunates who are dispossessed and expatriated, becomes something closer to the norm, an experience of crossing boundaries and charting new territories in defiance of the classic canonic enclosures".[9] Gloria Anzandula, the famed feminist Chicana scholar, drawing from her Mexican experience, theorized borderlands and border-crossing across cultures, sexualities, languages, and spiritualities.[10] Similarly, Homi Bhabha, one of the outstanding postcolonial thinkers of our time, advocates that we should regard ourselves as living in between spaces, and our identities should be constructed along a model of "hybridity".[11] He proposes that we should regard our homes as strange. The strangeness of home is a concept that invites us to be guests even in our own spaces, to occupy our own spaces with discomfort and to remain critical of the

---

[7] The global economy is a system noted for its policies of deregulation, privatization and liberalization, which reduces social welfare, creates insecurity, and separates families as increasingly people are forced to move in search of economic survival.

[8] Avtar Brah, "Diaspora, Border and Transnational Identities," in: Reina Lewis / Sara Mills (eds.), *Feminist Postcolonial Theory: A Reader* (Routledge: New York 2003), 613-634, here 613.

[9] Said, *Culture and Imperialism*, 317.

[10] Cf. Gloria Anzandula, *Borderlands / La Frontera: The New Mestiza* (Aunte Lute Books: San Francisco 1999).

[11] See Homi Bhabha, *The Location of Culture* (Routledge: New York 1994).

structures of what we call home. Bhabha also proposes the metaphor of the border, not as a place that brings us to an end, but one that invites us to look beyond our reality to another reality.[12] The border metaphor is a metaphor that places us in a migratory position, where we are all unsettled and where home is strange.

In her paper, "Diaspora, Border and Transnational Identities," Avtar Brah underlines the above positions when she challenges us to acknowledge that with current migrations we are experiencing "the homing of diaspora, the diaporising of home."[13] Given the massive movements that occur from all directions, Brah proposes that we should inhabit our homes and all spaces as "a diasporic space", which she describes as "the global condition of culture as a site of travel."[14] Brah describes the diaspora space as a conceptual category, "inhabited not only by those who migrated and their descendants, but equally by those who are constructed and represented as indigenous."[15] She proposes the diaspora space as "the site where the native is as much a diasporian as the diasporian is the native."[16] In short, we are all in the diaspora space, scattered; home is at the border where we encounter all sorts of cultures, where there is no settlement and where we are invited to look beyond our immediate homes and cultures to other realities that challenge and stretch our constructed realities. Home is indeed strange given the hybridity of our cultures and identities.

Biblical Studies at the Site of Travel

Biblical Studies is intertwined with these journeys of our world and the journeys of the word, both of the past and the present. According to Leticia Guardiola-Saenz, the biblical text is a borderless text,[17] and Jesus is a border-crosser.[18] Arguing that the "the biblical story itself invites its readers to identify with it and to act it out in history", I have argued that the biblical story is an

---

[12] Cf. Bhabha, *The Location*, 45.
[13] Brah, "Diaspora, Border," 623.
[14] Brah, "Diaspora, Border," 632.
[15] Brah, "Diaspora, Border," 632.
[16] Brah, "Diaspora, Border," 632.
[17] Cf. Leticia A. Guardiola-Saenz, "Borderless Women and Borderless Texts: A Cultural Reading of Matthew 15:21-28," in: *Semeia* 78 (1997), 69-81, here 71-72.
[18] Leticia A. Guardiola-Saenz, "Border-crossing and the Redemptive Power in John 7:53-8:11: A Cultural Reading of Jesus and the Accused," in: Musa W. Dube / John Staley (eds.), *John and Postcolonialism: Travel Space and Power* (Sheffield: Sheffield Academic Press 2002), 129-152.

unfinished story: it invites its own continuation in history, it resists the covers of our Bibles and writes itself on the pages of the earth. On these grounds, it is legitimate to hold that various biblical reader-actors from different moments in history should illumine the meaning and implications of the text for us.[19]

I wish it was all happy travel, where opportunities are available to all, boundaries are open to all, and bridges are laid for all, and the encounter with the Other is a justice-loving kiss. These journeys, however, are intertwined with the power relations that characterize our world – the so-called center and margins, developed and "underdeveloped", First and Two-thirds Worlds, colonizer and colonized. Border-crossing theorists and readers thus tell stories of contested power and concerted struggles to survive – wrenching power from boundary keepers, who will have doors closed behind them. In her reading of the woman with a demon-possessed daughter, Guardiola-Saenz says, "my reading is a story retold by the defeated, re-written from the inter-space of the postcolonial reader."[20]

For most contemporary Two-thirds World biblical readers and Christians, Jesus and the Bible arrived within their borders with colonizers. The Kenyan theorist Ngugi wa Thiongo thus holds that during the colonial era both Jesus and Shakespeare had brought light to the darkest Africa.[21] He insists that both the Bible and the needle were supposedly England's greatest gifts to Africa. He also points out that "the English, French, Portuguese came to the Third World to announce the Bible and the Sword."[22] In these statements Ngugi wa Thiongo makes connections between the Bible and colonial history – with its economic desires (needle), its literature (Shakespeare), its attack and suppression of the Other (sword). Ngugi wa Thiongo connects the biblical texts with modern colonial movements. Indeed when we study the 1884 Berlin Conference documents, where modern European colonialists gathered to slice the African continent up to distribute it among themselves without consulting or involving Africans, we realize that missionaries were acknowledged participants of the process.[23] Making connections between biblical texts and modern

---

[19] Musa W. Dube, "Towards a Postcolonial Feminist Interpretation of the Bible," in: *Semeia* 78 (1997), 11-26, here 12.

[20] Guardiola-Saenz, "Borderless Women," 74.

[21] Cf. Ngugi wa Thiongo, *Decolonising the Mind: The Politics of Language in African Literature* (James Currey: London 1986), 91.

[22] Ngugi wa Thiongo, *Decolonising the Mind*, 91.

[23] Cf. Musa W. Dube, *Postcolonial Feminist Interpretation of the Bible* (Chalice Press: St. Louis 2000), 3-6.

imperialism, in other words, does not need any special pleading. It is self-evident that biblical texts are entangled in this dance. According to Said: "Modern imperialism was so global and all-encompassing that virtually nothing escaped it [...] whether or not to look at the *connections between cultural texts and imperialism* is therefore to take a position already taken – either to study the connection in order to criticize it and think of alternatives for it, or not to study it in order to let it stand."[24]

In this paper, I seek to share my journeys with the "word" in biblical scholarship, as a child of modern colonialism, neo-colonialism and the contemporary global economy and as a black African woman scholar, who is mired within the continuous struggles for liberation, decolonization and depatriarchalization. I seek to share some of the boundaries I have sought to cross, the in-between spaces I have inhabited, and still inhabit, and some bridges I have crossed or tried to weave as a Two-thirds World Black African feminist scholar. I seek to share how I have been wrestling with the fact that the Bible was inseparably intertwined with the history of modern colonialism in Africa. This can only be a roughly summarized sketch tracing some of the journeys I have undertaken – for up to now, I am still trying to find a way through the maze. The sketches I wish to draw here, marking the questions I have borne as a Two-thirds World African feminist scholar, shall be addressed under the following sub-headings:

- Crossing the Greco-Roman Historical Boundaries
- Bridging the Boundaries of the Biblical Studies Curriculum
- Interrogating the Biblical Readers of Modern Colonial Times
- Interrogating the Ideological Boundaries of the Text
- Border-crossing the Academic Boundaries of Readers
- Re-reading the Colonized Bibles
- Bridging Methods of Studying Biblical Studies

Crossing the Greco-Roman Historical Boundaries
The first thing I confronted in the western academic biblical studies where I did my postgraduate studies in the 1990s, was that the boundaries of academic biblical studies excluded my questions. Whereas I was interested in doing biblical studies that engaged the modern colonial history and the biblical text's

---

[24] Said, *Culture and Imperialism*, 68 (emphasis added).

entanglement with this history, such a space was not readily available then. Instead as a biblical student my historical space of engagement with the biblical text was neatly placed in the Greco-Roman context. I studied the Greco-Roman history, culture, language, political structures and economic systems, and read the biblical texts within such a background. I was expected to read the text "objectively", searching for the original or the author's meaning. This approach yielded many fruitful harvests for me and remains vital, yet it bracketed many of the questions I came bearing to the field. It bracketed other histories of the biblical text.[25] Instead, the travelling biblical text had come to me, and many Two-thirds World communities of readers, marching with modern colonial travelers and garments. But because the standard historical context of studying the New Testament had been primarily defined as the ancient Greco-Roman context, and the reading method as historical criticism, my burning questions had no space of articulation.

At the core of my quest were the questions of: "How do I read the Bible as a *woman who was colonized through the Bible*?" and, "Why was it ethically acceptable for Bible readers, male and female, of modern colonialism to function hand in glove with colonizers of their countries?" For me, and other Two-thirds World women, the colonial oppression was equally significant as patriarchal oppression. Given the privileged status of the Greco-Roman context and historical criticism, my questions could pass as church history questions or history of interpretation. Yet, when I looked into the curriculum of church history in the western world, where I studied, church history seldom included the world-wide modern church history that brought Christianity to Two-thirds World countries. Perhaps modern church history was studied under missions, if at all. I must say that given the daunting walls of historical criticism, it was very helpful that I entered biblical scholarship when minority readers from Two-thirds Worlds and within the western metropolitan centers had begun to problematize the guild. The feminist framework of positing the personal as political, the narration of one's story, together with reader-response theories, provided windows of hope.

Accordingly, many minority and postcolonial scholars have problematized the focus on the Greco-Roman context as the privileged history for studying philosophy, biblical studies, literature, democracy, politics, and other related issues, pointing out that it is a Eurocentric approach that upholds the ideology

---

[25] Cf. Dube, "Towards a Postcolonial Feminist Interpretation of the Bible," 11-15.

of the superiority of the West.[26] In their book, *Unthinking Eurocentricism*, Ella Shohat and Robert Stam critique the academy for maintaining the colonizing Eurocentric heuristic posture that depicts Greece as the centre of all knowledge.[27] Two-thirds World scholars have crossed the boundaries of this privileged academic framework of study by using their own cultural/historical contexts (Liberation Theologies) and histories of the encounter of the biblical text working hand in glove with modern colonies.[28] Diasporic African American scholars have challenged the construction of and focus on the Greco-Roman context by, for example, highlighting ancient Egypt as another historical context for understanding biblical texts.[29] Others have pointed out that the historical-critical approach in academic biblical studies was hewn in the Enlightment period, which was also the height of modern imperialism; hence its assumptions perpetuate the same ideology.[30] Underlining the need to factor the entanglement of the biblical text with "worldly" journeys, Guardiola-Saenz points out that: "A cultural text is not confined to the borders of its written pages, but to the whole culture that embraces its interpretations [...]. A cultural text should be read not just for the history it reflects, but also for the history it has made: the political, moral, economic, and social consequences that the text has effected in the culture."[31]

My work still continues to investigate modern missionary letters, reports and books, to study their biblical interpretations, their perspectives towards the colonial projects of their mother countries and their construction of the Other. It investigates how colonial biblical readers translated indigenous cultures, religious spaces, gender, and their motivations. I have been reading Robert Moffat's *Missionary Labours and Scenes in Southern Africa* from 1842, and a

---

[26] Cf. Ella Shohat / Robert Stam, *Unthinking Eurocentrism: Multiculturalism and the Media* (Routledge: New York 1994), 55-94.

[27] Cf. Shohat / Stam, *Unthinking Eurocentrism,* 55-58.

[28] See Kwok Pui Lan, *Discovering the Bible in the Non-biblical World* (Orbis Press: Maryknoll 1995); Fernando F. Segovia, *Decolonizing Biblical Studies* (Orbis: Maryknoll 2000), and R. S. Sugirtharajah (ed.), *The Postcolonial Biblical Reader* (Blackwell Publishing: New York 2006).

[29] See Vincent Wimbush (ed.), *African Americans and the Bible: Sacred Texts and Social Textures* (Continuum: New York 2000) and more specifically in the same volume the article by Randall C. Bailey, "Academic Biblical Interpretations among African Americans in the United States," 696-711.

[30] Segovia, *Decolonizing,* 3-33, and Shawn Kelley, *Racializing Jesus: Race, Ideology and the Formation of Modern Biblical Scholarship* (Routledge: New York 2002).

[31] See Guardiola-Saenz, "Borderless Women," 72.

collection of papers and letters by John Mackenzie. Both missionaries worked among the Batswana ethnic groups over a long time.[32] The experience of reading such books is tantamount to what was succinctly named by Phyllis Trible as reading "Texts of Terror".[33] For a black African reader, it is a walk in a haunted house that features your very own "monsterfied" image, so that you do not want to look at yourself, you are afraid of yourself, you want to run away from yourself or simply despise yourself. To read such texts is a charring experience: a walk in a park of hellfire. The dilemma is whether to read or not read, and none of the choices is better. The challenge, for those who read, is how to read texts.[34] My advice is that one must enter such a colonizing literary jungle wearing the most efficient bullet-proof armor of decolonization that one can make.

Bridging the Boundaries of the Biblical Studies Curriculum
Of course, the questions and the observations raised here interrogate the boundaries of academic biblical scholarship and its curriculum. These observations question how biblical studies programs are designed: what they exclude and include, and the ideological purposes they serve.[35] It calls for interdisciplinary connections between various histories (ancient and modern) and various theological subjects (biblical studies with church histories, histories of interpretation and missions) and non-theological studies (economics and politics) and the integrations of various readers of the Bible, missionaries and academic readers. In a world where modern colonialism has created overlapping

---

[32] My initial analysis is found in Musa W. Dube, "Decolonizing the Darkness," in: Greg Carey / Lozado Francisco (eds.), *Soundings in Cultural Criticism: Perspectives and Methods in Culture, Power and Identity in the New Testament* (Fortress: Minneapolis 2013), 31-44, and Musa W. Dube, "The Bible in the Bush: The First 'Literate' Batswana Bible Readers," in: *Translation* 2 (Spring 2013), 79-103.

[33] See Phyllis Trible, *Texts of Terror: Literary-feminist Readings of Biblical Narratives* (Fortress Press: Minneapolis 1984).

[34] See Dube, *Postcolonial Feminist Interpretation*, 121-124, where I proposed a new reading strategy titled "Rahab's Reading Prism". I defined the strategy as "a postcolonial feminist eye of many angles and of seeing, reading, and hearing literary texts through resisting imperial and patriarchal oppressive structures and ideologies" (123).

[35] See Musa W. Dube, "Curriculum Transformation: Dreaming of Decolonization in Theological Education," in: D.N. Premnath (ed.), *Border Crossings: Cross-cultural Hermeneutics* (Orbis Press: New York 2007), 121-138, where I elaborate further on decolonizing theological education. See also the Fernando Segovia / Mary Ann Tolbert (eds.), *Teaching the Bible: The Discourses and Politics of Biblical Pedagogy* (Orbis Press: New York 1998).

territories and intertwined histories,[36] academic biblical studies must endeavor to cross multiple boundaries and live in the crossroads – for the biblical texts have long crossed multiple boundaries. The biblical guild needs to own up to the fact that the biblical text and its readers have already travelled and these journeys need to be factored into the curriculum and reading strategies. For me as a Two-thirds World scholar who has sojourned in western academic halls, the exclusion of our contexts, histories, and questions makes academic biblical studies a lonely journey, if not torturous and traumatic. It silences, shutting down our participatory learning by dismissing our questions. As I described it, it is tantamount to a long walk in a hall of mirrors that refuse to acknowledge our images, underlining that one belongs to suppressed knowledges.[37] Something must give.

Interrogating the Biblical Readers of Modern Colonial Times
Growing up in the context of the struggle for independence, debating societies often invited me and my fellow members of the Student Christian Movement to explain why we follow the faith of our oppressors, the colonizer. As I have said elsewhere,[38] evidence was largely against us as historical documents indicated that missionaries, that is, Bible readers, were not an ethical voice of resistance against the colonial projects of their mother countries. Indeed historical documents amply attest to missionaries as champions of colonialism. As Andrew Walls writes, "the missionary was spoken of in the vocabulary of the imperial pioneer."[39] Why did the modern colonial-time biblical reader fail to assume a prophetic and ethical role of resisting imperialism as an unacceptable economic and political system of exploiting Two-thirds World populations? How about the western scholars of that time?[40] This has been a major question to me. As Bible readers, I assumed they should have provided the ethical and prophetic voice of resistance. Yet one is at pains to find it, if it exists at all. And so by going with the faith of my colonizer, I could only be

---

[36] Cf. Said, *Culture and Imperialism*, 3-63.

[37] Cf. Musa W. Dube, "An Introduction: How We Have Come to 'Read With,'" in: *Semeia* 73 (1996), 7-17, here 10.

[38] Dube, *Postcolonial Feminist Interpretation*, 4-6.

[39] Andrew Walls, "British Missions," in: Torben Christensen / William Hutchinson (eds.), *Missionary Ideologies in the Imperialist Era: 1880-1920* (Aros: Aarhus 1982), 8-24, here 12.

[40] This question is best answered in Kelley, *Racializing Jesus*. Kelley's exploration highlights how modern scholar-thinkers did not escape from modern colonial ideology, and that their perspectives continue to inform contemporary academic biblical studies.

in the space of a collaborator, a betrayer. My agony brought me back to the biblical text. I sought to read again and to investigate the ideological angles of its travel narratives. I wanted to establish the reason for the failure of a prophetic voice among modern western biblical readers and scholars.

Interrogating the Ideological Boundaries of the Text
This investigation took three angles. First, I was eager to find out if the biblical texts sanctioned travel to foreign countries – if it is a borderless text – and if so, to access the standards it provided for meeting the Other who is different. I also sought to investigate how gender is constructed in such texts. I used the case studies of the Exodus and mission-oriented texts, studying how they sanction travel, crossing borders, how they construct the indigenous people, their lands and their cultures. In this investigation I wanted to find out if the biblical text stood a better chance of providing a counter-colonial ideology. My findings were not encouraging. Mission texts constructed the Other negatively – as a blank slate awaiting divine teachers (Matt 28:18-20), as ethically or morally lacking, and as women. The ideology of race was wrapped in gendered language. This is evident in the characters of Rahab (Josh 2), the Samaritan woman (John 4:1-42) or the mother with a demon-possessed daughter (Matt 15:21-28). Such characterization propounds an ideology that sanctions the suppression and oppression of the Other rather than encouraging relationships of liberating interdependence.

Second, I sought to analyze the biblical stance towards the imperialism of its time, to establish as much as I could if the Bible was a collaborative, resisting or revolting text towards the colonial powers of its time.[41] Since biblical texts were written under various imperial powers, it was important to investigate how this history impacted the production and ideological stance of biblical texts towards the empire and how it may inform future readers. The findings to this second question were varied, given that the biblical text rises from

---

[41] Dube, *Postcolonial Feminist Interpretation,* 127-155. Contemporary empire studies scholars in biblical studies have put up a spirited argument that biblical texts are anti-imperial. I just wish the modern missionary readers and scholars had interpreted the Bible from that perspective, then we would have a completely different story. Because they read it in resonance with the imperialism of their time and countries, this raises more questions; namely, why would almost all missionaries read the bible in agreement with colonialism, if biblical texts resisted the empire? Was the colonizing ideology in the text, the reader, or both? By and large, the function of the Bible as a colonizing book in modern colonialism is yet to be addressed by western empire studies scholars in biblical studies.

multiple contexts. Third, I also investigated the function of gender in the subjugation of the Other – both in the mission texts and colonizing narratives. As the above three cases highlight, female gender terminology was used to articulate the subjugation of the Other. Earlier feminist readers of these stories had sought to reconstruct the early Christian history as women's history, without problematising the colonizing ideology embedded in these texts. My reading of feminist interpretations of mission texts[42] brought me in sharp conflict with my feminist community of readers as I argued that our commitment to liberation is wanting if it does not pay equal attention to imperialism and how imperialism is manifested in the texts.[43] In my conclusion, I suggested, among other things, that feminist biblical readers should endeavor to also become decolonizing readers given that patriarchal resistance does not always translate into a decolonizing reading.

Simultaneously, I sought to read colonial classics such as *The Aeneid*, Rudyard Kipling's poem, "Take the White Man's Burden", and Joseph Conrad's *Heart of Darkness* to assess how they construct the Other who is the target of colonial desires.[44] In so doing I was making connections between the Bible and Shakespeare. The latter assisted me in searching for strategies of reading for decolonization, as suggested by Ngugi wa Thiongo. The assessment of the above named colonial classics enabled a comparison with biblical mission texts. There was much resonance between mission texts' presentation of the Other who is targeted for evangelism and how colonial literature constructed the colonized Other who is targeted for domination. I also analyzed texts of decolonizing writers such as Torontle Mositi's *The Victims*, and the Kenyan poet, Maina wa Kinyatti, whose title of a poem spoke loudly and clearly, namely, "May Imperialism Perish Forever".[45]

Border-crossing the Academic Boundaries of Readers

Taking a leaf from liberation readers who insisted on reading with base communities and in their contemporary contexts, I also sought to cross the boundaries of academic professional readers by reading with women from African

---

[42] Dube, *Postcolonial Feminist Interpretation*, 169-185.

[43] See Laura Donaldson, *Decolonizing Feminisms: Race, Gender, and Empire Building* (University of North Carolina Press: Chapel Hill 1992), who points out that addressing patriarchy does not substitute addressing the empire.

[44] Cf. Dube, *Postcolonial Feminist Interpretation*, 81-95.

[45] Cf. Dube, *Postcolonial Feminist Interpretation*, 97-109.

Independent Churches in Botswana.[46] The latter were church communities that historically resisted colonial Christianity by reading the Bible with and through African cultures, thus creating hybrid religions, cultures and resisting colonial domination. They rejected the colonial approach that regarded their indigenous traditions as evil. I wanted to read mission passages with them in search of decolonizing feminist ways of interpretations. And so off I went to the field. I spent time with small house churches, where they read the text, narrated the text, sang the text, danced the text and dramatized it, leaving me in a daze in my attempt to locate the interpretation of the passage. I had entered other boundaries of reading the text, outside the realm of western academic biblical studies halls. This approach was an attempt at shifting the voices of authority by crossing the accepted academic boundaries of the reader, to hear Other interpretations. I am currently continuing this work by reading the letters of the first literate Batswana and studying their response to missionary biblical teaching and the Setswana translated Bible.[47]

Re-reading the Colonized Bibles
In taking this journey, I was not only forced to confront Other ways of reading, I was also forced to read the Bible in indigenous languages. The process opened a whole new area for me in so far as reading for decolonization was concerned. I discovered that colonial ideology informed biblical translation in ways that I could never have imagined without reading the translated Setswana Bible.[48] While reading the story of the woman with a demon-possessed daughter with women from African Independent Churches, many readers insisted on reading one of the oldest versions of translation, done in 1903. I was forced to go shopping for the 1903 Wookey Bible to photocopy Matthew 15:21-28. Upon reading the passage, I discovered that the translator had used the Ancestors, Badimo, to translate the word "demons". Among Batswana and Bantu communities, stretching from Southern to Eastern Africa, Badimo are regarded as sacred figures, who re-present the interests of their surviving members and communities before God. So sacred is the position of Badimo that they had more attention than the higher God. In the 1903 Wookey Bible, their position

---

[46] Cf. Musa W. Dube, "Readings of *Semoya*: Batswana Women Interpretations of Matt. 15:21-28," in: *Semeia* 73 (1996), 111-129.

[47] Cf. Dube, "The Bible in the Bush," 79-103.

[48] Cf. Musa W. Dube, "Consuming a Colonial Cultural Bomb: Translating Badimo into 'Demons' in the Setswana Bible," in: *Journal for the Study of the New Testament* 21 (1999), 33-59.

had been transposed from sacred to evil. It was shocking. My ground shook. This translation was a "text of terror". Here I was invited to spin back to 1857, when the first Setswana Bible was completed and placed in the hands of trusting believers. The first Batswana readers discovered that according to their Setswana Bible, "Jesus went casting out Badimo!" What a perfect piece of evidence that Batswana, and all other Bantu people, were lost and in "darkness". It was written in the Bible! Translation theory cannot pretend that it is all about seeking dynamic or formal equivalences and staying faithful to the original meaning or source. For these reasons, I categorize such translations as "colonized Bibles".

Yet this translation was not only colonizing. It was also patriachalizing, for while the Ancestors (Badimo) were communities of the Living Dead that included both women and men, the Badimo were now relegated to the evil space. The colonizing ideology behind the translation sought to distance readers from their own cultural beliefs. Second, while the names of God are gender neutral in Bantu languages, in the Setswana Bible translation they assume male gender. Modimo, the Setswana name for God, becomes "rara wa rona yo o ko legodimong," that is "our father who art in heaven". Jesus was also male – replacing the gender-neutral and communal role of Badimo. Through these translations, Batswana, Bantu peoples and women had lost their place in the sacred space. The impact over the last two centuries has been to intensify patriarchy in the sacred space as well as in society.

Working with the Circle of Concerned African Women Theologians[49] and African biblical scholars in general,[50] we are continuing to re-read our colonized Bibles, to expose how modern colonialism informed indigenous translations, to rethink translation theory, and to consider how Bible translations

---

[49] See Dora Mbuwayesango, "How Local Divine Powers Were Supressed: A Case of Mwari of the Shona," 63-76, and Seratwa Ntloedibe Kuswani, "Translating the Divine: The Case of Modimo in the Setswana Bible," 77-100, both in: Musa W. Dube (ed.), *Other Ways of Reading: African Women and the Bible* (SBL: Atlanta 2000).

[50] Cf. Aloo Mojola, "How the Bible is Received in Communities: A Brief Overview with Particular Reference to East Africa," in: Phillip L. Wickeri (ed.), *Scripture, Community and Mission: Essays in Honor of Preman Niles* (Christian Council of Asia: Hong Kong 2002), 1-17, whose work is most instructive in this area. A summarized version of various other African scholars exploring colonized Bible translations can be found in Musa W. Dube, "The Scramble for Africa as the Biblical Scramble for Africa: Postcolonial Perspectives," in: Musa W. Dube / Andrew Mbuvi / Dora Mbuwayesango (eds.), *Postcolonial Perspectives in African Biblical Interpretations* (SBL: Atlanta 2012), 1-29, here 11-15.

could be enriched by our gender inclusive languages. This is one area where there could be an enriching project between African feminist scholars and earlier western feminist research on gender inclusive translations of the Bible. This project of re-reading our colonized Bible also calls for a shift in the pedagogical contents of biblical studies.[51] Whereas a good biblical studies program often required all postgraduate students to learn biblical languages and two European languages such as German, French or Spanish, such a requirement was not only further colonization for most of us – it also did not enable Two-thirds World biblical scholars to carry out the necessary research within their communities. Given that Christianity, and hence a large portion of Bible readers, have shifted toward the Two-thirds World, a review of biblical programs is necessary. Then languages of the latter, which were first used to translate Bibles, can be featured. This will enable informed research and the review of colonized Bibles that are still the daily bread of many African communities.

Bridging Methods of Studying Biblical Studies

As said earlier, my paper does not seek to be exhaustive, but to provide a summarized sketch. In my conclusion, I want to describe the project, "Other Ways of Reading: African Women and the Bible",[52] which became a book. In this volume, I worked with various members of the Circle of Concerned African Women Theologians to challenge and cross the theoretical and methodological boundaries of biblical studies. Integrating African folktales, divination styles, African storytelling techniques, poetry, enculturation and histories of various colonial experiences, we sought to challenge the predominantly Eurocentric methods of biblical interpretation and African gender-insensitive ways of reading. We were proposing other ways of reading. This project highlights that theories and methods of reading are themselves context-specific. Much as we learn methods of reading from the First World, the First World, too, can learn and apply our frameworks. Unless theoretical and methodological frameworks of reading are generated from various contexts, exclusively western methods maintain the Eurocentric colonial ideology.[53]

---

[51] See Dube, "The Scramble for Africa," 11-15.

[52] Initially the plan was to produce three volumes on methods, translation and a commentary, but due to lack of sufficient human resources, the three areas were collated together into one volume.

[53] Cf. Shohat / Stam, *Unthinking Eurocentrism*, 55-94.

Yet by bringing African folktales to be read with biblical stories – not as inferior and lesser traditions – the volume also sought to challenge the colonizing ideology held in mission texts and practices that treat the Other as a blank slate. In the Christian reading of the Bible, all other cultures and religious beliefs were lacking, evil and/or awaiting the pinnacle of salvation – namely the Christian gospel. Women and scholars from Two-thirds Worlds live more often than not in multi-faith and multi-religious contexts.[54] They have embraced Christianity and the biblical texts through and within a historical context that dismissed and denigrated their indigenous beliefs, but they remain within multiple traditions. It is no longer possible for us to pretend that the biblical text has not done many rounds, slept around and sired many mixed children. The biblical text has created many contact zones in the modern colonial history. In my view, if we study that Bible alone, we come very close to asserting that it still has the right to annihilate other traditions. I also do not believe that studying the Bible through various methods and theories sufficiently counters the history of the biblical text that claimed the right to dismiss other religious and cultural beliefs.[55] A postcolonial feminist reading thus seeks to work at the crossroads of various traditions in a hybrid space.

It might seem logical for people in former colonial contexts to explore multi-faith hermeneutics. Yet if we take Brah's observation seriously, namely, that the massive movements of people towards all directions place the contemporary world in a state of a diasporian identity for both those who have moved and those who have remained in their native homes (because one's neighborhood is now a hub of various cultures and religions). Brah's observation implies that all departments, including biblical studies, religion and theology, should review their programs accordingly. Islam, Hindusim, African indigenous religions and other religions are no longer found only in specific geographic-cultural spaces. Rather, they have journeyed into all directions with the contemporary movement of people. Thus if one wants to study African Indigenous Religions one may have to go to Cuba, Brazil, or the USA,[56] and if one wants

---

[54] Cf. Dube, *Postcolonial Feminist Interpretation*, 31-34.

[55] Cf. Canaan Banana, "The Case for a New Bible," in: I. Mukonyora / J. L. Cox / F. J. Verstraelen (eds.). *'Rewriting the Bible': The Real Issues: Perspectives from within Biblical and Religious Studies in Zimbabwe* (Mambo Press: Gweru 1993), 17-32, who makes the argument that the current Bible must be extended to include sacred traditions and norms of communities where the Bible has journeyed and tabernacled.

[56] See Jacob Olupona / Terry Rey (eds.), *Orisa Devotion as World Religion: The Globalization of Yoruba Religious Culture* (The University of Wisconsin Press: Madison 2008).

to study African Pentecostalism, one may have go to London or Brussels.[57] This is what constitutes "the global condition of culture as a site of travel", and "the site where the native is as much diasporian as the diasporian is the native", as posited by Brah.[58] Academic biblical studies should be true to this context by dancing with this complexity.

The sketches of journeys, border-crossings and bridges described in this paper remain at the margins. They remain unsettled and unsettling energies between the boundaries, inviting more border-crossing towards relationships of liberating interdependence in the academic biblical guild.

El artículo destaca los cruces de múltiples fronteras del mundo postcolonial y las posteriores identidades diaspóricas globales. Nacido dentro de la historia colonial moderna, la escritora marca el camino de la lectura de un libro que ha sido colonizado, y la continuidad de la colonización de la ideología en el estudio académico de la Biblia. Propone descolonizar los estudios bíblicos de su eurocentrismo, un enfoque exclusivo centrado en el antiguo mundo grecorromano. Los estudios bíblicos se problematizan, ya que ponen entre paréntesis preguntas sobre el colonialismo moderno. Las actitudes de los textos bíblicos de misión hacia el otro y hacia el imperialismo de su tiempo se deben investigar; el uso del género para articular posiciones de desigualdad debe ser explorado, y la propuesta de otras maneras de leer la Biblia también. En un intento de matizar tanto al colonizador como al lector de la Biblia colonizada de los tiempos modernos. La investigación actual de la escritora descubre aspectos del contexto colonial moderno, buscando identificar las estrategias de dominación, la resistencia, la colaboración y el surgimiento de la hibridez en el espacio de encuentro colonial actual.

The article underlines multiple-border crossings of the postcolonial world and the subsequent global diasporian identities. Born within the modern colonial history, the writer maps the journey of reading a book that had colonized her, and the continuity of colonizing ideology in the academic study of the Bible. Proposing to decolonize biblical studies from its Eurocentricism, the exclusive focus on the ancient Greco-Roman world in the study of biblical studies is problematized, since it brackets questions about modern colonialism; biblical mission texts' attitudes towards the Other and towards the imperialism of their time are investigated; the use of gender to articulate positions of inequality is explored, and other ways of reading the Bible are proposed. In a bid to profile both the colonizing and the

---

[57] See Kwabena Asamoah-Gyadu, "From Prophetism to Pentecostalism: Religious Innovation in Africa and African Religious Scholarship," in: Afe Adogame (ed.), *Christianity in Africa and the Diaspora: The Appropriation of a Scattered Heritage* (Continuum: London 2008), 161-175.

[58] Brah, "Diaspora, Border," 632.

colonized Bible reader of modern times the writer's current research reads letters of the modern colonial context, seeking to identify strategies of domination, resistance, collaboration and the emergence of hybridity in the modern colonial contact zone.

Der Beitrag unterstreicht die Grenzüberschreitungen der postkolonialen Welt und die daraus folgenden globalen Diasporaidentitäten. In der modernen Kolonialgeschichte geboren zeichnet die Autorin ihre Reise des Lesens des Buches, das sie kolonialisiert hat, auf, wie auch die bleibende kolonialisierende Ideologie in akademischen Bibelwissenschaften. Um biblische Studien von ihrem Eurozentrismus zu dekolonialisieren, problematisiert die Autorin den ausschließlichen Fokus auf die klassische griechisch-römische Welt in den Bibelwissenschaften; sie untersucht die Haltung in biblischen Missionstexten gegenüber den Anderen und dem Imperialismus ihrer Zeit; sie erforscht die Verwendung von Geschlecht, um Positionen von Ungleichheit zu artikulieren, und schlägt andere Wege, die Bibel zu lesen, vor. Mit dem Ziel, sowohl die kolonialisierenden und die kolonialisierten Bibel-LeserInnen der Moderne zu profilieren, liest die Autorin in ihrer aktuellen Forschung Briefe aus dem modernen kolonialen Kontext, um Strategien von Dominierung, Widerstand, Kollaboration und das Erscheinen von Hybridität in der modernen kolonialen Kontaktzone zu identifizieren.

Musa W. Dube is a Humboldtian awardee (2011) and a biblical scholar based at the University of Botswana. She studied New Testament at the University of Durham (UK) and the University of Vanderbilt (USA). Her research interests include: gender, postcolonial, translation and HIV&AIDS studies. She is the author of *Postcolonial Feminist Interpretation of the Bible* (Chalice Press, 2000).

Journal of the European Society of Women in Theological Research 22 (2014) 157-171.
doi: 10.2143/ESWTR.22.0.3040796

Andrea Taschl-Erber

Messianische Prophetinnen: Frauenstimmen in der Ouvertüre des Lukasevangeliums

Im Dialog mit ersttestamentlichen Befreiungstraditionen

Die Frage nach einer biblischen Fundierung feministisch-befreiungstheologischer Kritik an Macht- und Herrschaftsstrukturen richtet den Fokus auch auf weibliche Rollenmodelle in beiden Testamenten: Welche Visionen von Befreiung entwerfen Frauen in der Bibel als utopische Gegenentwürfe gegenüber vielfach erfahrener sozioökonomischer Ungerechtigkeit und politischer Unterdrückung? Inwiefern reflektieren diese Figuren mit ihrer kritischen Prophetie authentische Frauenstimmen[1] in ihrem Protest gegenüber den herrschenden Verhältnissen? Entfalten jene Visionen in bleibender Aktualität ihre transformative Kraft in Geschichte und Gegenwart – oder verlieren sie ihr systemveränderndes Potential infolge spiritualisierender und individualisierender Auslegungen? Inwieweit werden ersttestamentliche Frauenstimmen im Neuen Testament rezipiert, so dass sich ausgehend von den biblischen Texten ein Kontinuum prophetischer Sozialkritik und politischen Widerstands von Frauen aufzeigen lässt?

Angesichts der prominenten Positionierung namentlich eingeführter weiblicher Erzählfiguren, die einen vergleichsweise breiten narrativen Raum für ihre Worte und Handlungen erhalten, erscheint die Ouvertüre des Lukasevangeliums als exemplarischer Text, um die Frage nach deren Botschaft jenseits ideologischer Geschlechterkonstruktionen innerhalb der androzentrischen Darstellung und in späteren patriarchal geprägten Rezeptionen zu stellen.[2] Dabei

---

[1] Mit Athalya Brenner und Fokkelien van Dijk-Hemmes verstehe ich darunter „traces of textualized women's traditions" (Athalya Brenner, „Introduction," in: Athalya Brenner / Fokkelien van Dijk-Hemmes, *On Gendering Texts: Female and Male Voices in the Hebrew Bible* [Brill: Leiden 1993], Biblical Interpretation Series 1, 1-13, hier 7).

[2] Für einen exegetischen Durchgang durch Lk 1-2 in feministischer Perspektive siehe Andrea Taschl-Erber, „Subversive Erinnerung: Feministisch-kritische Lektüre von Mt 1-2 und Lk 1-2," in: Claire Clivaz / Andreas Dettwiler / Luc Devillers / Enrico Norelli (Hg.), *Infancy Gospels:*

folgt eine Lektüre, welche Lk 1-2 in Dialog mit ersttestamentlichen Frauentraditionen bringt, quer durch die Schriften Israels den Spuren einer Erinnerung daran, inwieweit Rettungs- und Befreiungserfahrungen mit Frauengestalten verbunden sind, seien es Prophetinnen, Widerstandskämpferinnen, große Mütter großer Söhne etc. Aufgrund ihrer „Interfiguralität"[3] mit ihren ersttestamentlichen Vorbildern gewinnen die Protagonistinnen in Lk 1-2 (Elisabet und Maria sowie die Prophetin Hanna) schließlich mehr Profil, die Intertexte eröffnen neue und erweiterte Sinnhorizonte.[4] Indem ein Diskurs mit ihnen hergestellt wird, lassen sich politische Aussagen im Raum der interferierenden Texte stärker konturieren. Gerade im Hinblick auf die Vielstimmigkeit des Lk, wo sich ganz unterschiedliche Stimmen Gehör verschaffen und emanzipatorische Aufbrüche neben patriarchale Ansprüche treten,[5] erhalten die im Text laut werdenden Frauenstimmen durch die intertextuelle Lektüre einen kräftigeren Klang und mehr Gewicht.

So möchte ich im Folgenden aus dem dicht gesponnenen Netz intertextueller Bezüge zu ersttestamentlichen Texten, Themen und Figuren in Lk 1-2 einige herauslösen, in denen kraftvolle Frauenstimmen und -traditionen ans Licht treten. Insbesondere bietet sich ein Vergleich des *Magnificat* (Lk 1,46-55) mit anderen Liedern an, die Frauenfiguren in den Mund gelegt sind: Mirjam

---

    Stories and Identities (Mohr Siebeck: Tübingen 2011), Wissenschaftliche Untersuchungen zum Neuen Testament 281, 231-256.

[3]   Siehe Wolfgang G. Müller, „Interfigurality: A Study on the Interdependence of Literary Figures," in: Heinrich F. Plett (Hg.), *Intertextuality* (de Gruyter: Berlin 1991), Research in Text Theory 15, 101-121.

[4]   Grundsätzlich muss ein rezeptionsorientierter Ansatz die produktionsästhetische Intertextualität (intendierte Bezüge) nicht außer Acht lassen, da diese ja auch durch Referenzsignale die Rezeption steuert (vgl. Georg Steins, *Die ‚Bindung Isaaks' im Kanon [Gen 22]: Grundlagen und Programm einer kanonisch-intertextuellen Lektüre: Mit einer Spezialbibliographie zu Gen 22* [Herder: Freiburg i. Br. 1998], Herders Biblische Studien 20, 95); doch liegt diese hier nicht in meinem Fokus. Hinsichtlich der zugrunde liegenden Methodologie siehe meine ausführlichere Darstellung: Andrea Taschl-Erber, „Rettungsgeschichten und subversive Frauenpower: Eine intertextuelle Lektüre von Lk 1 vor dem Hintergrund ersttestamentlicher Frauentraditionen," in: *Studien zum Neuen Testament und seiner Umwelt* 38 (2013), 97-145.

[5]   Anstatt gegenüber früheren Tendenzen, Lk als besonders frauenfreundliches Evangelium zu sehen, nun den Blick nur mehr auf seine patriarchale Seite zu lenken, gilt es dessen Heterogenität nicht vorschnell in positiver oder negativer Hinsicht aufzulösen, sondern die differierenden Stimmen im Text wahr- und ernst zu nehmen und diese in einer pluriformen gemeindlichen Praxis zu verorten, die im Ringen um egalitäre Prinzipien nicht konfliktfrei war.

(Ex 15), Debora (Ri 5),[6] Hanna (1 Sam 2), Judit (Jdt 16). Welche theologischen Akzente werden hier gesetzt? Und warum werden bestimmte theologische Aussagen mit Frauen verbunden?

Mirjam

In Ex 15 wird die vorangegangene Erzählung der Rettung am Schilfmeer auf einer Meta-Ebene theologisch reflektiert und poetisch „verdichtet". Wie die ausdrücklich als „Prophetin" bezeichnete Mirjam, die „politische Führungs-figur beim Exodus",[7] die in Ex 15,20 zum ersten Mal namentlich erwähnt wird und so gerade mit der hier artikulierten Befreiungserfahrung besonders verknüpft ist, und Mose stimmt Maria ein Loblied auf Gott als Retter (vgl. Lk 1,47; Ex 15,2) an.

Dass es sich in Ex 15 um einen parallelen Gesang von Mose und Mirjam handelt (wobei Mirjam in der kanonischen Endfassung, die durch eine andro-zentrische Redaktion gegangen ist,[8] die Antiphon übernimmt: V. 21), erinnert in gewisser Weise an die Diskussion, welcher Frauenfigur in Lk 1 das *Magnificat* zuzuschreiben ist: In der altlateinischen Textüberlieferung fungiert auch Elisabet als Sprecherin. Der Hymnus ist in die „gynozentrische" Szene des Besuchs Marias bei Elisabet (Lk 1,39-56) eingebettet, in der allein die Erfahrungen, Deutungen und Hoffnungen von Frauen fokussiert werden. Anstatt des stereotypen Motivs weiblicher Konkurrenz (siehe Sara/Hagar, Rahel/ Lea, Hanna/Peninna) bestimmen hier gegenseitige Anerkennung, Unterstüt-zung und Solidarität (wie etwa bei Rut und Noomi)[9] die Darstellung. So erweist sich das *Magnificat* im Rahmen dieser Begegnungsszene als gemeinsames

---

6   Das Lied Deboras muss in dieser Reihe natürlich erwähnt werden, doch konzentriere ich mich im Folgenden auf die anderen Texte, die stärkere Anknüpfungspunkte für eine intertextuelle Lektüre des lk Evangelienanfangs bieten.

7   So der Titel des Beitrags von Mercedes García Bachmann, „Mirjam als politische Führungs-figur beim Exodus," in: Irmtraud Fischer / Mercedes Navarro Puerto / Andrea Taschl-Erber (Hg.), *Tora* (Kohlhammer: Stuttgart 2010), Die Bibel und die Frauen: Eine exegetisch-kultur-geschichtliche Enzyklopädie 1/1, 305-346.

8   Dazu etwa Fokkelien van Dijk-Hemmes, „Traces of Women's Texts in the Hebrew Bible," in: Athalya Brenner / Fokkelien van Dijk-Hemmes, *On Gendering Texts: Female and Male Voices in the Hebrew Bible* (Brill: Leiden 1993), Biblical Interpretation Series 1, 17-109, hier 38-40.

9   Bezüglich intertextueller Verbindungen zum Rutbuch siehe den entsprechenden Abschnitt in Taschl-Erber, „Rettungsgeschichten," 133-142. Auch bei Moses Geburt in Ex 2 ist die Koope-ration von Frauen von entscheidender Bedeutung.

Lied zweier geisterfüllter[10] Prophetinnen, die gemeinschaftlich ihre Befreiungserfahrungen formulieren.[11]

Generell weist Namensgleichheit oder -ähnlichkeit deutlich auf eine Interfiguralität hin: Bereits Marias programmatischer Name ruft also Mirjam, die Prophetin des Exodus, in Erinnerung und bringt „die Hoffnung auf einen neuen Exodus" zum Ausdruck.[12] Des Weiteren zeigt ein Vergleich der Verkündigungserzählung in Lk 1,26-38 mit den Berufungsgeschichten ersttestamentlicher Führungspersonen und Propheten, wie etwa Gideon (Ri 6), Mose (Ex 3) oder Jeremia (Jer 1), dass eine „Verschränkung von Geburtsankündigung und Berufung" vorliegt.[13] Marias Einführung in den Erzählzusammenhang des Lk

---

[10] Dass Gottes Geistkraft über sie kommt, wird Maria bereits in Lk 1,35 vom Engel zugesagt; Elisabet wird vor der Deutung der verspürten Kindsbewegung in V. 41 von der Geistkraft erfüllt. Zum Konnex mit Prophetie siehe auch Lk 1,67: Zacharias „wurde vom heiligen Geist erfüllt und begann prophetisch zu reden"; nach der Ankündigung in 1,15 wird Johannes bereits vom Mutterleib an mit Geist erfüllt; ebenso ruht auf Simeon die Geistkraft, die ihn zur Prophetie befähigt (2,25-35).

[11] Vgl. Claudia Janssen / Regene Lamb, „Das Evangelium nach Lukas: Die Erniedrigten werden erhöht," in: Luise Schottroff / Marie-Theres Wacker (Hg.), *Kompendium Feministische Bibelauslegung* (Gütersloher Verlagshaus: Gütersloh 1998), 513-526, hier 519; Claudia Janssen, „Maria und Elisabet singen ...: Das Magnificat im Kontext der Begegnung einer alten und einer jungen Frau: Evangelium nach Lukas 1,39-56," in: Claudia Janssen / Beate Wehn (Hg.), *Wie Freiheit entsteht: Sozialgeschichtliche Bibelauslegungen* (Gütersloher Verlagshaus: Gütersloh 1999), 178-183.

[12] Kerstin Schiffner, *Lukas liest Exodus: Eine Untersuchung zur Aufnahme ersttestamentlicher Befreiungsgeschichte im lukanischen Werk als Schrift-Lektüre* (Kohlhammer: Stuttgart 2008), Beiträge zur Wissenschaft vom Alten und Neuen Testament 172, 277. Schiffner arbeitet im lk Porträt Marias eine Stilisierung ihrer Figur anhand der Prophetin Mirjam heraus (ebd., 259-296). Zusätzlich zieht sie die Traumvision Mirjams in Pseudo-Philos *Liber Antiquitatum Biblicarum* (LAB 9,10), die Mose vor seiner Geburt als Retter des Gottesvolkes ankündigt, als Parallele zur Verkündigungsszene in Lk 1 heran (ebd., 285-287). Zum Namen siehe ihre ausführliche Darstellung ebd., 259-278.

[13] Walter Radl, *Der Ursprung Jesu: Traditionsgeschichtliche Untersuchungen zu Lukas 1-2* (Herder: Freiburg i. Br. 1996), Herders Biblische Studien 7, 281; vgl. auch Jane Schaberg, *The Illegitimacy of Jesus: A Feminist Theological Interpretation of the Infancy Narratives* (Sheffield Academic Press: Sheffield 1995 [Erstausgabe: Harper & Row: San Francisco 1987; erweiterte Neuausgabe: Sheffield Phoenix Press: Sheffield 2006]), 128-132; Schiffner, *Lukas*, 281-285; Dietrich Rusam, *Das Alte Testament bei Lukas* (de Gruyter: Berlin 2003), Beihefte zur Zeitschrift für die neutestamentliche Wissenschaft 112, 46-47; sowie Bea Wyler, „Mary's Call," in: Athalya Brenner (Hg.), *A Feminist Companion to the Hebrew Bible in the New Testament* (Sheffield Academic Press: Sheffield 1996), The Feminist Companion to the Bible 10, 136-148.

wird so als prophetische Berufung stilisiert, wenngleich sie (im Unterschied zu Hanna in Lk 2,36) nicht explizit als Prophetin tituliert wird.

Ihre Erfahrung des rettenden Handelns Gottes, welcher „auf die Erniedrigung seiner Sklavin" gesehen habe (Lk 1,48), knüpft zudem an die Exoduserzählung an. Denn bei der Berufung des Mose eröffnet ihm JHWH: „Ich habe das Elend meines Volkes in Ägypten gesehen" (Ex 3,7; vgl. auch V. 9.16). Auch weitere zentrale Motive der Exodusüberlieferung werden im *Magnificat* aufgenommen.[14] Vor diesem Hintergrund tritt Maria als Prophetin der Befreiung auf: Ihre Rettungserfahrung besingt sie als Zeichen für den radikalen Umsturz der sozialen und politischen Verhältnisse durch die Gottheit, welche in der Geschichte Israels immer wieder in erbarmender Treue ihre befreiende Macht erwiesen hat.

Hanna

Die doppelte Geburtsgeschichte in der Eröffnung des Lk knüpft aber auch eng an entsprechende ersttestamentliche Texte an. Mit der Wiederaufnahme des Motivs überwundener Unfruchtbarkeit reiht sich der Evangelienanfang des Lk in eine Erzähltradition ein, nach der die Gottheit in kritischen Phasen der Geschichte des Volkes – als Gott nicht nur der „Väter", sondern auch der Mütter Israels – Partei für verzweifelte und in einem patriarchalen System gedemütigte Frauen ergreift und mit ihren Segenszusagen gleichzeitig die auf dem Spiel stehende Zukunft des Gottesvolkes sichert.[15] Die Rolle der Väter tritt dabei in den Hintergrund, da die für den weiteren Lauf der Heilsgeschichte bedeutsamen Kinder „ihre Existenz mehr dem rettenden Eingreifen Gottes für die Frauen als der männlichen Potenz verdanken."[16]

---

[14] Vgl. dazu Schiffner, *Lukas*, 232-236.

[15] Zur Geschichte des Motivs der (zunächst) unfruchtbaren Frau siehe etwa Mary Callaway, *Sing, o Barren One: A Study in Comparative Midrash* (Scholars Press: Atlanta 1986), Society of Biblical Literature: Dissertation Series 91; Athalya Brenner, „Female Social Behaviour: Two Descriptive Patterns within the ‚Birth of the Hero' Paradigm," in: Athalya Brenner (Hg.), *A Feminist Companion to Genesis* (Sheffield Academic Press: Sheffield 1993), The Feminist Companion to the Bible 2, 204-221 [zuerst erschienen in: *Vetus Testamentum* 36 (1986), 257-273]; Claudia Janssen, *Elisabet und Hanna – zwei widerständige alte Frauen in neutestamentlicher Zeit: Eine sozialgeschichtliche Untersuchung* (Grünewald: Mainz 1998), 80-115.

[16] Irmtraud Fischer, *Die Erzeltern Israels: Feministisch-theologische Studien zu Genesis 12-36* (de Gruyter: Berlin 1994), Beihefte zur Zeitschrift für die alttestamentliche Wissenschaft 222, 90. Vgl. Yairah Amit, „‚Manoah Promptly Followed His Wife' (Judges 13.11): On the Place of the Woman in Birth Narratives," in: Athalya Brenner (Hg.), *A Feminist Companion to Judges* (Sheffield Academic Press: Sheffield 1993), The Feminist Companion to the Bible 4,

Nach motivisch-sprachlichen und inhaltlich-strukturellen Anleihen in den Erzählkreisen um Abraham/Sara/Hagar, Rebekka/Isaak[17] und Jakob/Rahel/Lea sowie in der Geburtsverheißung an die Mutter Simsons in Ri 13[18] rückt insbesondere die Hanna-Tradition in 1 Sam 1-2 ins Zentrum der Aufmerksamkeit. Schon die – namentliche – Vorstellung von Zacharias und Elisabet gleich nach dem Proömium (Lk 1,1-4) ähnelt dem Buchanfang von 1 Sam (wobei in Lk 1,5 auch Elisabet eine Genealogie erhält).[19] Elkana hat freilich zwei Frauen, von denen Hanna, die er liebt (1 Sam 1,5; vgl. Rahel: Gen 29,18.20.30), wie Elisabet unfruchtbar ist (vgl. Lk 1,7; 1 Sam 1,2).[20]

In den Kränkungen durch Elkanas Zweitfrau Peninna (nach 1 Sam 1,6-7 MT)[21] manifestiert sich der patriarchale Normencodex, der den Wert von Frauen an ihren Söhnen misst;[22] analog spricht Elisabet retrospektiv von ihrer „Schande unter den Menschen" (Lk 1,25), von der sie Gott befreit habe.[23] Auch nicht Elkanas größere Zuwendung (mit welcher er zur Eskalation der Situation beiträgt) lindert Hannas Leid, zumal ihn bloß seine eigene Perspektive leitet: „Bin ich dir nicht mehr wert als zehn Söhne?" (1 Sam 1,8).[24]

146-156, hier 156: „Biblical birth narratives have a striking tendency to assign a peripheral and secondary role to the father."

[17] Die starke Ahnfrau des Nordreichs ist mit ihrem aktiven Part viel deutlicher konturiert als Isaak.

[18] Zu den vielfältigen Motivverflechtungen mit den Genesis-Erzählungen sowie Ri 13 siehe Taschl-Erber, „Rettungsgeschichten," 101-112.

[19] Elisabet stammt ebenfalls aus priesterlichem Geschlecht („aus den Töchtern Aarons"; vgl. auch den Namen von Aarons Frau in Ex 6,23). Hingegen bleibt die Frau des Manoach in Ri 13,2 namenlos.

[20] Vgl. außerdem Gen 11,30 (Sara); 25,21 (Rebekka); 29,31 (Rahel); Ri 13,2-3 (Simsons Mutter).

[21] Die Septuaginta differiert hier.

[22] Dazu Luise Schottroff, *Lydias ungeduldige Schwestern: Feministische Sozialgeschichte des frühen Christentums* (Gütersloher Verlagshaus: Gütersloh 1994), 271: „Der biblische Text wälzt damit die patriarchale Schuld gegenüber Hanna auf eine Frau ab."

[23] Οὕτως μοι πεποίηκεν κύριος ἐν ἡμέραις αἷς ἐπεῖδεν ἀφελεῖν ὄνειδός μου ἐν ἀνθρώποις. Lk 1,25 knüpft an die Septuaginta-Version von Gen 29,31 an: Ebenso dankt Rahel nach ihrer ersten Geburt für die hinweggenommene „Schande" der Kinderlosigkeit (Ἀφεῖλεν ὁ θεός μου τὸ ὄνειδος […]).

[24] Siehe die kritische Analyse bei Yairah Amit, „,Am I Not More Devoted To You Than Ten Sons?' (1 Samuel 1.8): Male and Female Interpretations," in: Athalya Brenner (Hg.), *A Feminist Companion to Samuel and Kings* (Sheffield Academic Press: Sheffield 1994), The Feminist Companion to the Bible 5, 68-76, hier 74-75; Lillian R. Klein, „Hannah: Marginalized Victim and Social Redeemer," in: Athalya Brenner (Hg.), *A Feminist Companion to Samuel and Kings* (Sheffield Academic Press: Sheffield 1994), The Feminist Companion to the Bible 5, 77-92, hier 86-89.

Doch Hanna „steht auf" (1 Sam 1,9) und tritt aktiv für die Veränderung ihrer Situation ein. Im Tempel wendet sie sich an JHWH[25] und verspricht den erbetenen Sohn der Gottheit zu weihen (vgl. dazu Ex 13,2; Num 6,5; Ri 13,5[26]), „wenn du auf die Erniedrigung deiner Sklavin schaust" (1 Sam 1,11; in Anlehnung an die Exodusmotivik); die Textfassung der Septuaginta ist im *Magnificat* (Lk 1,48) wörtlich wiederaufgenommen.[27] Ähnlich deutet Lea, die ungeliebte Frau Jakobs, die Geburt ihres ersten Sohnes Ruben in Gen 29,32,[28] wie sich auch an die Geburtsankündigung an Hagar, Saras ägyptische Sklavin, in Gen 16,11 die Begründung anschließt: „Denn die Gottheit hat auf deine Erniedrigung hingehört."[29] Das *Hinschauen* Gottes spielt ebenso bei Elisabets theologischer Deutung ihrer Schwangerschaft in Lk 1,25 eine wichtige Rolle: „Denn so hat die Gottheit mir getan in den Tagen, in denen sie darauf schaute (ἐπεῖδεν), meine Schande unter den Menschen fortzunehmen." Hier klingt ferner die Gotteserfahrung Hagars in Gen 16,13 (siehe wiederum die Septuaginta-Version) an: „Du bist die Gottheit, die nach mir geschaut hat."[30]

Wie Hanna gleich nach der Tempelszene schwanger wird, erfüllt sich auch für Elisabet die göttliche Geburtsverheißung im Tempel unmittelbar darauf (vgl. Lk 1,23-25; 1 Sam 19-20); freilich ist Gabriels Botschaft in Lk 1,8-22 an Zacharias adressiert. Erst das jenem auferlegte Schweigen gibt in Lk 1 die Bühne für die Frauen frei, um die Rede- und Handlungsinitiative zu ergreifen, so dass auch ihre Sicht der Geschehnisse laut werden kann. Dagegen ist Hannas Part von Beginn an viel aktiver: Sie erhält weit mehr Gesprächszeit als die anderen Akteure in der Ouvertüre von 1 Sam und ist in alle Dialoge involviert. Ihre stumme Kommunikation mit Gott im Tempel entzieht sich männlicher Zuhörerschaft, Vermittlung und Kontrolle (so dass auch der Priester Eli ihr Verhalten missdeutet: 1 Sam 1,12-14).[31] In vergleichbarer Weise wird jedoch in der zur

---

[25] Vgl. Rebekka in Gen 25,22, worauf sie ein Völkerorakel erhält.

[26] Auch dass Hanna gegenüber dem Vorwurf des Priesters Eli beteuert, sie habe weder Wein noch Bier getrunken (siehe 1 Sam 1,14-15), erinnert an Ri 13, wo der Engel die Mutter Simsons ermahnt, weder Wein noch Bier zu trinken, da ihr Sohn von Geburt an ein geweihter Nasiräer sein werde (siehe V. 4.7.14); vgl. dazu Num 6,3 (siehe aber auch Lev 10,9). Elisabets Sohn Johannes steht also in der Tradition von Simson und Samuel: vgl. Lk 1,15.

[27] 1 Sam 1,11 LXX: [...] ἐὰν ἐπιβλέπων ἐπιβλέψῃς ἐπὶ τὴν ταπείνωσιν τῆς δούλης σου [...]. Vgl. Lk 1,48: ὅτι ἐπέβλεψεν ἐπὶ τὴν ταπείνωσιν τῆς δούλης αὐτοῦ.

[28] Gen 29,32 LXX: Διότι εἶδέν μου κύριος τὴν ταπείνωσιν [...].

[29] Gen 16,11 LXX: [...] ὅτι ἐπήκουσεν κύριος τῇ ταπεινώσει σου.

[30] Gen 16,13 LXX: Σὺ ὁ θεὸς ὁ ἐπιδών με.

[31] Hingegen bekommt – wie Zacharias in Lk 1 – in Gen 17 *Abraham* die göttliche Verheißung, dass seine Frau ihm einen Sohn gebären werde (vgl. Lk 1,13; Gen 17,19). In Gen 17,16 und vor allem

Engelerscheinung des Zacharias parallel komponierten Verkündigungsszene in Lk 1,26-38 Maria selbst zur unmittelbaren Empfängerin der Offenbarung (im Unterschied zu Mt 1,20-25; vgl. aber Gen 16,11; Ri 13,3-5).

Als Hanna ihrem Sohn den Namen Samuel gibt, bringt sie eine erste theologische Reflexion ein (1 Sam 1,20; vgl. auch bei der Erfüllung ihres Gelübdes V. 27), wie auch Elisabet – im Kontrast zu Zacharias' Reaktion auf die Geburtsverheißung (vgl. Lk 1,18) – ihre Schwangerschaft sogleich als Handeln Gottes deutet (Lk 1,25).[32] In Hannas verallgemeinerndem Lobgesang[33] (1 Sam 2,1-10) spiegelt ihre eigene Erfahrung der Hilfe Gottes (vgl. insbesondere V. 5)[34] vergleichbare Erfahrungen von Gottes Parteilichkeit gegenüber Erniedrigten in vielfältigen Leidenssituationen (vgl. Ps 113,7-9). Ihre Aussagen „gewinnen dadurch zugleich eine öffentliche und politische Dimension",[35] Hanna wird zur Symbolfigur für das notleidende und auf Rettung hoffende Volk.[36]

Nicht zuletzt wegen der messianischen Ausrichtung des Schlussverses wird sie in der jüdischen Rezeptionsgeschichte zur Prophetin,[37] welche die Befreiung des

---

18,10 liegt der Fokus zwar stärker auf Sara, dennoch werden die Ankündigungen dem Ehemann mitgeteilt. So wird durch redaktionelle Enteignung von Frauenerfahrungen Abraham „zum Gottesmittler für Sara" (Irmtraud Fischer, „Genesis 12-50: Die Ursprungsgeschichte Israels als Frauengeschichte," in: Luise Schottroff / Marie-Theres Wacker [Hg.], *Kompendium Feministische Bibelauslegung* [Gütersloher Verlagshaus: Gütersloh 1998], 12–25, hier 15).

[32] Gerade in Gebeten, Gelübden und Dankliedern rund um Schwangerschaft und Geburt sowie den Deutungen zur Namensgebung treten oft „female voices" zu Tage (dazu van Dijk-Hemmes, „Traces," 90-103).

[33] Gemäß seinem jetzigen Kontext lässt sich der Hymnus durchaus als Danklied einer Frau nach einer Geburt verstehen, zumal der Dank über eine glückliche Geburt auch als Triumph über den siegreichen Kampf um Leben und Tod formuliert werden kann. So liest sich V. 6 vor dem Hintergrund eventueller Geburtskomplikationen in einem spezifischen Sinn, verweist im Kontext der umgebenden Verse jedenfalls auf die Erfahrung, der Leben spendenden/nehmenden Macht Gottes ausgeliefert zu sein. In Jes 42,13-14 dient der Vergleich eines schreienden Kriegshelden mit einer schreienden Gebärenden als Bild für JHWH, so dass schon von hier aus Vorsicht gegenüber genderspezifischen Klischees in der Gattungsbestimmung (Danklied versus Siegeslied) angebracht ist (vgl. van Dijk-Hemmes, „Traces," 93-97).

[34] Angesichts der zuvor erfahrenen Demütigungen durch eine feindlich erlebte Umgebung lässt sich auch die Spitze gegen freche Reden sowie die anvisierte Umkehr der Verhältnisse im Kontext situieren.

[35] Willy Schottroff, „Der Lobgesang der Hanna," in: Luise Schottroff / Johannes Thiele (Hg.), *Gotteslehrerinnen* (Kreuz-Verlag: Stuttgart 1989), 24-35, hier 29.

[36] Siehe die parallele Formulierung in 1 Sam 1,11/9,16 (außerdem Dtn 26,7). Vgl. auch Janssen, *Elisabet,* 103.

[37] Siehe im babylonischen Talmud den Traktat *Megilla* 14b (Sara, Mirjam, Debora, Hanna, Abigajil, Hulda, Ester).

Volkes verkündet. So tritt in der erweiterten Fassung ihres Liedes im *Targum Jonathan* eine Aktualisierung im Blick auf die Befreiung Jerusalems (das mit einer unfruchtbaren Frau verglichen wird)[38] von der römischen Besatzungsmacht zu Tage.[39] Ein Reflex dieser Tradition kommt offenbar in Lk 2,36-38 bei der hochbetagten Witwe[40] Hanna (vgl. wieder den programmatischen Namen) zum Vorschein, die als Einzige der neutestamentlichen Frauengestalten explizit als „Prophetin" tituliert wird[41] und Gott im Tempel dient[42] (vgl. den Tempelkontext in 1 Sam). Anlässlich der Darstellung Jesu im Tempel[43] proklamiert sie – im religiös-politischen Widerstand gegen die mit Rom kooperierende Tempelhierarchie – öffentlich die messianische Rolle des Kindes (ohne dass allerdings ihre Worte referiert werden; vgl. demgegenüber die Prophetie Simeons: Lk 2,28-35).[44]

An Hannas Lied lehnt sich in Aufbau und Motivik das *Magnificat* an, das ebenso mit freudigem Jubel über die Rettungserfahrung einsetzt. Auch hier wird der individuelle Dank der Sprecherin (Lk 1,46-50), der in Gottes Hinsehen auf die Notsituation gründet, in eine überindividuelle Ebene eingebettet (V. 51-55); von Maria als „Sklavin Gottes"[45] (V. 48; vgl. bereits V. 38) verlagert sich der Blick auf Israel als „Gottesknecht"[46] (V. 54). Wie Hanna repräsentiert

---

[38] Vgl. die Zionsmetaphorik bei Deuterojesaja, wo die Figur der unfruchtbaren Frau eine kollektive Dimension erhält, oder auch später in 4 Esra 9-10.

[39] Für Übersetzungen siehe Joan E. Cook, *Hannah's Desire, God's Design: Early Interpretations of the Story of Hannah* (Sheffield Academic Press: Sheffield 1999), Journal for the Study of the Old Testament: Supplement Series 282, 78-79; W. Schottroff, „Lobgesang," 33-34.

[40] Vgl. insbesondere Jdt 16,22-23.

[41] Vgl. demgegenüber Apg 21,9 (partizipiale Charakterisierung der Töchter des Philippus); Offb 2,20 (polemisch bezüglich Isebel).

[42] Vgl. die am Eingang des Offenbarungszelts Dienst tuenden Frauen in Ex 38,8; 1 Sam 2,22.

[43] Die Eröffnung des Lk ist von Tempelszenen gerahmt: siehe Lk 1,8-22/2,22-52.

[44] Apg 2,17-18 entsprechend (als Wiederaufnahme von Joel 3,1-2) zeigt sich paarweise männlich-weibliche Prophetie.

[45] Traditionelle Übersetzungen von δούλη κυρίου lieferten im Verlauf einer auf die Unterordnung von Frauen zielenden Rezeptionsgeschichte ein klassisches Beispiel für einen Genderbias in Form geschlechtlich differenzierter Interpretationen: vgl. gegenüber der „Magd des Herrn" als Paradigma demütigen Gehorsams (auch gegenüber anderen „Herren") das männliche Äquivalent eines „Gottesknechts" (in der Septuaginta: δοῦλος κυρίου), etwa für Mose, Josua, David, Salomo, Propheten, Abraham, Isaak und Jakob/Israel; siehe auch Lk 2,29 (Simeon): mit Apg 2,18 lassen sich die „GottesdienerInnen" als ProphetInnen verstehen. SklavIn (nur) von Gott – und von niemandem sonst – zu sein (vgl. etwa Lev 25,55), erweist sich freilich auch in politischer Zielrichtung als herrschaftskritisches Programm.

[46] Der griechische Begriff παῖς kann auch „Kind" bedeuten, aber aufgrund der parallelen Charakterisierung Marias bleibe ich bei dem traditionellen Terminus (vgl. dazu etwa in der Septuaginta Jes 41,8-9; 42,1; 44,1-2.21).

Maria also Israel, ihre Erfahrung reflektiert zeichenhaft die des Volkes. Eine wichtige thematische Verbindung der beiden Strophen erfolgt über Gottes Erbarmen (ἔλεος, V. 50.54), das sich in der Befreiungsgeschichte Israels immer wieder Bahn bricht als „Erhöhung der Erniedrigten" (vgl. die in der Reihe von sieben Aorist-Indikativen in V. 51-54 zentrale Aussage ὕψωσεν ταπεινούς in V. 52,[47] korrelierend mit 2 Sam 1,7). Die konkrete Erfahrung von „Erniedrigung" (Lk 1,48: nicht „Niedrigkeit" als demütige Haltung oder Gesinnung; vgl. 1 Sam 1,11) seitens der Beterin wird im Liedzusammenhang des *Magnificat* nicht näher expliziert, entspricht aber der Situation der Gedemütigten, Hungernden und Leidenden im Gegenüber zu den „Mächtigen" und „Reichen" im Kontext der politischen, ökonomischen und sozialen Gewalt- und Unterdrückungserfahrungen Israels während der römischen Besatzung.

In beiden Hymnen verkörpert die Sprecherin als Typus der Armen JHWHs die Erfahrungen und Hoffnungen der „Erniedrigten" (ταπεινοί) – gerade auch als Frau – und entwirft die prophetische Vision des radikalen Umsturzes der Macht- und Herrschaftsverhältnisse in einer messianischen Utopie sozioökonomischer Gerechtigkeit und politischer Befreiung. Für das vielstimmige neutestamentliche Zeugnis über Maria ist damit als wichtige Facette festzuhalten: Als Erste – noch vor Jesu Antrittsrede (vgl. Lk 4,18-19) – verkündet sie im Eröffnungskapitel des Lk das Evangelium der Armen als ein Evangelium (auch und insbesondere) von Frauen.

Judit

Als „Gesegnete unter den Frauen" (Lk 1,42) steht Maria ferner in der Tradition von Jaël (vgl. im Debora-Lied Ri 5,24) und Judit (vgl. Jdt 13,18), zwei aktiven Widerstandskämpferinnen, die sich als Retterinnen für Israel erwiesen haben, deren Rezeptionsgeschichte sich jedoch vor allem auf ihre Gewalttat, die Tötung des feindlichen Heerführers, konzentrierte.[48] Ihr Lied (Jdt 16,1-17)

---

[47] Vgl. Norbert Lohfink, *Lobgesänge der Armen: Studien zum Magnifikat, den Hodajot von Qumran und einigen späten Psalmen* (Katholisches Bibelwerk: Stuttgart 1990), Stuttgarter Bibelstudien 143, 16.

[48] Siehe die Beiträge von Sigrid Eder, „Gewalt im Geschlechterverhältnis: Jaël, Sisera und die Konstruktionen von Weiblichkeit und Männlichkeit im aktuellen Gewaltdiskurs"; Agnethe Siquans, „Die Macht der Rezeption: Eckpunkte der patristischen Juditinterpretation"; Elisabeth Birnbaum, „Dimensionen des Juditbuches und ihre Bedeutung für die neuzeitliche Rezeption," in: Irmtraud Fischer (Hg.), *Macht – Gewalt – Krieg im Alten Testament: Gesellschaftliche Problematik und das Problem ihrer Repräsentation* (Herder: Freiburg i. Br. 2013), Quaestiones disputatae 254, 83-106; 171-197; 198-224.

stimmt Judit zum Lobpreis der rettenden Gottheit an – die „durch die Hand einer Frau" (V. 5; intertextuell mit Ri 4,9 verknüpft) gehandelt hat.

Auch im Juditbuch kommt die biblische Armentheologie zur Sprache: In Judits Gebet[49] vor ihrer Tat (9,11) wie in ihrem Lied[50] (16,11) findet sich ein Rekurs auf die „Erniedrigten". Das in Psalmen und Prophetie, im Hannalied wie im *Magnificat* benannte Unrecht wird hier „in den Gewaltkontext des Krieges gerückt [...] als Instrument von Unterdrückung [...]."[51] Da häufig auch sexuelle Gewalt gegenüber Frauen als „Erniedrigung" verbalisiert wird,[52] tritt gleichzeitig ein geschlechtsspezifischer Aspekt vielfältiger Gewalterfahrungen im Rahmen von Krieg und militärischer Besatzung ans Licht (entsprechend werden auch in Jdt 16,4 Kriegsgräuel aus der Sicht der Zivilbevölkerung repräsentiert).[53]

Im Dialog mit der Textwelt der Septuaginta vermittelt das Juditbuch eine kriegskritische Theologie:[54] Die Charakterisierung der Gottheit als eine, die „den Kriegen ein Ende setzt" (Jdt 9,7-8; 16,2), deren „Macht in der Gewaltunterbrechung besteht",[55] statt eines Kriegshelden rezipiert beispielsweise die Septuaginta-Version von Ex 15,3 (vgl. auch Jes 42,13 LXX im Unterschied zur hebräischen Fassung des MT). Der imperialen Macht Assurs, die durch militärische Gewalt demonstriert wird,[56] steht die Macht des Gottes Israels gegenüber, welche nicht durch die „Mächtigen" repräsentiert wird, da jener ein „Gott der Erniedrigten, Beistand der Geringen, Helfer der Schwachen, Beschützer der Resignierten, Retter der Hoffnungslosen" ist, wie Jdt 9,11

---

[49] Wie in Judits resümierendem Lied erfolgt auch in diesem reflektierenden Text (9,2-14) eine theologische Interpretation der erzählten Ereignisse (hier prospektiv).

[50] Auch Judit spricht als Verkörperung des Volkes/Zions.

[51] Claudia Rakel, *Judit – über Schönheit, Macht und Widerstand im Krieg: Eine feministisch-intertextuelle Lektüre* (de Gruyter: Berlin 2003), Beihefte zur Zeitschrift für die alttestamentliche Wissenschaft 334, 140.

[52] Vgl. die Belege des Verbs ταπεινόω in Gen 34,2 (Dina); Dtn 21,14; 22,24.29 (Gesetzestexte); Ri 19,24; 20,5 (Nebenfrau des Leviten); 2 Sam 13,12.14.22.32 (Tamar); Klgl 5,11 (Frauen in Zion, Jungfrauen in Städten Judas); Ez 22,10-11 (Gräuel in Jerusalem). Siehe auch Jane Schabergs These einer illegitimen Herkunft Jesu aufgrund einer Vergewaltigung Marias: Schaberg, *Illegitimacy*.

[53] Von sexueller Gewalt ist auch Judit im feindlichen Lager bedroht.

[54] Vgl. Rakel, *Judit*, 1; außerdem ebd., 12: „Das Juditbuch tritt auf diese Weise z. B. in ein Streitgespräch etwa mit den Makkabäerbüchern ein, wenn es um die Frage geht, wie Widerstand zu denken ist."

[55] Rakel, *Judit*, 170.

[56] Der Großkönig wird in Jdt 2,5 als „der Herr der ganzen Erde" tituliert.

programmatisch formuliert. Nicht Heeresgewalt und Manneskraft bringen die Rettung, sondern eine Frau, die ihre Stärke von Gott erhält. Damit werden patriarchale Ideale und Werte auf den Kopf gestellt. Traditionelle Geschlechter-konstruktionen (männliche Gewalt – weibliche Ohnmacht) werden reproduziert und gleichzeitig durchbrochen. So verkörpert Judit, herkömmlichen Gender-stereotypen entsprechend, das schwache und ohnmächtige Gottesvolk, jedoch gegenüber dem feindlichen Heerführer als Repräsentanten der Gewalt-macht Assurs die rettende Macht der Gottheit Israels, die für die Machtlosen und Gewaltopfer eintritt und die scheinbar Ohnmächtigen zum Widerstand ermächtigt. Holofernes, der durch Judits Schönheit[57] buchstäblich seinen Kopf verliert, fällt durch sein eigenes Schwert.

Das Juditbuch „vermag den Diskurs der Gewalt nicht vollkommen zu durchbrechen",[58] reiht sich aber in eine kriegskritische Tradition[59] ein – die in der Jesusüberlieferung (gegenüber anderen zeitgenössischen Entwürfen, die βασιλεία τοῦ θεοῦ, die „Gottesherrschaft", zu verwirklichen) wieder aufge-nommen wird.[60] Die Geburt des Frieden bringenden Retters in Armut (Lk 2) realisiert dieses theologische Programm (als Kontrastvision gegenüber gän-giger Herrscherideologie, insbesondere der Kolonialmacht Rom: vgl. die Inschrift von Priene mit dem „Evangelium" des Geburtstages von Kaiser Augustus),[61] wie auch die Fortsetzung der Jesusgeschichte im gekreuzigten Messias einen provokanten Gegenentwurf zu herkömmlichen Macht- und Herrschaftsdiskursen bietet.

---

[57] „Im Juditbuch wird den scheinbar Ohnmächtigen die Möglichkeit zum Widerstand gegen Gewalt ausgerechnet am Ort der Ausbeutung selbst gegeben: in der Schönheit des von Gewalt bedrohten weiblichen Körpers [...]" (Rakel, *Judit*, 170-171).

[58] Rakel, *Judit*, 145.

[59] Vgl. Jes 2,4/Mi 4,3; Hos 2,20; Sach 9,9-10; Ps 46,10; Ps 76,4.

[60] Siehe beispielsweise die Rezeption von Sach 9,9-10. Vorsicht ist freilich gegenüber einer antijüdischen Sichtweise angebracht, die biblische Gewalttexte nur im Bereich des AT verortet und dieses als Kontrastfolie zum NT konstruiert: vgl. dazu etwa die grundsätzlichen Überle-gungen bei Gerlinde Baumann, „Gewalt im Alten Testament: Grundlinien der Forschung – hermeneutische Überlegungen – Anregungen," in: Irmtraud Fischer (Hg.), *Macht – Gewalt – Krieg im Alten Testament: Gesellschaftliche Problematik und das Problem ihrer Repräsentation* (Herder: Freiburg i. Br. 2013), Quaestiones disputatae 254, 29-52, hier 48-49.

[61] Ein „Gegenbild zu kaiserlicher Herrlichkeit" sieht hier auch Silke Petersen, „Maria aus Naza-ret: Eine Geschichte der Verwandlung," in: Marinella Perroni / Mercedes Navarro Puerto (Hg.), *Evangelien: Erzählungen und Geschichte* (deutsche Ausgabe des Bandes hg. v. Irmtraud Fischer / Andrea Taschl-Erber; Kohlhammer: Stuttgart 2011), Die Bibel und die Frauen: Eine exegetisch-kulturgeschichtliche Enzyklopädie 2/1, 320-339, hier 337.

Schlussbilanz

In der Interfiguralität mit Prophetinnen und Widerstandskämpferinnen des Ersten Testaments zeigen sich Elisabet, Maria und Hanna in der Ouvertüre des Lk als Rollenmodelle einer gegen die herrschenden Machtverhältnisse protestierenden Prophetie, deren fundamentale Kritik des sozialen und politischen Systems die Grundlinien der Jesusbewegung antizipiert. Wie seine ersttestamentlichen Vorbilder zeichnet das *Magnificat* das Bild einer Gottheit, die in treuem Erbarmen auf die Not der Unterdrückten sieht und ihnen machtvoll Gerechtigkeit und Befreiung verschafft; die eingespielte Exodusüberlieferung ruft dabei auch eine gesellschaftspolitische Verpflichtung in Erinnerung. Das Widerstandsdokument gegen soziale Unterdrückung und Gewalterfahrungen durch die römische Kolonialmacht setzt nicht auf militärische Gewalt, sondern auf die Macht der rettenden Gottheit, welche die Machtlosen und scheinbar Ohnmächtigen zum Widerstand ermächtigt. Individualisierende, spiritualisierende oder allegorisierende Lesarten verkürzen freilich die politische Dimension des Textes und berauben ihn seiner systemverändernden Kraft.

Es sind Frauenfiguren, mit denen sich solche Formulierungen der Hoffnung und des Widerstands verbinden. In diesen Stimmen tritt eine weibliche Sub- bzw. Gegenkultur zu Tage, welche die dominierende Ordnung herausfordert und subversives Potential beinhaltet. So steht Gott auch in der Eröffnung des Lk auf der Seite der Frauen, in deren Rettungs- und Befreiungserfahrungen sich die Hoffnungen der Erniedrigten exemplarisch erfüllen. Die Rettung des Volkes nimmt jeweils bei einer Frau ihren Anfang.[62] Exoduserfahrungen und Neubeginn in der Geschichte des Volkes sind eng mit Frauengestalten verknüpft.

Die heilsschwangere „Zeit der Mütter"[63] am Evangelienanfang des Lk, welche die „Unfruchtbarkeit" überwindet und die messianische Zukunft eröffnet, gibt Frauen den Raum, ihre Erfahrungen des „Hinsehens" Gottes auf die „Erniedrigung" der Gedemütigten und ihre damit verbundenen widerständigen

---

[62] Vgl. Luise Schottroff, „Marias Leben und Marias Prophetien – Menschwerdung der Gerechtigkeit Gottes," in: Luise Schottroff / Johannes Thiele (Hg.), *Gotteslehrerinnen* (Kreuz-Verlag: Stuttgart 1989), 35-45, hier 40; Schottroff, *Schwestern*, 282.

[63] Brigitte Kahl spricht von der „countertime of the mothers" im Sinne eines „anti-patriarchal break of time" als Voraussetzung des messianischen Neuanfangs (Brigitte Kahl, „Reading Luke against Luke: Non-uniformity of Text, Hermeneutics of Conspiracy and the ‚Scriptural Principle' in Luke 1," in: Amy-Jill Levine / Marianne Blickenstaff [Hg.], *A Feminist Companion to Luke* [Sheffield Academic Press: London 2002], Feminist Companion to the New Testament and Early Christian Writings 3, 70-88, hier 83).

Visionen mit prophetischer Autorität zu verkünden. Auch wenn nicht ausschließlich Frauenstimmen in der Ouvertüre des Lk – und noch weniger im Rest des Evangeliums – zu Wort kommen,[64] sind sie als mahnende Gegenstimmen ebenso im weiteren Verlauf der Evangelienerzählung mitzuhören.[65]

Una lectura intertextual de la apertura de Lucas nos descubre la memoria subversiva, arraigada en las tradiciones en el primer testamento, su crítica social profética y la resistencia política de las mujeres. La *interfigurality* con las profetas como Miriam (Ex 15) y Ana (1Sam 1-2) y con la lucha resistente de Judith, hace de Isabel, María y Ana, en Lc 1-2, modelos de una profecía que protesta contra las relaciones opresivas de poder y dominación. Como documento de la resistencia contra la represión social así como la violencia perpetrada por el imperio colonial romano, el Magnificat contiene – al igual que los ejemplos del primer Testamento (canciones de Miriam, de Deborah, Ana y Judith) – partiendo de la mirada de Dios sobre los oprimidos una visión mesiánica de liberación política y la justicia socioeconómica, que se apoya en el poder y la resistencia de quienes parecen indefensos y empodera a aquellas personas sin poder.

An intertextual reading of the opening of Luke discovers the subversive memory, rooted in traditions in the First Testament, of prophetic social criticism and political resistance by women. Their interfigurality with prophets such as Miriam (Ex 15) and Hannah (1Sam 1-2) as well as resistance fighter Judith, renders Elisabeth, Mary and Hannah in Lk 1-2 role models of a prophecy that protests against oppressive relationships of power and domination. Like its models from the First Testament (Miriam's, Deborah's, Hannah's and Judith's songs), the Magnificat departs from God, who looks at the "oppressed", and develops, as a document of resistance against social oppression and the experience of violence perpetrated by the Roman colonial power, a messianic vision of political liberation and socio-economic justice counting on the power and the resistance of those who appear helpless and empowering those without power.

Einer intertextuellen Lektüre der Ouvertüre des Lukasevangeliums erschließt sich eine in ersttestamentlichen Traditionen wurzelnde subversive Erinnerung an prophetische Sozialkritik und politischen Widerstand durch Frauen. In der Interfiguralität mit Prophetinnen wie Mirjam (Ex 15) und Hanna (1 Sam 1-2) sowie der Widerstandskämpferin Judit erweisen sich Elisabet, Maria und Hanna in Lk 1-2 als Rollenmodelle

---

[64] Bereits in Lk 2 verstummen die Frauenstimmen: dazu Taschl-Erber, „Erinnerung," 246-249.

[65] Siehe auch Kahl, „Reading Luke," 87: „The narrative structure inscribes [...] the subversive memory of a ‚different' time and order into the subsequent synthesis as a permanently opposing element. [...] Luke allows himself to be read ‚from back to front'; he provides, in a way, the impetus for a feminist-critical relecture of Luke against Luke."

einer gegenüber oppressiven Macht- und Herrschaftsverhältnissen protestierenden Prophetie. Als Widerstandsdokument gegen soziale Unterdrückung sowie die Gewalterfahrungen durch die römische Kolonialmacht entwirft das *Magnificat* wie seine ersttestamentlichen Vorbilder (siehe die Lieder Mirjams, Deboras, Hannas und Judits) ausgehend von Gottes Hinsehen auf die „Erniedrigten" eine messianische Vision politischer Befreiung und sozioökonomischer Gerechtigkeit, welche auf die Macht und den Widerstand der scheinbar Ohnmächtigen setzt und Machtlose ermächtigt.

Andrea Taschl-Erber studierte Katholische Theologie und Klassische Philologie (Griechisch) an der Universität Wien, wo sie 2006 im Rahmen einer Stelle als Vertragsassistentin am Institut für Neutestamentliche Bibelwissenschaft promovierte. Seit 2013 arbeitet sie als Universitätsassistentin am Institut für Alttestamentliche Bibelwissenschaft an der Universität Graz, nachdem sie hier bereits 2007-2011 das internationale Projekt „Die Bibel und die Frauen" betreute.

Journal of the European Society of Women in Theological Research 22 (2014) 173-186.
doi: 10.2143/ESWTR.22.0.3040797

Eleonora Hof

Re-imagining World Christianity: Challenging Territorial Essentialism

In spring 2013, while visiting Kenya and Tanzania, I attended an English language church service in Moshi, a town at the foot of Mount Kilimanjaro. The service was led by an enthusiastic, extrovert pastor, who was most happy to welcome visitors from abroad. His strong accent was unmistakably from the southern United States. Worship started with songs that were well known to me, since they were all favorites from the contemporary evangelical worship scene and written by well-known worship leaders such as Michael W. Smith and Matt Redman. Moreover, these songs were accompanied by startling visuals in bright colors in a powerpoint presentation. The sermon was a solid expository preaching on Hebrews accompanied by reading from the archaic sounding, not revised King James Version. A handful of Tanzanians were present, but most of the attendees were expatriates. I asked about possible relationships with other congregations in Moshi, but apparently they did not fancy any connections with other churches. I left the church feeling on the one hand welcomed as a guest, but on the other hand confused about what I had just witnessed.[1]

It is the goal of this article to use this particular story, which took place in a specific locality, as a tool to scrutinize and critique prevalent conceptions of World Christianity. In addition, I will use this story to argue for an imaginary of World Christianity which includes the continuing missionary presence of the western world in the Two-thirds Worlds in the topography of World Christianity. Only by consciously expanding our framework will it be possible to pair careful analysis with a plea for resistance. Resistance is here taken as attending to issues of power and injustice and identifying patterns that need to be addressed in order to promote change. The abundance of similar stories like

---

[1]   See for a photo essay of the church service http://www.flickr.com/photos/28938702@N05/sets/ 72157636573708553/, 19 February 2014.

the one I have recounted shows that by no means do we live in a postmissionary time,[2] as has been advocated by some scholars.[3] Instead, one witnesses a continuing influx of missionaries who are "planting churches" without any regard for local theologies, ecumenical cooperation or local ownership. In the practice of the church in Moshi, a considerable amount of the common knowledge and practice of ecumenical circles is negated. It has been the merit of Robert Wuthnow, a sociologist of religion, to point out the sheer size and quantity of American foreign missionary endeavors.[4] Yet, in some influential missiological works, the effects of these American efforts are downplayed or ignored. For example, Lamin Sanneh, well-known for stressing the infinite translatability of the Christian faith,[5] emphasizes how non-western Christianity is advancing "without Western organizational structures".[6] Granted, Wuthnow is not a missiologist and explicitly claims not to aim to make a contribution to the field of missiology, but it is nevertheless regrettable that his valuable insights to this field have not been extensively discussed by missiologists.[7]

---

[2] See Robert Wuthnow, *Boundless Faith: The Global Outreach of American Churches* (University of California Press: Berkeley 2009).

[3] See Roland Löffler, "Introduction: Robinson Crusoe Tries Again or: Werner Ustorf's Way of Developing Missiology into a Research Concept of Global and Pluralistic Christianity," in: Werner Ustorf, *Robinson Crusoe Tries Again: Missiology and European Constructions of 'Self' and 'Other' in a Global World 1789-2010*, edited by Roland Löffler (Vandenhoeck & Ruprecht: Göttingen 2010), Research in Contemporary Religion 9, 7-20, here 9; Bert Hoedemaker, *Met Anderen tot Christus: Zending in een Postmissionair Tijdperk* (Boekencentrum: Zoetermeer 2000).

[4] Roughly 40.000 U.S. citizens were employed as full-time missionaries in foreign countries in 2001. In addition, 350.000 U.S. citizens undertook a short term mission trip (ranging from between two weeks and a year). U.S. churches spent $3,7 billion on foreign ministries; cf. Wuthnow, *Boundless Faith*, 23.

[5] See Lamin Sanneh, *Translating the Message: The Missionary Impact on Culture* (Orbis Books: Maryknoll 2009, 2nd rev. and ext. ed.), American Society of Missiology Series 42.

[6] Lamin Sanneh, *Whose Religion Is Christianity?: The Gospel beyond the West* (Eerdmans: Grand Rapids 2003), 3. See for the further agenda of Sanneh: "I have decided to give priority to indigenous response and local appropriation over against missionary transmission and direction, and accordingly have reversed the argument by speaking of the *indigenous discovery of Christianity* rather than the *Christian discovery of indigenous societies*" (10, emphasis in the original).

[7] The absence of any substantial discussion has been noted and lamented by Robert Priest. Robert Priest, "Robert Wuthnow and the Global Christianity Paradigm". (http://www.missiologymatters. com/2012/10/28/robert-wuthnow-and-the-global-christianity-paradigm/, 23 April 2013).

Three Imaginaries of World Christianity

The emerging field of World Christianity is in its most basic form the study of the Christian presence and witness on a global scale.[8] This field of study follows its own presuppositions, agendas, claims and interests and is therefore by no means a neutral and value-free endeavor. In order to develop my own working definition of World Christianity, I propose a schematic overview of three ways of imagining World Christianity. These imaginaries are value-laden and provide each a different lens for interpreting data on Christian presence and witness.

The first imaginary could be characterized by the implicit or explicit dominance of the West. World Christianity is imagined as the exotic and unfamiliar branch of Christianity. The West is therefore tacitly omitted from the world in World Christianity. This usage is comparable to the concept of world music,[9] which designates everything that is exotic and does not belong to the mainstream.[10] A tell-tale sign of (unconscious) West-centrism is that non-western theologians and theologies are labeled "native" or "indigenous". These adjectives are reserved for non-western, non-normative and non-mainstream theologies. As a result, the normativity of western Christianity remains unchallenged since there is no conceptual framework available which aids this challenge.

The second imaginary is characterized by the emphasis it places on a geographical ordering of the world in World Christianity, plotting Christian presence visibly on the map of the world. An example of this is the popular evangelical image of the 10/40 window, the area between ten degrees and forty degrees north. Included in this window are North Africa, the Middle East, Central Asia, China, India and South-East Asia.[11] Plotting "unreached people

---

[8] See Dale Irvin, "World Christianity: An Introduction," in: *The Journal of World Christianity* 1 (2008), 1-26.

[9] The analysis and criticism of the construction of world music runs remarkably parallel to the criticism leveled against this imaginary of World Christianity. See John Connell / Chris Gibson, "World Music: Deterritorializing Place and Identity," in: *Progress in Human Geography* 28 (2004), 342-361.

[10] See Namsoon Kang, "Whose/Which World in World Christianity?: Toward World Christianity as Christianity of Worldly-Responsibility," in: Andrew Walls / Akintunde Akinade (eds.), *A New Day: Essays on World Christianity in Honor of Lamin Sanneh* (Peter Lang: New York 2010), 31-49. Kang cites the work of Mark Noll as a representative of this view; see Mark Noll, *The New Shape of World Christianity: How American Experience Reflects Global Faith* (InterVarsity Press: Downers Grove 2009).

[11] See Luis Bush, "The AD2000 Movement as a Great Commission Catalyst", in: Jonathan Bonk (ed.), *Between Past and Future: Evangelical Mission Entering the Twenty-First Century* (Pasadena: William Carey Library 2003), Evangelical Missiological Society Series 10, 17-36, here 21.

groups" on the map of the world is also an indication of this geographical approach. The website of the Joshua Project provides an abundance of maps which charter these "unreached people groups".[12] The material on their webpage can be seen as the evangelical-conservative version of this second imaginary, which does not explicitly address the root causes of continued western dominance. In academic textbooks, the geographic approach can also be found, but it presents itself in contrast with the first imaginary. The dominance of the West is rejected since the West is treated as "just" one of the geographic regions where Christianity is present. This approach is characterized by its attempt to avoid the West-centrism that plagued the first imaginary.[13]

The third imaginary moves beyond the other two approaches by attempting to avoid the West-centrism of the first imaginary and the geographical reductionism of the second imaginary. Instead, it emphasizes the importance of transnational ties in the shaping of World Christianity. Foregrounding transnational ties enables a keen attention for the way power relationships are shaped. It also highlights the complex character of these transnational connections and therefore actively resists reductionism.[14]

These three imaginaries can be perceived in a chronological order in which the second imaginary gained dominance after the first imaginary. I have the impression that at this present moment there might be, at least in academia, a shift taking place from the second imaginary towards the third, given the growing interest in transnational ties in the shaping of World Christianity. Yet the observation of such a shift is tentative. As becomes clear from the literature cited, all three perspectives are also simultaneously present.

Challenging Territorial Essentialism

The second imaginary of World Christianity, as it presents itself in academic literature, is, in my opinion, plagued by a number of difficulties, which prohibit sustained interaction with the continuing reality of missionary encounters.

---

[12] See http://joshuaproject.net/great-commission-maps.php, 8 October 2013.

[13] See Dyron Daughrity, *The Changing World of Christianity: The Global History of a Borderless Religion* (Peter Lang: New York 2010); Sebastian Kim / Kirsteen Kim, *Christianity as a World Religion* (Continuum: London 2008).

[14] See for representatives of this view the following works: Hilde Nielssen / Inger Marie Okkenhaug / Karina Hestad Skeie (eds.), *Protestant Missions and Local Encounters in the Nineteenth and Twentieth Centuries: Unto the Ends of the World* (Brill: Leiden 2011), Studies in Christian Mission 40; Charles Farhadian / Robert Hefner (eds.), *Introducing World Christianity* (John Wiley: Malden 2012).

I use the analytical tool of the category of "territorial essentialism", a term coined by Dorottya Nagy, to outline the reasons for the deficiency of this imaginary.[15] I identify three consequences of adopting the second imaginary. Territorial essentialism is defined as the naturalization of a given territory by making it the primary lens of interpretation. This naturalization can take place through the unwarranted emphasis on a certain locality such as a country or a continent. Naturalization is complete when it is hardly possible to acknowledge the necessary contingency of this locality.

I will outline the logics of territorial essentialism with reference to the second imaginary of World Christianity. Nagy criticizes the authors of a standard textbook on World Christianity for succumbing to "continental narrowness", given their essentialization of the continents.[16] I add to Nagy's observation that their cartography does not adequately reflect the European hegemony which leads to the present continental divisions.[17] The easy acceptance of the current continental division as "just so" fails to do justice to the power dimensions that played a decisive role in imagining the continents. The fallacy of naturalism needs to be countered by an emphasis on the contingency of continental divisions. The acknowledgment of contingency creates room to investigate the possibility of unjust power relationships.

After having outlined the nature of territorial essentialism, I now proceed to specify in more detail why this approach is unhelpful in the analysis of World

---

[15] See Dorottya Nagy, "Where Is China in World Christianity?," in: *Diversities* 12 (2010), 70-83, here 74. See also her dissertation on Chinese migrant communities in Hungary. Dorottya Nagy, *Migration and Theology: The Case of Chinese Christian Communities in Hungary and Romania in the Globalisation-Context* (Boekencentrum: Zoetermeer 2009), Mission 50. The terminology of "territorial essentialism", which Nagy coined for missiology, surfaces as well in another discipline, namely media studies. Interestingly enough, the usage here seems to be quite similar to our present purposes. Andreas Hepp, *Cultures of Mediatization*, transl. Keith Tribe (Cambridge: Polity Press, 2013), 139.

[16] See Kim / Kim, *Christianity as a World Religion*. The essentialization of the continents shows itself primarily in the outline of the book which is structured according to the division of the continents. In a private conversation, Kim repudiated the charge of essentialization of the continents because the book shows a sustained concern for stressing transnational ties and the importance of denominational differences which cut across continents.

[17] See Ali Mazrui, "The Re-invention of Africa: Edward Said, V. Y. Mudimbe, and Beyond," in: *Research in African Literatures* 36 (2005), 68-82, here 74-75. Roughly the same observation could be made about Christianity as a world religion. There is nothing natural about the present division of the major world religions, as Tomoko Masuzawa has argued. Tomoko Masuzawa, *The Invention of World Religions: Or, How European Universalism Was Preserved in the Language of Pluralism* (University of Chicago Press: Chicago 2005).

Christianity. Here I take territorial essentialism to be an essential characteristic of the second imaginary of World Christianity, and my criticism will therefore extend to this imaginary as a whole. First, this imaginary lends itself too easily to a triumphalist narrative. Second, it reduces the complexities of World Christianity to a level playing field, leaving no room for critiquing unjust power relationships. Third, it gives rise to imagine missions as "working among" certain nations, religions or ethnic tribes, whereby these entities become bounded wholes.

In the first place, a triumphalist narrative celebrates the growth of Christianity across the globe as a way of avoiding complicated questions about the entanglement of mission and (neo-)colonial realities. Ironically, the continuity of missionary encounters is written out of the story of World Christianity. By continually stressing local agency and local theologies, there remains less room to challenge the not-so-local aspects of neocolonial influence. A triumphalist narrative of World Christianity has the capacity to function as a "quick fix" that takes recourse to bypassing continued missionary efforts. Then World Christianity provides a celebratory narrative with a happy ending. Although I am clearly overstating matters here, this narrative runs like this: "After we got through the ugly and nasty colonial period when missions and empire were harmfully entangled with each other, we finally entered the state of postcolonial bliss where non-western forms of Christianity are flourishing." If local agency becomes a dogma, there is hardly any room left for analyzing this type of neocolonial missionary encounters, an example of which I have recounted at the beginning of my paper.

Second, when Christianity is interpreted primarily through the category of country, continent or ethnic tribe, the danger is that all these forms of Christianity are considered to be on the same level. The characteristics of Christianity in Africa or Christianity in North America are then the objects of study. Structural inequalities and power differentials are consequently difficult to account for.[18] A complicating factor is that theologically speaking, there is indeed a fundamental equivalence among Christian communities. According to the image described in the letter to the Ephesians, all are reconciled in one body with Christ as its head.[19] Moreover, Christian faith is polycentric. There is no definitive Christian heartland and it is always a possibility that Christian

---

[18] See also Wuthnow, *Boundless Faith*, 2.

[19] The Ephesian vision has gained popularity through the work of Andrew Walls; see Andrew Walls, "The Ephesian Moment: At a Crossroads in Christian History," in: Andrew Walls, *The*

presence disappears in a certain context.[20] Yet, when this principle is taken out of its context, it might seem as if there is no potential for resistance, since Christian presence and witness flows freely. The potential for resistance should not be located in a different theological way of interpreting the fundamental equality of World Christianity. Instead, it could be located in aiming at bringing together both the theological fundament of unity in Christianity on a global scale and attention to real and harmful inequalities and the abuse of power.

Last, the geographic conception of World Christianity could easily give rise to, continue or encourage a common way of speaking in mission organizations about working "among" a certain ethnic tribe, religion or nation.[21] It is precisely the preposition "among" that is problematic, given that it carries with it an association that peoples are bounded wholes with a stable and definable identity. This approach cannot account for diversity, conflict and ambiguity within the perceived cultural or ethnic blocks. If one opts for a non-territorial framework of interpreting World Christianity, it becomes clear that the interpretation of the world according to the concepts of boundedness and self-containedness is not adequate.[22]

Cross-cultural Process in Christian History: Studies in the Transmission and Appropriation of Faith (Orbis Books: Maryknoll 2002), 72-81.

[20] See Andrew Walls, "Christianity in the Non-western World: A Study in the Serial Nature of Christian Expansion," in: Andrew Walls, *The Cross-cultural Process in Christian History: Studies in the Transmission and Appropriation of Faith* (Orbis Books: Maryknoll 2002), 27-48; Andrew Walls, *The Missionary Movement in Christian History: Studies in Transmission of Faith* (Orbis Books: Maryknoll 1996).

[21] For example: mission among Buddhists; among Muslim peoples; among the unreached (people groups). See Kevin Greeson, "Church Planting Movements among Muslim Peoples," in: *Church Planting Movements* (2011). (http://www.missionfrontiers.org/issue/article/church-planting-movements-among-muslim-peoples, 7 October 2013); Oluseyi Ige, "Overcoming Practical Barriers to Serving among the Unreached". (http://svm2.net/abandonedtimes/overcoming-practical-barriers-to-serving-among-the-unreached/, 7 October 2013); Charlie Fletcher, "Dark Clouds and Silver Linings: Mission among Buddhists". (http://www.ridley.edu.au/index.php/blog/post/dark-clouds-and-silver-linings-mission-among-buddhists/, 7 October 2013); http://usa.ntm.org/, 7 October 2013.

[22] Dale Irvin detects this way of reasoning in discourse about "the rural, the village, the countryside, or even the nation". Dale Irvin, "The Church, the Urban, and the Global: Mission in an Age of Global Cities," in: *International Bulletin of Missionary Research* 33 (2009), 177-182, here 179. See also the analytical work of Kathryn Tanner: Kathryn Tanner, *Theories of Culture: A New Agenda for Theology* (Fortress: Minneapolis 1997).

Alternative Topographies

I locate myself within the emerging third imaginary of World Christianity. As this framework begins to show its contours, I want to contribute to this type of understanding World Christianity by writing missionary encounters into the story of World Christianity and by providing an alternative topography. I argue with Claire Brickell that more attention should be paid to contemporary mission efforts. Here, the field of geography might provide us with important clues for interpreting the reordering of the world in World Christianity.[23]

Thus far I have outlined three different conceptions of World Christianity and I have argued how territorial essentialism is impeding the analysis of currents within World Christianity. I would like to add the gendered nature of World Christianity to the equation, and use gender awareness as a critical tool in deconstructing masculinist readings of World Christianity. As has been remarked by Philip Jenkins in an often quoted statement on the first page of his book *The Next Christendom*: "If we want to visualize a 'typical' contemporary Christian, we should think of a woman living in a village in Nigeria, or in a Brazilian *favela*."[24] A typical Christian is apparently a woman, yet little analysis has been carried out on how this affects World Christianity. In her important study, *World Christianity as a Women's Movement*, Dana Robert calculates how World Christianity is, in terms of statistics, a women's movement.[25] This means that conversion rates of women to Christianity are high and that the majority of Christians worldwide are female.[26] She therefore calls for the sustained inclusion of the gender factor in World Christianity. She rightly considers it problematic that the experience of women within contemporary Christianity remains under the radar since it is subsumed under the larger interpretative framework of World Christianity. I consider the study of gender within World Christianity a distinct field of inquiry, in line with the

---

[23] See Claire Brickell, "Geographies of Contemporary Christian Mission(aries)," in: *Geography Compass* 6 (2012), 725-739.

[24] Philip Jenkins, *The Next Christendom: The Coming of Global Christianity* (Oxford University Press: Oxford 2011, 3rd rev. and ext. ed.), 1-2.

[25] See Dana Robert, "World Christianity as a Women's Movement," in: *International Bulletin of Missionary Research* 30 (2006), 180-188. See also: Dana Robert, "Women in World Mission: Controversies and Challenges from a North American Perspective," in: *International Review of Mission* 93 (2004), 50-61.

[26] Robert does not attempt to provide the percentage by which women outnumber men in World Christianity. Her evidence is constructed from various and piecemeal sources which prohibit providing more exact data.

analysis of women and mission, a field which has recently witnessed an upsurge in interest. These studies have mostly taken a historic angle.[27] In addition, a mission theology is being developed from a feminist perspective.[28] Furthermore, there has been an enormous investment to broaden feminist concerns beyond first-world matters.[29] Yet, I still detect a gap in literature, and this gap concerns the gendering of World Christianity. The 2013 study by Adriaan van Klinken of masculinities in African Christianity will likely spark further interest in this topic.[30] In addition, Namsoon Kang has argued for the priority of gender justice within contemporary Christianity. However, her work has a strong normative bend, which I support in itself, but which pays less attention to the actual dynamics of contemporary World Christianity.[31]

We are therefore left with few clues about what is happening in contemporary mission encounters. We do have some predictions concerning the import of conservative gender roles from North America and the controversies following in its wake, but these are often motivated by fear rather than solid analysis.[32] What I have witnessed in my encounter in Moshi, Tanzania, could indeed confirm a conservative dynamic, given that patriarchal values are an integral part of the preaching of this particular American pastor: in his sermon, the pastor assigned to himself the primary responsibility for leading the church.

---

[27] See Susan Smith, *Women in Mission: From the New Testament to Today* (Orbis Books: Maryknoll 2007); Gunilla Gunner / Karin Sarja, "Paradoxes and Challenges: Gender Perspectives in Mission History," in: Volker Küster (ed.), *Mission Revisited: Between Mission History and Intercultural Theory: Essays in Honour of Pieter N. Holtrop* (LIT Verlag: Münster 2011), Contact Zone: Explorations in Intercultural Theology 10, 119-126; Mary Taylor Huber / Nancy Lutkehaus (eds.), *Gendered Missions: Women and Men in Missionary Discourse and Practice* (University of Michigan Press: Ann Arbor 1999); Fiona Bowie / Deborah Kirkwood / Shirley Ardener (eds.), *Women and Missions: Past and Present: Anthropological and Historical Perceptions* (Berg: Providence 1993).

[28] See Katja Heidemanns, "Missiology of Risk?: Explorations in Mission Theology from a German Feminist Perspective," in: *International Review of Mission* 93 (2004), 105-118; Letty Russell, "God, Gold, Glory and Gender: A Postcolonial View of Mission," in: *International Review of Mission* 93 (2004), 39-49.

[29] See Rosemary Radford Ruether, "Feminism in World Christianity," in: Arvind Sharma / Katherine Young (eds.), *Feminism and World Religions* (State University of New York Press: Albany 1999), 214-247.

[30] See Adriaan van Klinken, *Transforming Masculinities in African Christianity: Gender Controversies in Times of AIDS* (Ashgate: Farnham 2013).

[31] See Namsoon Kang, "The Centrality of Gender Justice in Prophetic Christianity and the Mission of the Church Reconsidered," in: *International Review of Mission* 94 (2005), 278-289.

[32] See the section on gender and sexuality in Jenkins, *The Next Christendom*, 231-235.

Moreover, it became clear that his wife's role was to be in charge of the women's and children's ministry.

How then can we go about finding a way to use gender as a critical tool in order to refine our understanding of World Christianity? Is it true that the prevalent stories of travelling, sea voyages and exploration provide us with a masculinist script, as Kwok Pui-lan suggests?[33] Drawing on insights from diasporic[34] and borderland discourses,[35] I argue that the interpretation of World Christianity will be different if instead of these masculinist scripts, pointers of a female (diasporic) subject will be employed. Consequently, the trope that is used in assessing World Christianity shifts from attention to travelling and exploration towards the storyteller. Storytelling provides room for negotiation, displacement, ambivalence, rupture and continuity, and the strategies of identity negotiation. By its very nature it disrupts complacent narratives of bounded identities based upon the conflation of ethnicity and a specific geographic location.

Returning to Mount Kilimanjaro

How could this specific church in Northern Tanzania, with which I started this paper, inform and shape our understanding of World Christianity? Here, I will develop further the issue of spatiality and argue that "missionary geopolitics" play a formative role in this story.

The study of spatiality has recently witnessed an upsurge within religious studies, theology in general, missiology, postcolonial studies and the study of World Christianity.[36] Within missiology one can detect a shift from interpreting texts to interpreting places.[37] This attention to the spatial dimension has a profound potential for resistance since it enables to focus on the imaginary that underlies specific spatial constructions. Taking postcolonial theory

---

[33] See Kwok Pui-lan, *Postcolonial Imagination and Feminist Theology* (Westminster John Knox: Louisville 2005), 46.

[34] See Nagy, *Migration and Theology*.

[35] See Gloria Anzaldúa, *Borderlands / La Frontera: The New Mestiza* (Aunt Lute Books: San Francisco 1987).

[36] For an analysis from the perspective of religious studies: Thomas Tweed, *Crossing and Dwelling: A Theory of Religion* (Harvard University Press: Cambridge 2008). For an analysis from a theological perspective: John Inge, *A Christian Theology of Place* (Ashgate: Aldershot 2003).

[37] Marion Grau, *Rethinking Mission in the Postcolony: Salvation, Society and Subversion* (T&T Clark: London 2011).

into account, one could assert that: "There is no better place to locate and test postcolonial theory than in the streets of the postcolony."[38] Analytical space cannot remain disconnected from what is actually happening on the streets. I will therefore focus on this particular street, in this town at the feet of Mount Kilimanjaro, on a specific Sunday morning. The brand-new church, located in one of the more affluent parts of town, is characterized by the absence of local languages and any form of local leadership structures. It engages in a form of unmaking of history by neglecting the prior history of Christianity in Moshi through its deliberate act of eschewing all ecumenical contacts.[39] This contested place, where history is repressed and future continuity is uncertain, nevertheless does not float in space without connections. A decisive continuity with colonial approaches to mission is witnessed, given the lack of regard for local agency, theology and leadership. Here, in the streets of the postcolony, colonial attitudes are hauntingly present. It is precisely because of this continuing presence, which is by no means unique for this particular locality, that I have attempted to write this story into the concept of World Christianity.

The close reading of this particular locality ties in with a concern for "missionary geopolitics". This term, coined by Brickell, writing from the perspective of geographical studies, emphatically inserts the missionary within the discourse on religion, (trans)nationalism and migration.[40] Unfortunately, the figure of the missionary does hardly feature in this field of research, which might be explained by the fact that missionaries elude categories of migrants, such as migrant workers, expatriates, business elites and students. Inspired by Brickell, the study of "missionary geopolitics" provides a necessary and timely field of inquiry. For the particular context I have been reviewing, the town of Moshi at the feet of Mount Kilimanjaro[41] acquires additional meaning. The Kilimanjaro region has historically served as a site of pervasive colonial fantasies of a supposedly African essence and has proved to be an influential symbol of the exotic nature of Africa. It is a contested site with dense layers

---

[38] Tinyiko Sam Maluleke, "Postcolonial Mission: Oxymoron or New Paradigm?," in: *Swedish Missiological Themes* 95 (2007), 503-528, here 511.

[39] See for a short overview of the history of Christianity in Moshi: Bengt Sundkler / Christopher Steed, *A History of the Church in Africa* (Cambridge University Press: Cambridge 2000), 540-551.

[40] See Brickell, "Geographies of Contemporary Christian Mission(aries)", 728.

[41] The town of Moshi serves as an operating base for trekking tours to Kilimanjaro and hosts therefore many tourists before or after their trek. Mount Kilimanjaro dominates the city skyline when weather is clear.

of meaning.[42] This observation is confirmed by other mission agencies who ascribe special meaning to the mountain.[43] A historic constellation which pairs exoticism with discovery and adventure is part of the legacy of the mountain area. Given this legacy which has infused the region with meaning, desire and fantasy, I argue, with Kang, for a "geopolitical sensitivity". This sensitivity serves as a tool to discover "alternatives to theological/cultural/geopolitical imperialism and appropriation".[44] It is exactly here where the category of resistance comes to the fore again.

In this paper I have focused mainly on developing analytical tools in order to scrutinize contemporary missionary encounters within World Christianity. I have argued that these encounters should not be written out of history by maintaining the fiction of a post-missionary time, but instead should be seen as an integral (albeit for many undesired) part of World Christianity. This makes World Christianity a space that is all the more contested, where migration in many forms, including that of foreign missionaries as western agents, exerts considerable influence and continues to generate polydox forms of witness and encounter in highly complex settings.[45]

Esta historia de un culto en Tanzania dirigida por misioneros norteamericanos va a servir como herramienta para explorar, criticar y ampliar los imaginarios frecuentes del Cristianismo Mundial. La primera idea nos recuerda que Occidente deja fuera al resto del mundo cristiano al mantener la normatividad teológica occidental. En segundo lugar, existe un imaginario geográfico que interpreta el mundo cristiano de acuerdo a las divisiones continental/área. La última idea subraya los lazos transnacionales y su complejidad y quiere estar atenta a la manera en que se forman las relaciones de poder. El esencialismo territorial, que es una estrategia común en las

---

[42] François Bart / Milline Mbonile / François Devenne (eds.), *Mount Kilimanjaro: Mountain, Memory, Modernity* (Mkuki na Nyota Publishers: Dar es Salaam 2006).

[43] See for a contemporary example of the lure that Mount Kilimanjaro provides the 2013 trekking tour to Mount Kilimanjaro by the organization of "Climbing for Christ". See for another contemporary example the 2013 Kilimanjaro Trek organized by Mission Africa to raise awareness and support for their mission. In this instance, Mount Kilimanjaro serves as a representation for the whole of the continent (http://www.missionafrica.org.uk/opportunities/54/climb-kilimanjaro-2013, 10 October 2013).

[44] See Namsoon Kang, "Out of Places: Asian Feminist Theology of Dislocation," in: Jione Havea / Clive Pearson (eds.), *Out of Place: Doing Theology on the Crosscultural Brink* (Equinox: London, 2011), 105-128, here 126.

[45] See for an exploration of the subjects of polydox trajectories within contemporary Christianity the work of Marion Grau: Grau, *Rethinking Mission in the Postcolony*.

dos primeras discusiones, dificulta el estudio de la totalidad del cristianismo a nivel mundial. Esto es definido como la naturalización de un determinado territorio, usando ese territorio como objeto principal de la interpretación. Estos tres problemas relacionados desde esta perspectiva se pueden analizar entendiendo que el esencialismo territorial podría dar lugar a un discurso triunfalista, desde la perspectiva de este cristianismo mundial, que entiende una igualdad de condiciones en las distintas geografías, y puede llevar a considerar a las culturas como realidades acotadas. Utilizando el género como categoría crítica, nos ponemos como reto imaginar un cristianismo mundial, cambiar los intereses y explorar las narraciones de historias. Éstas proporcionan espacios de cierta ambivalencia para el desplazamiento, la ruptura, la continuidad y las estrategias de negociación de identidad. En conclusión, propongo una revisión de la geopolítica de los misioneros a la luz de la continua presencia misionera de Occidente.

The story of a church service in Tanzania led by American missionaries is used as a tool to explore, critique and expand prevalent imaginaries of World Christianity. The first imaginary tacitly leaves out the West in World Christianity by continuing western theological normativity. Second, there is a geographic imaginary that interprets World Christianity according to continental / regional divisions. The last imaginary stresses transnational ties and their complexity and is attentive to the way in which power relationships are shaped. Territorial essentialism, which is a common strategy in the first two imaginaries, nevertheless hampers the study of World Christianity. It is defined as the naturalization of a given territory by using it as the primary lens of interpretation. Three problems connected to this strategy are discussed: territorial essentialism could give rise to a triumphalist discourse, it imagines World Christianity as a level playing field, and it can lead to considering cultures as bounded wholes. Using gender as a critical category, tropes of imagining World Christianity are challenged, shifting attention from travelling and exploration towards storytelling. Storytelling provides room for ambivalence, displacement, rupture, continuity, and the strategies of identity negotiation. In conclusion, I argue for a sustained emphasis on missionary geopolitics in the light of the continued missionary presence of the West.

Die Geschichte eines Gottesdienstes in Tansania unter der Leitung von amerikanischen Missionaren wird als Mittel verwendet, um vorherrschende Vorstellungen von Weltchristenheit zu untersuchen, kritisieren und auszuweiten. Das erste Imaginäre schließt stillschweigend den Westen aus der Weltchristenheit aus, indem eine westliche theologische Normativität weiterverfolgt wird. Zweitens gibt es ein geographisches Imaginäres, das die Weltchristenheit nach kontinentalen, regionalen Unterscheidungen interpretiert. Das letzte Imaginäre unterstreicht transnationale Verbindungen und ihre Komplexität und zeigt ein feines Gespür dafür, wie Machtverhältnisse gebildet werden. Territorialer Essentialismus, eine häufige Strategie in den beiden ersten Imaginären, behindert das Studium der Weltchristenheit. Er wird als die Naturalisierung eines bestimmten Territoriums durch seine Verwendung als vorherrschende Interpretationsperspektive definiert. Drei damit zusammenhängende Probleme werden diskutiert: Territorialer Essentialismus kann zu einem triumphalistischen Diskurs führen; er kann die Weltchristenheit so darstellen, als ob gleiche Voraussetzungen für alle bestünden; und er kann dazu führen, dass Kulturen als geschlossenes Ganzes gesehen werden. Der Gebrauch von Gender als kritische Kategorie stellt Metaphern, wie Weltchristenheit vorgestellt wird, in Frage, indem die Aufmerksamkeit von Reisen und Erforschung zum Erzählen hin verschoben wird. Erzählen schafft Raum für Ambivalenz, Verlagerung, Bruch, Kontinuität und Strategien der Verhandlung von Identitäten. Zum Schluss plädiere ich für die Betonung der missionarischen Geopolitik angesichts der fortdauernden missionarischen Präsenz des Westens.

Eleonora Dorothea Hof is a PhD Student at the Protestant Theological University in Amsterdam, The Netherlands. She is currently writing her dissertation about a theology of mission in the age of World Christianity.

Journal of the European Society of Women in Theological Research 22 (2014) 187-198.
doi: 10.2143/ESWTR.22.0.3040798

Mayra Rivera

A Labyrinth of Incarnations: The Social Materiality of Bodies

The title of this essay comes from an article by the postcolonial theorist Edward Said. Commenting on the phenomenology of Maurice Merleau-Ponty, Said observed, "Society [...] is a true labyrinth of incarnations." A labyrinth, he adds, "because of a complexity that has no discernible end or beginning, and an 'incarnation' because implicit gestural language and outward expression are inseparable, united as man himself is in an indissoluble bond between body and soul."[1] Said was referring specifically to Maurice Merleau-Ponty's attention to the body's constitutive belonging to the world. The body is in and of the world, Merleau-Ponty would say. Yet Said's elegant formulation invites a deeper exploration of the complex relationship between "society" and "incarnation", and between the theological and social dimensions of corporeality. How can we envision those labyrinths, those networks without beginning or end through which discourses, cultures, and practices become flesh?

I suggest that an exploration of social-material incarnations should characterize a new phase in theologies of the body. I trace the development of this insight in theologies of the body of the past three decades and end with some suggestions for future directions.

Bodies in Christianity

The body appeared in religious studies in the second half of the twentieth century. Defiantly. At least that is how we scholars of religion like to tell the story of the scholarly turn to the body. We know it is hardly the first time that Christian thinkers have been puzzled and challenged by corporeal phenomena. Miraculous feedings and healings, the power of relics, the transformations produced by ascetic practices, and many other such phenomena have been the subject of formative debates throughout Christian history. But here I refer to the body in the twenty-first century. In this context, we tend to associate the

---

[1] Edward W. Said, "Labyrinth of Incarnations: The Essays of Maurice Merleau-Ponty," in: *The Kenyon Review* 29.1 (1967), 54-68, here 67.

body with eroticism and sexuality. The large and growing corpus of literature on Christianity and the body includes a substantial number of works on the role of Christianity in occluding, forbidding and/or inciting sexual desires.[2] Still, there are other stories that have also shaped present-day visions of the body – accounts of multitudes bearing wounds inflicted in the name of the people, the nation, and the economy. Images of human bodies all but destroyed by concentration camps, the atomic bomb, or hunger represent the shattering of myths of human progress. If these bodies reveal anything, it is the likelihood of corporeal destruction.

Recognition of human vulnerability led early liberation thinkers to the Christian body. They sought to bring attention to its material needs – basic necessities such as food, health, and protection against violence. For Latin American liberation philosopher Enrique Dussel, this orientation required an ethics grounded in corporeality.[3] Thus Dussel turned to Hebrew Scriptures, Greek literature, and the New Testament in search of models for a corporeal anthropology that avoided the separation between body and soul.[4] As long as the essence of human life was assumed to reside in an immaterial principle such as the soul, he argued, material necessities would be deemed secondary or derivative, merely supporting something more lasting and true.

It was clear that theologies concerned with poverty and violence could not ignore the body; neither could those confronting sexism. But these problems required different strategies. Liberationists argued that the bodies of the poor were mostly absent from modern theological discussions of salvation. Thus they sought to bring attention to the cries of the hungry. In contrast, the bodies of women were written into the texts that subordinated them. Discourses about gender and sexuality – like those about race – deployed the body as a foundation of knowledge and a source of unquestionable truth. In order to unsettle that logic, feminists tried to liberate themselves from the body-as-foundation

---

[2]   For example, Carter Heyward considered "the erotic […] our most fully embodied experience of the love of God" (Carter Heyward, *Touching Our Strength: The Erotic as Power and the Love of God* [Harper: San Francisco 1989], 99).

[3]   The philosophical responses to the atrocities of the Shoah deeply influenced the development of Latin American liberation thought, particularly through Dussel's engagement with Emmanuel Levinas.

[4]   See Enrique Dussel, *El Humanismo semita: Estructuras intencionales radicales del pueblo de Israel y otros semitas* (Editorial Universitaria de Buenos Aires: Buenos Aires 1969); Enrique Dussel, *El Humanismo helénico* (Editorial Universitaria de Buenos Aires: Buenos Aires 1975).

– from biological essentialisms. If genders are culturally constructed, then we can transform them. But would that mean abandoning the body?

Clearly not. Part of the theoretical task has been to question the idea of "nature" and "body" as passive or immutable and to question the dualisms on which the opposition between materiality and transcendence rests. The body/spirit dualism was one of the main targets of these projects, which would reach the heart of Christian doctrine. For, as Rosemary Radford Ruether memorably argued, "the disembodied nature of the […] divine […] has served as a linchpin of the Western masculinist symbolic."[5] Feminist theologians have tracked biological essentialisms and spirit/matter dualisms, in all their versions, to deconstruct them. They have also sought to provide alternative visions of the relationship between divinity and materiality, such as the influential metaphor of the universe as the body of God. The works of Sallie McFague and Ivone Gebara are examples of this effort to overcome the image of a distant God that would not come close to the messiness of our lives and our bodies.[6] Developing the images of intimacy between the divine and the cosmos, feminists have offered other models that assert the fundamental "relational" (instead of dualistic) structure of the cosmos.[7]

Reclaiming the value of bodies further entailed attending to elements of human experience that had been dismissed as irrelevant because too carnal for theological reflection. Sexuality has been the preferred site for such reappraisals of corporeal experience, yet recent theologies of food, dance, and the like have had similar aims.[8] These theologies imagine the body as created and embraced by the divine, its pains and desires inseparable from its spiritual longings. A vision of divinity as close and intimate is the basis for insisting that theology take seriously not just the body in general, but also the specific experiences of feeling hungry, relishing the sun, tasting food, enjoying sexuality.

Yet this path now presents us with new challenges. Some of these challenges have to do with the limits of the ways we have sought to theologize the

---

[5] Rosemary Radford Ruether, *Sexism and God-talk: Toward a Feminist Theology* (Beacon Press: Boston 1983), 269.

[6] See Sallie McFague, *The Body of God* (Fortress Press: Minneapolis 1993); Ivone Gebara, *Longing for Running Water: Ecofeminism and Liberation* (Fortress Press: Minneapolis 1999).

[7] See, for example, Laurel Schneider, *Beyond Monotheism: A Theology of Multiplicity* (Routledge: London 2008).

[8] See, for example, Angel F. Méndez-Montoya, *The Theology of Food: Eating and the Eucharist* (Wiley-Blackwell: Oxford 2009); Norman Wirzba, *Food and Faith: A Theology of Eating* (Cambridge University Press: Cambridge 2011).

body. Others emerge from broader cultural changes in understandings and experiences of corporality.

Approaches in Theologies of the Body

The goal of the feminist theologies that I mentioned before could be described as liberating bodily experience and knowledge from forms of Christianity that suppress it. This is a common way of representing works about eroticism and sexuality, for instance; affirming forms of carnal desire is seen as inherently liberative. Who would complain? I won't. But I am interested in careful analyses of our visions of liberation and the role we give to theology in articulating those visions. For instance, I worry that speaking about Christianity as simply repressing sexuality or the body may lead to construing secular views of corporeality as *de facto* liberative. Therefore we need to take a critical look not only at *negative* views of the body in Christian theology, but also at *celebratory* views of the body in secular culture – especially those that present themselves as liberative.

Mark Jordan's work on Michel Foucault analyzes the complex relationship between Christian and secular views of sexuality and it turns a critical eye toward theology. Foucault noted that we tell ourselves that we talk of sex because we have overcome previous repressions. But we shall be suspicious of this narrative. Power does not always repress speech; it often demands or incites it. The story of a previous repression conveniently makes "the mere fact that one is speaking about it" appear as "a deliberate transgression."[9] For Foucault, this self-serving narrative is not a clear break from theology, but rather its adaptation. Foucault argues, with irony, "[w]hat sustains our eagerness to speak of sex in terms of repression is doubtless this opportunity to speak out against the powers that be, to utter truths and promise bliss, to link together enlightenment, liberation, and manifold pleasures."[10] That is, we enjoy describing pleasure as enlightenment and liberation. Our discourses bring together "the fervor of knowledge, the determination to change the laws, and the longing for the garden of earthly delights."[11] Sex-talk is thus couched as liberation and takes the place of redemption – as a garden of delights. Commenting on these and other passages, Jordan observes that here Foucault

---

[9] Michel Foucault, *The History of Sexuality*, trans. Robert Hurley (Pantheon: New York 1978), vol. 1: *An Introduction*, 6.

[10] Foucault, *An Introduction*, 7.

[11] Foucault, *An Introduction*, 7.

alludes to the "religious images or concepts that might survive into secular speech about sex."[12] But Foucault is much more interested "in the continuity of the energies of religious rhetoric. The idea that speech about sex tells its truth in order to overturn unjust oppression and open a new future is not just a prophetic idea, it reactivates the rhetoric of prophecy," Jordan writes.[13]

Perhaps theologians would not be troubled by the suggestion that "sexuality" bears the marks of Christianity. But even where Christian influence is not considered as a contamination to be avoided, the continuity of discourses about sexuality with the religious prophetic ideas should at least problematize narratives that portray talk of sex as a sign of liberation. To what extent is the very category of sexuality part of a modern project that approaches bodies as objects from which we are to extract information: male or female, white or colored, heterosexual or homosexual, and so on? The logic that undergirds such an approach to corporeality is not disrupted by multiplying the categories of sexuality – layered with gender and racial labels – and/or by treating such categories as positive attributes, Jordan argues. "What is needed is an epistemic shift [...] treating [bodies] as something other than objects of [...] knowledge."[14] The challenge is to think differently about corporeality itself.

The need for caution regarding cultural presuppositions about the body and liberation extends beyond categories of sexuality to include celebrations of bodily forms. We are now accustomed to the proliferation of body images around us – not only representations of bodies as objects of scientific knowledge, but also as objects of desire. These images are instrumental in teaching us what is regarded as a normal and therefore a desirable and desired body. Those are the bodies we cannot *not* want. Depictions of bodies that deviate from the norm are most often used to induce an urge to correct them, to eliminate divergences in others or in ourselves. And the more we believe in the perfectability of bodies, the narrower the standards for normalcy become. The representation of bodily splendor may appear to be the opposite of the devaluation of corporeality. But those glorified bodies merely displace the devaluation – to particular people and to specific elements of corporeality.

---

[12] Mark Jordan, "Sexuality and the After-life of Christianity," in: Mark Jordan, *Convulsing Bodies: Religion and Resistance in Foucault* (Stanford University Press: Stanford, forthcoming).

[13] Jordan, "Sexuality and the After-life of Christianity," (forthcoming).

[14] Mark Jordan, "Foucault's Ironies and the Important Earnestness of Theory," in: *Foucault Studies* 14 (2012), 7-19, here 17.

Theologian Sharon Betcher analyzes the problem of the idealization of bodies drawing from postcolonial and disability studies.[15] She observes that the celebration of idealized, perfect bodies and the desire to be re-created in their image implies imagining bodies unaffected by transience, weakness, and vulnerability. These rejected aspects of human corporeality tend to be projected onto others – particularly people with disabilities – as if their bodies were the only vulnerable ones! Betcher further argues that feminist theology has not effectively challenged these patterns of corporeal idealization, thus failing to disrupt "disability abjection".[16]

For Betcher the problem is "*the* body". As a theoretical category "the body" fosters an illusion of completeness and wholeness easily naturalized, objectified, and normalized. "The body" evokes the unattainable stability that norms demand but that corporeality cannot mirror. Retrievals of "the body" can even exacerbate racialization and ableism, for instance. Betcher suggests, "Whereas 'body' can invite the hallucinatory delusion of wholeness, and thus the temptation to believe in agential mastery and control, flesh [...] admits our exposure, our vulnerability one to another, if also to bios."[17] I will return to the flesh at the end of the article. For now let's take to heart Jordan's and Betcher's words of caution about the ambivalence of both "sexuality" and "the body".

Postcolonial theory proves helpful in diagnosing ambivalence, and its analyses of the ideological weight of representations of bodies are crucial. We have become familiar, for example, with comparisons of the measurements of people's skulls, the size of which were construed as evidence for the evolutionary progress of each race. Bodies were organized by "race" and each race was characterized according to its purported distance from the animal. Modern/colonial categorizations of bodies based on physical data were clearly an exercise of power. Postcolonial theory helped us understand that those images did not represent, but rather produced the idea of race, and that constructions of race relied on views about gender. The markers of a properly evolved race included abiding by the categories of gender and sexuality assumed as appropriate by the colonial system. Discourses about bodies naturalized and thus justified hierarchies of power, tying social categories such as

---

[15] Cf. Sharon V. Betcher, "Becoming Flesh of My Flesh: Feminist and Disability Theologies on the Edge of Posthumanist Discourse," in: *Journal of Feminist Studies in Religion* 26.2 (2010), 107-118.

[16] Betcher, "Becoming Flesh of My Flesh," 107.

[17] Sharon V. Betcher, *Spirit and the Politics of Disablement* (Fortress Press: Minneapolis 2007), 108.

gender, race, and class to visible bodily traits.[18] The contribution of post-colonial theory to the study of corporeality lies in uncovering how discursive practices define and position people in society. Important as this project has been for understanding mechanisms of power, its focus on representation has come at the expense of engagements with other dimensions of corporeality.

Scholars are increasingly seeking approaches to corporeality that allow them to move beyond the focus on discourse to materiality – to elements of corporeality that are not reducible to signification. What concepts do we use to think about how ideologies become policies and practices that produce social-material environments, that become flesh? What theories might help us see, for example, how nationalist and racial ideologies motivate and shape the displacement of manufacturing processes or military bases to the global south, which produce occupational hazards and toxic environments, which in turn transform the bodies of those affected sometimes for two or three generations? Or how practices of racialization restrict access to economic resources, increase levels of stress, which in turn affect bodily processes and thus susceptibility to illnesses?

A turn to materiality would not mean abandoning attention to the social, but rather deepening our understanding of the reach of social relations. For even when the body is invoked to create and justify social hierarchies, social constructions do not remain immaterial. Constructions of gender, sexuality, and race shape social structures that shape environments and thus our bodies. Re-thinking corporeal materiality entails building on the insights of poststructuralist approaches, particularly about the constitutive relationship between corporeality and discourse. These analyses are grounded in the conviction that words do not mirror what is, or express the thoughts and desires of a person, but rather shape reality and subjectivity. Discursive practices incite passions, create and negate identities, entice our interest in theologizing the body. In this sense, poststructuralist approaches already consider words as intricately connected to the experiences of bodies. As Judith Butler has argued, even the claims that bodies exceed language must be understood as linguistic statements, as discursive.[19] To assume otherwise would imply claiming an extra-cultural, universal,

---

[18] Postcolonial theory also helps us analyze the formation of new race-gender identities through the notions of hybridity and mimicry, how the colonized are compelled to perform given identities with unexpected results. But those analyses of identities tend to focus on cultures and behaviors, not on bodies. Cf. Homi K. Bhabha, *The Location of Culture* (Routledge: London 1994).

[19] See Judith Butler, *Bodies That Matter: On the Discursive Limits of 'Sex'* (Routledge: New York 1993).

absolute foundation for a particular view of reality, a type of argument that feminists have challenged in their efforts to de-naturalize gender assumptions. Scholars calling for a renewed attention to materiality – many of whom are feminist theorists – do not abandon these insights about the role of discourse. Yet they explore not only the efficacy of words to shape materiality, but also the productivity of materiality.[20]

Cultural Changes

The recent scholarly interest in materiality as a dynamic element of our environment and our bodies is much more than the result of our having exhausted the prevalent methodologies. Rather, this interest responds to broader cultural changes prompted by developments in science and technology. New scientific notions of materiality are transforming theories in the humanities and beyond. Instead of passive matter characterized by inertia, on which humans act unilaterally, materiality is described in terms of forces and energies in complex networks of relations. Theories focus on *processes* of materialization – not just on a stuff called *matter*.[21]

We understand materiality differently. And we are experiencing new material phenomena as technological advances become part of our everyday engagements with the world. Even though biological essentialisms have not disappeared, we are believers in the transformability of the body, in the power of fitness regimes or meditation practices, drug enhancement or genetic modification. Organ transplants and stem cell experiments have captured the imagination of writers, producers, and philosophers who wrestle with the significance of such exchanges of bodily matter, where part of one body becomes part of another. But new technologies force us to think beyond the exchange between humans to include the participation of the non-human – animals, bacteria, and inorganic matter – in

---

[20] See, for instance, Diana Coole / Samantha Frost (eds.), *New Materialisms: Ontology, Agency, and Politics* (Duke University Press: Durham 2010); Stacy Alaimo / Susan Hekman (eds.), *Material Feminisms* (Indiana University Press: Bloomington 2008).

[21] We see research focusing on how the everyday practices of raising children may lower testosterone in men, for instance; how meditation transforms a body to produce a relaxation response; how particular bodily positions increase testosterone levels. These examples focus on the influence of practices in bodily changes rather than the stability associated with genetic traits. This implies an understanding that material processes respond to human agency, but this does not imply that human agency can determine the results unilaterally. The complex transformations produced by global warming are a frightening reminder that humans cannot fully control the outcome of the material practices in which we engage.

the production and reproduction of corporeal matter. The boundaries between human and non-human flesh are porous and provisional.

So are the divisions between socio-economic and biological processes. The use of new reproductive technologies, the proliferation of genetic testing and treatments, the debates about cloning, etc. are all foregrounding not only the productivity and malleability of materiality, but also how the potentialities opened by these technologies are enmeshed in social and economic relations. Social factors influence what technologies are developed and who has access to them. Money, as much as biology and technology, influences who can reproduce or live longer. At the same time, technological practices and discourses reshape understandings of subjectivity and communal relations.[22] The processes of material transformation and becoming are deeply, if ambiguously relational. The emerging vision is one where bodies are not simply *located* in society – as suggested by the common phrase "social location" – but *constituted* in relation to the world.

Theories of corporeality for the twenty-first century must be attentive to those changes in understandings and practices of materiality. As Judith Butler argues,

> if we are to make broader social and political claims about rights of protection and entitlements to persistence and flourishing, we will first have to be supported by a *new bodily ontology*, one that implies the rethinking of precariousness, vulnerability, injurability, interdependency, exposure, bodily persistence and desire, work and the claims of language and social belonging.[23]

What can theology contribute to this task of developing a new bodily ontology to ground broader social and political claims about human flourishing?

Flesh

In my current research, I have turned toward Christian understandings of "flesh" to suggest new visions of our bodily materiality.[24] "Flesh" helps me

---

[22] Nicolas Rose describes, for example, the impact of genetic testing on conceptions of communities. By changing the criteria for identity from collective histories and shared cultural practices to biological indicators, the bases for claiming to be part of a community are significantly transformed. Nikolas Rose, *The Politics of Life Itself: Biomedicine, Power, and Subjectivity in the Twenty-first Century* (Princeton University Press: Princeton 2007).

[23] Judith Butler, "On This Occasion...," in: Roland Faber / Michael Halewood / Deena Lin (eds.), *Butler on Whitehead: On the Occasion* (Lexington Books: Lanham 2012), 3-18, here 12 (italics mine).

[24] See Mayra Rivera, "Unsettling Flesh," in: *Journal of Feminist Studies in Religion* 26.2 (2010), 119-123; Mayra Rivera, "Flesh of the World: Corporeality in Relation," in: *Concilium* (2/2013), 51-60.

focus on the material elements of corporeality more consistently than the term "body" does. The difference between body and flesh reflects the terms' distinct semantic histories and affective charges and is detectable even in the common usage of the terms. "Body" tends to denote an entity complete in itself, formed and visible to those around it, whereas "flesh" evokes the materiality of bodies. Of the two terms, it is "flesh" that carries the most ambiguous connotations: of lust, instinct, sinfulness, disease, and death. Tellingly, flesh is also feminized. It is no accident that the most material term is also the most devalued. It is our materiality we fear, even while we are enchanted by star-like bodies, by bodies without flesh.

This turn to flesh is consonant with Dussel's argument, which I mentioned at the beginning, that a liberationist ethics should be grounded in a carnal anthropology. From his exploration of ancient sources, Dussel concluded that only a model based on the relationship between flesh and spirit – rather than body and soul – could lead to an integral anthropology and thus ground an ethics of liberation. Dussel wrote: "John said: 'the word became flesh'. A Greek would have said: 'the word took a body' – which is radically different."[25] I too return to John in search for Christian metaphors of carnal corporeality. Dussel's goal was to keep spirit and flesh closely together by challenging the idea of an autonomous soul, which was only loosely connected to the body. My main purpose is to keep corporeality close to the materiality of the world.

Flesh helps me focus on materiality, but both flesh and materiality must be rethought. The materiality to which I am alluding is not something given and unchangeable, belonging to nature and protected from culture. Nor is it passive stuff neatly contained within the skin. It is an element connecting bodies to one another, connecting human bodies to the elements and the earth. As Rubem Alves says, "My flesh overflows and fertilizes the world; the world overflows and my body receives it."[26] While experienced intimately, this flesh is not inherently turned into itself. It is exposed, constituted through relationships, materially weaving you in me and me in you.

These relational traits of carnality may ground theories of corporality that unsettle the desire to conform to objectifying standards for individual bodies.

---

[25] Dussel, *El Humanismo semita*, 28 (my translation). Dussel returns to this anthropological issue in more recent works, arguing that a critical ethics derived from the experience of victims would be based on a "carnal corporeality" and not on the soul (Enrique Dussel, *Ética de la liberación: En la edad de la Globalización y de la exclusión* [Trotta: Madrid 2002]).

[26] Rubem Alves, *I Believe in the Resurrection of the Body* (Wipf & Stock: Eugene 1986), 8.

Instead they can foster more dynamic visions for the flourishing of diverse forms and capacities of human embodiment. That is why Betcher counsels scholars to "learn to think flesh without 'the body'."[27] A view of carnal corporeality would emphasize becoming, and the need for societies to provide the conditions to sustain the vitality of flesh.

Exposure to others is also a source of vulnerability – clearly biological, but also social. Indeed, the becoming of flesh is always already social. Our materiality is woven by the elements that surround us, but also of words. Words mark, wound, elevate, or shatter bodies; gender norms "surface as [...] styles of flesh."[28] Laws prohibit or authorize practices that infect bodies, produce illness and death. Literally.

At its best, a theology of the flesh would avoid separating vulnerability from the life-giving qualities of carnality. Christian flesh is both the clay of creation and the matter of incarnation. Neither rotten nor invulnerable, Christian flesh may ground theologies attuned to the human capacity to endure pain as part of life, as the very possibility of experiencing passion with other fleshly beings.

Society is a labyrinth of incarnations. Theologizing flesh requires wrestling with the changing social-material processes that constitute bodies and our discourses about them. We will need to be mindful of the term's ambiguous history and be critical of the cultural ideals that inform our theologies and still strive to respond to the ethical challenges of our times.

Este ensayo hace un llamado a las teologías del cuerpo a examinar encarnaciones socio- materiales. Primero explora la contribución de las teologías de liberación y feministas en la "vuelta al cuerpo" en los estudios religiosos. En estas teologías, el cuerpo se convierte en el concepto central desde el cual analizan la desigualdad social, la vulnerabilidad humana, la relacionalidad, el dolor y el deseo. Este artículo presenta las limitaciones de representaciones simplistas del cristianismo como represivo y las visiones seculares como intrínsecamente liberadoras, señala la necesidad de pensar la corporeidad evitando tanto la reducción de los cuerpos a objetos como su idealización. Con este propósito es necesario moverse del énfasis teológico en el discurso hacia la materialidad. El pensamiento postcolonial analiza las construcciones sociales e ideológicas de los cuerpos, pero no sus procesos de materialización donde los factores biológicos, sociales y económicos se entrelazan. Repensar la carne y la materialidad como metáforas de desbordamiento, entretejido, y exposición

---

[27] Betcher, "Becoming Flesh of My Flesh," 110.
[28] Judith Butler, "Sex and Gender in Simone De Beauvoir's *Second Sex*," in: *Yale French Studies* 72 (1986), 35-49, here 48.

contribuyen a desarrollar visiones más abarcadoras de la relaciones que constituyen la vida.

This essay calls for theologies of the body to examine social-material incarnations. It explores the "turn to the body" in religious studies, beginning with the ways that it builds upon liberationist and feminist theological movements. The body becomes a site for thinking through social inequality, human vulnerability, relationality, pain, and desire. This paper argues that something is missed when Christianity is simplistically construed as sexually repressive, and non-religious views of the body as intrinsically liberative. The challenge, this essay argues, is to think corporeality in a mode that refuses both objectifying knowledge, and idealizations that deny vulnerability. For these purposes, it is necessary to shift theological emphasis from discourse to materiality. Postcolonial theory analyzes the social and ideological constructions of bodies, but not the processes of materialization where biological, social, and economic factors interlace. Flesh and materiality rethought in this way – as overflowing, interweaving, and exposed – deepen the accounts of the relationships that constitute life.

Dieser Beitrag fordert Körper-Theologien dazu auf, sozio-materielle Inkarnationen zu analysieren. Er untersucht die "Wende zum Körper" in den Religionswissenschaften, angefangen davon, wie sie auf befreiungstheologische und feministisch-theologische Bewegungen aufbaut. Der Körper wird der Ort des Nachdenkens über soziale Ungerechtigkeit, menschliche Verletzlichkeit, Beziehungshaftigkeit, Schmerz und Begehren. Dieser Beitrag argumentiert, dass etwas nicht wahrgenommen wird, wenn das Christentum vereinfacht als sexuell repressiv und nicht-religiöse Perspektiven auf den Körper als inhärent befreiend dargestellt werden. Die Herausforderung, so die These dieses Artikels, ist, Körperlichkeit so zu denken, dass sowohl objektivierendes Wissen als auch Idealisierungen, die Verletzlichkeit verleugnen, zurückgewiesen werden. Deshalb ist es notwendig, den theologischen Schwerpunkt von Diskurs zu Materialität zu verschieben. Postkoloniale Theorie analysiert die soziale und ideologische Konstruktion von Körpern, aber nicht die Prozesse von Materialisierung, in denen biologische, soziale und ökonomische Faktoren verknüpft sind. Wenn Fleisch und Materialität so neu gedacht werden – als überfließend, verknüpft und bloß gestellt –, vertieft das unser Verständnis von Beziehungen, die Leben begründen.

Mayra Rivera is Associate Professor of Theology at Harvard Divinity School. She is author of *The Touch of Transcendence: A Postcolonial Theology of God* (2007) and co-editor of *Planetary Loves: Spivak, Postcoloniality, and Theology* (2010) and *Postcolonial Theologies: Divinity and Empire* (2004).

Journal of the European Society of Women in Theological Research 22 (2014) 199-214.
doi: 10.2143/ESWTR.22.0.3040799

Montserrat Escribano-Cárcel y Neus Forcano i Aparicio

Aportaciones de la neuroteología feminista, de las teologías *queer* y postcoloniales para una nueva concepción de la subjetividad ética

Una teología capaz de irrumpir en el espacio público

Aunque Europa y el mundo occidental han vivido desde la Modernidad una progresiva secularización y una separación entre religión y Estado, se constata, a comienzos del siglo XXI, que las religiones emergen con fuerza y provocan polémica en el espacio público. Es lo que algunos expertos han convenido en llamar la desprivatización de la religión.[1] En países referentes de la laicidad del estado como Francia, se han podido constatar reacciones violentas recientes en las calles de París en contra de la ley de matrimonio para parejas homosexuales que se aprobó en el Parlamento en mayo del 2013. Con la crisis financiera y la desestabilización del estado del bienestar, en muchas social-democracias europeas aparecen discursos religiosos ortodoxos en connivencia con el poder neoliberal; pero también y paralelamente, personas y comunidades creyentes se han sumado a los movimientos políticos reivindicativos para solucionar la precariedad laboral, quejarse de la pérdida de prestaciones sociales y han reaccionado ante el desmantelamiento de la democracia y los servicios públicos básicos en el ágora pública.

Si la teología se entiende como una reflexión acerca de la experiencia espiritual, la propia y la de la comunidad, y de la reflexión sobre qué concepción de Dios, de la realidad y del ser humano se tiene, podemos preguntarnos: ¿qué aportan hoy las teologías feminista, *queer* y postcolonial a la concepción de "ser persona", de "libertad" y de "comunidad"? ¿Pueden estas teologías contribuir al cambio social y a la renovación democrática?

En el contexto de las movilizaciones ciudadanas como la del 15-M, o del movimiento *Occupy Wall Street* en Estados Unidos, donde una mayoría plural del 99% confluye en estrategias de lucha para conseguir justicia social

---

[1] Cf. José Casanova, "Religión, política e igualdad de género," en: *Iglesia Viva* 251 (2012), 9-40.

frente a las élites poderosas del 1%,[2] el reto y el sueño que planteamos es si será capaz la reflexión teológica de romper la barrera de lo sagrado y lo profano, de abandonar su reducto académico y de especialización, para implicarse en la vida cotidiana y saltar a la arena pública. Al mismo tiempo, también nos preguntamos si sabrá la teología dialogar y enriquecerse de los avances de las neurociencias para entender y aportar sus propios matices al sujeto ético.

Nuestra identidad neurobiológica

¿Qué son las neurociencias?

En la actualidad, estamos asistiendo a un conocimiento que se despliega con una enorme proyección, se trata de las "neurociencias". Su interés abarca el estudio de todo el sistema nervioso y el de los componentes que la incluyen: la espina dorsal, las redes de células nerviosas sensoriales que recorren todo nuestro cuerpo y el órgano que más atenciones está recibiendo, el cerebro. Este órgano a pesar de tratarse de una masa gelatinosa de apenas un kilo cuatrocientos gramos, está resultando extremadamente complejo. El protagonismo del cerebro comenzó gracias a estudios como el del médico e histólogo Santiago Ramón y Cajal (1862-1939) que logró describir un gran número de estructuras del sistema nervioso relacionadas con el cerebro. Pero su mayor descubrimiento fue percibir la unicidad de cada una de estas células que llamamos "neuronas", intuir las conexiones que se realizaban entre ellas y aventurar la importancia que debía suponer esta realidad para el ser humano. Este descubrimiento supuso un punto y aparte y permitió que las neurociencias modernas se desplegaran en innumerables disciplinas. Pero también desde la perspectiva teológica supuso descubrir la existencia de unas bases neuronales que refrendaban el principio de unicidad personal querida por la divinidad y afirmada desde la antropología teológica.

A partir del trabajo de Ramón y Cajal, los y las neurocientíficas han podido descifrar parte de la extensa morfología y de la asombrosa actividad de las neuronas. Cada una de estas células, sabemos ahora que establece contacto con otras neuronas próximas a través de unas fibras, llamadas dendritas, formando estructuras parecidas a densos matorrales. Previamente a las observaciones de

---

[2] Cf. Joerg Rieger / Kwok Pui-lan, *Occupy Religion: Theology of the Multitude* (Rowman & Littlefield Publishers: Lanham 2013).

Ramón y Cajal[3] se pensaba que el sistema nervioso era un continuo sin divisiones que formaba una especie de tejido extendido. Sin embargo, este médico mostró que entre las neuronas existía discreción y que, a través de las dendritas, estas células establecían conexiones con el resto. Hoy sabemos que tienen, además de la función de conectarse, también la de canalizar o bien inhibir, las señales eléctricas que reciben. Las neuronas disponen a su vez de unos cables largos y sinuosos, llamados axones, a través de los cuales transmiten la información. Así, cada célula nerviosa es capaz de establecer entre mil y diez mil contactos con otras neuronas. A los puntos de contacto entre unas y otras se les denomina sinapsis y pueden a su vez estar activas o permanecer sin actividad. Las neurociencias nos recuerdan que albergamos más de cien mil millones de neuronas que, siguiendo una instrucción genética precisa, muestran una morfología variada. Así, las neuronas ocupan posiciones muy distintas, mantienen una extremada actividad y al agruparse, configuran enormes redes de transmisión de información. Además, ahora sabemos que nuestro cerebro establece cada segundo de nuestra vida un millón de nuevas conexiones. De ahí que, la gran cantidad de neuronas que tenemos junto a su enorme variabilidad, además de su capacidad de establecer sinapsis y las posibilidades de transmisión de información con el resto, hacen que el número de estados diferentes que nuestro cerebro puede albergar sea, sencillamente, apabullante y, como dice el neurólogo V. S. Ramachandran, supera de lejos el número de partículas elementales que encontramos en el universo conocido. [4]

Tal como lo define una de las primeras instituciones para el estudio de esta disciplina, la *Society for Neuroscience,*[5] este nuevo campo del saber llamado neurociencias incluye el estudio de las moléculas, las neuronas y de todos los procesos que se llevan a cabo en y entre las células nerviosas de las que ahora, poco a poco, comenzamos a comprender sus formas de organización, de comunicación y los modos en que establecen las "redes neuronales". Pero, además de su preocupación por una descripción fisiológica y biológica cada vez más precisa, las neurociencias estudian también cómo el sistema nervioso realiza

---

[3] Santiago Ramón y Cajal mostró sus descubrimientos en la *Anatomische Gesellschaft* (Sociedad anatómica alemana) celebrada en la ciudad de Berlín, el año 1889. Publicó estos resultados en: Santiago Ramón y Cajal, *Manual de histología normal y técnica micrográfica* (Nicolás Moya: Madrid 1889).

[4] Cf. Vilayanur S. Ramachandran, *Lo que el cerebro nos dice: Los misterios de la mente humana al descubierto* (Planeta: Barcelona 2012).

[5] Cf. http://www.sfn.

cada una de las funciones que desarrollamos a lo largo de nuestra vida: hablar, movernos, recordar, proyectar el futuro, rezar, enamorarnos o reír. Muchas de ellas, las realizamos de modo simultáneo, lo que hace más complejo aún nuestro cerebro. Aunque todas se localizan en áreas específicas de nuestro cerebro, situadas en alguno de los dos hemisferios, llamados lóbulos, actúan como ámbitos de funcionamiento independientes aunque mantienen una estrecha conexión entre sí. El reto, ahora, es conocer mejor cada una de estas áreas, cómo se realizan las conexiones neuronales[6] (conectoma), y comprender cómo nuestras experiencias y el contexto hacen que seamos seres únicos e irrepetibles y en continuo cambio.

El conocimiento y desarrollo de las neurociencias han tenido un impacto inmediato, especialmente sobre la ciencia médica. Principalmente, tras ser declarada la década de los noventa del siglo XX como la "Década del cerebro".[7] Desde entonces, el gran número de investigaciones y de financiación destinada a este respecto han potenciado tanto el conocimiento médico como sus aplicaciones. El resultado es que estamos ante algunos avances importantes en enfermedades como la esquizofrenia, las psicosis, el autismo, el Alzheimer, los trasplantes de órganos o las terapias regenerativas que afectan a millones de personas y cuya repercusión social se prevé aún mayor durante el siglo XXI.

Pero además de las posibilidades que se abren para las ciencias médicas, ha supuesto también la consolidación de áreas de investigación ya iniciadas anteriormente como las ciencias cognitivas. Al mismo tiempo, también están propiciando en nuestros días la aparición de otras ramas nuevas del conocimiento como son: la neurofilosofía,[8] la neuroeconomía,[9] la neuroeducación,[10]

---

[6]   Cf. Sebastian Seung, *Connectome: How The Brain's Wiring Makes us Who We Are* (Penguin Books: London 2012).

[7]   El 1 de enero de 1990, el entonces presidente de los Estados Unidos de Norteamérica, George H.W. Bush, hizo la presentación pública de la resolución 6158 en la que señalaba los próximos diez años como "Década del cerebro". El objetivo era incrementar la implicación política y social en la investigación neurocientífica y concienciar a la opinión pública acerca de la importancia de las enfermedades neurológicas y microquirúrgicas. Ver Edward R. Laws, "The Decade of the Brain: 1990 to 2000," en: *Neurosurgery* 47 (2000), 1257-1260.

[8]   Cf. Patricia S. Churchland, *El cerebro moral: Lo que la neurociencia nos cuenta sobre la moralidad* (Paidós: Barcelona 2012).

[9]   Cf. Paul W. Glimcher / Colin F. Camerer / Ernst Fehr / Rusell A. Poldrack (eds.), *Neuroeconomics: Decision Making and the Brain* (Elsevier: London 2009). También ver: Jesús Conill-Sancho, "Neuroeconomía y Neuromárketing: ¿Más allá de la racionalidad maximizadora?," en: Adela Cortina (ed.), *Neurofilosofía Práctica* (Comares: Granada 2012), 39-64.

[10] Cf. Francisco Mora, *Neuroeducación* (Alianza Editorial: Madrid 2013).

la neuroética,[11] la neurorreligión,[12] o la neuroteología·[13] por nombrar solo algunas. Aunque la que más nos interesa en estos momentos sea esta última, por tratarse de un conocimiento que surge de la interacción entre los resultados alcanzados por las neurociencias y las distintas perspectivas teológicas recogida a lo largo de una dilatada tradición de pensamiento. En nuestro caso, la perspectiva neuroteológica que queremos construir la insertamos en la corriente de pensamiento crítico feminista y en las perspectivas liberacionistas que se abrieron tras el nacimiento de la llamada teología de la liberación.

Características de las neurociencias aplicadas a la neuroteología feminista
La novedad que presenta las neurociencias nos ofrece la oportunidad de recoger algunas características que, desde esa perspectiva teológica feminista que soñamos, podríamos asumir críticamente como herramientas metodológicas. Nuestra pretensión ética es lograr dialogar e influir sobre las neurociencias y, a la vez, aportar nuestro conocimiento y metodologías a las propuestas neurocientíficas que están perfilando qué es un ser humano y cómo se configura su identidad. Por ello, recogemos ahora algunas de las características que aporta el conocimiento neurocientífico y que creemos que, si son incluidas en nuestra reflexión neuroteológica feminista, pueden ser de gran utilidad. Algunas de estas son:

a) La primera es la *novedad*. Como sabemos, la investigación del sistema nervioso ha abierto un enorme espectro de ciencias y saberes. Esto ha posibilitado un conocimiento cada vez más preciso, gracias al desarrollo de nuevos métodos y de técnicas de investigación. Al mismo tiempo, las neurociencias están dibujando y presentando grandes interrogantes sobre el ser humano tales como su unicidad, la conciencia o la posibilidad de su libertad que nos obligan a repensarlas desde nuestra perspectiva teológica

---

[11] Cf. Adela Cortina, *Neuroética y neuropolítica: Sugerencias para la educación moral* (Tecnos: Madrid 2011). También: Kathinka Evers, *Neuroética: Cuando la materia se despierta* (Katz: Madrid 2010).

[12] Cf. Andrew Newberg / Eugene D'Aquili / Vince Rause, *Why God Won't Go Away: Brain Science and the Biology of Belief* (Ballantine Books: New York 2001); Patrick McNamara (ed.), *Where God and Science Meet. How Brain and Evolutionary Studies Alter Our Understanding of Religion* (Praeger: Westport 2006), vol. 1. También: Pius-Ramón Tragan (ed.), *Neurociencias y espíritu: ¿Abiertos a una vida eterna? Actas de las X Jornadas Universitarias de Cultura humanística en Montserrat* (Verbo Divino: Estella 2012).

[13] Cf. Andrew Newberg, *Principles of Neurotheology* (Ashgate: Farnham 2012).

feminista. Así, nuestra aportación puede evidenciar materialismos o dualismos por parte de las neurociencias y reclamar entonces posibilidades éticas y perspectivas diversas necesarias para el conocimiento.

b) Otras características que manifiestan las neurociencias son su carácter *interdisciplinar* y *transversal*. Es por ello que cualquier ámbito de conocimiento puede ser ahora necesario para responder a las enormes preguntas que se están planteando acerca del conjunto del sistema nervioso, especialmente del cerebro, y de las visiones antropológicas que se derivan de su estudio. Entre las neurociencias no resulta ya extraño que figuren disciplinas en principio tan distantes como la informática o la teología. Tanto la interdisciplinariedad como la transversalidad intentan dar una respuesta ética a complejas cuestiones que van más allá de la mera descripción fisiológica. Profundizar entonces en la comprensión que tenemos sobre nosotras mismas lleva, necessariamente, a plantear cuestiones filosóficas y teológicas de gran calado. A pesar de que durante mucho tiempo, cuestiones como el sujeto, la conciencia, el alma o la libertad han permanecido excluidas de los llamados espacios científicos, ahora ya no pueden permanecen al margen bajo el argumento sesgado de que no encajan en los límites de una disciplina concreta. Esto sería, como señala el teólogo Philip Clayton, no ver el bosque por fijarse en los árboles.[14]

c) La última característica que queremos destacar es la *trans-disciplinariedad*. Esta característica surge al poner en común perspectivas, conocimientos, métodos y análisis de ámbitos diferentes de conocimiento. Así sucede con la neuroteología en la que pretendemos leer desde una perspectiva neurocientífica la teología y también al contrario. Por ello, la consecuencia no es sencillamente una perspectiva interdisciplinar, sino que la novedad reside ahora en que asistimos a una disciplina nueva. La neuroteología, tal como la concebimos, es un cruce entre conocimientos diversos y no un mero acercamiento de ámbitos distintos. Esta apuesta va más allá de una propuesta de diálogo entre las ciencias y la teología – como aconsejó el Concilio ecuménico Vaticano II. El resultado ahora es un *conocimiento liminal*. Este término tiene la osadía de desdibujar las fronteras iniciales de las que partía. Así cada una de las disciplinas, tanto las neurociencias como las teologías pueden ver ampliados y corregidos sus conocimientos. Otro ejemplo interesante de esta posibilidad liminal lo vemos también en el

---

[14] Cf. Philip Clayton, *En busca de la libertad: La emergencia del espíritu en el mundo natural* (Verbo Divino: Estella 2011).

neurofemismo, disciplina muy interesante sin duda para nosotras, y de la que estamos viendo ya el aviso que lanza a la comunidad científica al reclamar una necesaria *re-queerificación* del conocimiento cerebral.[15]

Estas características están convirtiendo a las neurociencias en un conocimiento multiplicativo, que está cambiando el modo de hacer ciencia y la comprensión que tenemos de las personas. Los límites experimentales iniciales en los que surgieron las ciencias se han traspasado, instalándose ahora el enfoque neuronal en la práctica totalidad de las áreas de conocimiento y de todos los ámbitos de conocimiento que se ocupan de comprender el comportamiento humano y sus posibilidades de mejoramiento (*human enhancement*). Esta celeridad exige que nos movamos con cautela, que cuestionemos los presupuestos antropológicos que se manejan en los métodos y modos de concebir al ser humano y a la vez, que afirmemos con rotundidad la necesidad de unos fundamentos éticamente cordiales[16] que permitan el florecimiento de todos los seres humanos.

Nuestra neuroidentidad plástica

Actualmente, gracias al desarrollo de técnicas de medición no invasivas como la tomografía por emisión de positrones (PET), la electroencefalografía (EEG) o la imagen por resonancia magnética funcional (IRMF) es posible visualizar y percibir a través de imágenes el volumen de determinadas regiones del cerebro. Desde los años noventa del pasado siglo estas técnicas se efectúan mientras el cerebro realiza una actividad. En los últimos años se están aplicando en personas que sufren trastornos o bien que no pueden desempeñar actividades motoras. Para diferentes campos de investigación, como la psicología, la antropología, la filosofía o la teología, la introducción de estas técnicas pueden, por primera vez, valorar la actividad de nuestro sistema nervioso y medir estados cerebrales relevantes.[17] Esto significa, al menos para la neuroteología feminista que queremos desarrollar, que además del gran interés técnico que

---

[15] Cf. Isabelle Dussauge / Anelis Kaiser, "Re-queering the Brain," en: Robyn Bluhm / Anne Jaap Jacobson / Heide Lene Mainbom, *Neurofeminism: Issues at the Intersection of Feminist Theory and Cognitive Science* (Palgrave Macmillan: Basingstoke 2012), 121-144.

[16] Cf. Adela Cortina, *Neuroética y neuropolítica: Sugerencias para la educación moral* (Tecnos: Madrid 2011).

[17] Cf. Kathinka Evers / Mario Sigman, "Lectura de la mente: Una perspectiva neurofilosófica," en: *Recerca* 13 (2013), 43-62.

supone, es posible ahora indagar por primera vez la mente de modo más directo y descodificar parte de nuestra experiencia subjetiva.

Nos asomamos a perspectivas diferentes que posibilitan un conocimiento distinto sobre quiénes somos y cuáles son las bases fisiológicas que determinan nuestra neuroidentidad. Sin embargo, la complejidad de nuestro comportamiento, a pesar de estar diseñado por un código genético preciso e informado por nuestro sistema nervioso, no queda nunca circunscrito a este marco, sino que permanece expuesto siempre a un contexto histórico. Esta posibilidad nos permite desear e ir siempre más allá, como nos recuerda la teología cristiana. Así, el ser humano se entiende como un ser histórico, abierto a un final.[18]

Pero no podemos olvidar que el deseo y la trascendencia humana se inician en la carnalidad, en nuestra capacidad somática. De este modo, la experiencia vivida en nuestro cuerpo altera, modela y configura la estructura de nuestro cerebro. Neurobiólogos, como Eric R. Kandel, están probando que nuestro sistema nervioso no es estático, sino extraordinariamente dinámico.[19]

Precisamente, las experiencias humanas que sentimos a través del cuerpo se inscriben en nuestro cerebro dejando huellas únicas que generan nuestra unicidad. Estas huellas psíquicas y sinápticas se establecen en redes neuronales gracias a la plasticidad que manifiesta nuestro cerebro y dependen no solo de nuestra determinación genética, sino de la relación que las personas mantienen con su realidad. De ahí que hablemos también de un cerebro social y cooperativo.[20]

Por un cerebro despierto y cordial

La plasticidad neuronal se convierte en una de las cualidades más interesantes y también en una perspectiva hermenéutica posible para comprender la realidad del ser humano. Para nosotras, la antropología cristiana que brota de la concepción trinitaria de la divinidad, supone una visión enormemente dinámica de la creación y del ser humano. Esta comprensión teológica del ser humano recoge el pensamiento ofrecido por la tradición cristiana, como

---

[18] Cf. Montserrat Escribano-Cárcel, "La Neuroética fundamental y nuestra comprensión de la realidad: Posibilidades de transformación también en lo religioso," en: Francisco Javier López Frías / Paulina Morales Aguilera / Marta Gil Blasco (eds.), *Bioética, Neuroética, Libertad y Justicia* (Comares: Granada 2013), 881-893.

[19] Cf. Eric R. Kandel, "Cellular Mechanisms of Learning and the Biological Basis of Individuality," en: Eric R. Kandel / James Schwartz / Thomas Jessell, *Principles of Neural Science* (McGraw-Hill: New York 2000), 1247-1289.

[20] Cf. François Ansermet / Pierre Magistretti, *A cada cual su cerebro: Plasticidad neuronal e inconsciente* (Katz: Madrid 2006).

veremos a continuación, y a la vez, trata de ponerlo en diálogo crítico con el conocimiento neurocientífico. Por ello, el encuentro entre ambas se presenta ahora como un *loci theologici* (lugar teológico), es decir, un espacio pertinente desde el cual repensar categorías centrales para esta disciplina como son: la experiencia religiosa, la libertad, la conversión (*metanoia*), o la misma idea de persona. Tenemos la certeza de que movilizar los horizontes hermenéuticos desde los cuales pensamos nos obliga a mirar desde otras perspectivas, a ampliar las visiones académicas iniciales y a ahondar en nuestras perspectivas políticas.[21]

Debido al carácter transdisciplinar que muestra la neuroteología feminista, el espacio liminal que resulta entre el conocimiento neurológico y el teológico hace que pueda ser especialmente fecundo y movilizador para ambas disciplinas. Aunque apenas estamos intuyendo los caminos por los que discurrirá la neuroteología feminista, sabemos ya que, como toda teología, se trata de un modo peculiar de producir conocimiento, nunca es objetivo ni debe obviar el contexto en el que surge. De ahí que nuestra propuesta parta de las posibilidades que ofrecen las teologías feministas críticas, las teologías postcoloniales,[22] las teologías *queer*,[23] la bio-teología[24] y las teologías constructivas.[25]

Uno de los problemas a los que ha de hacer frente la neuroteología feminista es que, a pesar de los asombrosos resultados que cada día ofrecen las neurociencias, se trata aún de un conocimiento muy incipiente. Lo que sabemos de la actividad neuronal es insuficiente para proponer, por ejemplo, otras metáforas más apropiadas que vayan más allá de las actuales y que giran entorno a sistemas mecánicos como los ordenadores. Entender nuestro cerebro o saber cómo interpretarlo para modificarlo es un conocimiento poco más que seminal en la actualidad. Sin embargo, hay una pregunta fundante que no debe cesar

---

[21] Cf. Montserrat Escribano, "Teología feminista como instancia crítica de las religiones en el espacio público: La propuesta de Elisabeth Schüssler Fiorenza," en: *Contrastes. Revista Internacional de Filosofía* 18 (2013), 305-320.

[22] Cf. Kwok Pui-lan, *Postcolonial Imagination and Feminist Theology* (Westminster John Knox Press: Louisville 2005). También: Mayra Rivera Rivera, *The Touch of Transcendence: A Postcolonial Theology of God* (Westminster John Knox Press: Louisville 2007).

[23] Cf. Marcella Althus-Reid / Lisa Isherwood (eds.), *Controversies in Body Theology* (SCM Press: London 2008).

[24] Cf. Ulrike Auga, "No Other Means? Fundamentalisms, Religion, Survival, and Biopolitical Counterdiscourses," en: Ulrike Auga / Christina von Braun / Claudia Bruns / Jana Husmann (eds.), *Fundamentalism and Gender: Scripture – Body – Community* (Pickwick Publications: Eugene 2013), 264-288.

[25] Cf. Rieger / Pui-Lan, *Occupy Religion*.

y que repetitivamente debe formularse y es: ¿qué debemos hacer con nuestro cerebro?[26]

La teología *queer*, tal como la plantean Lisa Isherwood y Marcella Althus-Reid, nos ayudan a fijar algunos de estos puntos de apoyo críticos.[27] Su propuesta teológica es una apuesta radical por una teología centrada en los modos en que amamos, nos relacionamos, tanto como individuos o como sociedad, y a la vez, por aquello que el amor puede hacer en nosotras mismas y en nuestro mundo. Quizá esta perspectiva permita a la neuroteología feminista ahondar sobre los modos en los que se almacenan las huellas que en nuestro cerebro plástico dejan las experiencias. Pero, especialmente, puede cuestionar qué puede significar el Amor desde una concepción teológica como esta, que no olvida lo carnal y somático vista desde una perspectiva también política. Al mismo tiempo, puede preguntarse qué sentido alberga hoy en día ese Amor dentro de una institución como la Iglesia y si aún puede ayudarnos a tomar partido por las dolientes y a frenar decisiones biopolíticas en medio de un sistema capitalista atroz.

Estamos llamadas a responder de modo personal, institucional y político a cuestiones como: ¿qué hemos hecho de nuestra plasticidad? Es decir, cuál ha sido nuestra responsabilidad ante la vida recibida y cómo hemos sostenido la de los demás que se nos han hecho prójimos. La neuroteología no puede ser tan solo un mecanismo de producción de conocimiento, ni una disciplina que ofrezca una metodología más o menos novedosa. Tampoco puede ser un ámbito estático de conocimiento, sino un espacio que movilice nuestras sinapsis, que cree paradigmas resistentes y que provoque lecturas incómodas. Siendo esto así, quizá podamos llegar a ser neuronalmente cordiales.

Aportaciones de la teología trinitaria clásica a la noción de "persona"

La aportación de la reflexión teológica sobre el concepto de Dios es básica para comprender qué tipo de antropología se dibuja desde una tradición religiosa concreta. Como decía Tomás de Aquino, "hablar de Dios es siempre insuficiente" – porque el lenguaje humano no puede abarcarlo ni limitarlo – "pero no es indiferente" – ya que las palabras y las imágenes que utilizamos se corresponden a un modo de interpretar y ver la realidad, y de hecho, la

---

[26] Cf. Catherine Malabou, *What Should We Do With our Brain?* (Fordham University Press: New York 2008).

[27] Cf. Marcella Althus-Reid / Lisa Isherwood, "Thinking Theology and Queer Theory," en: *Feminist Theology* 15 (2007), 302-314.

configuran y transforman. El convencimiento del poder creador de la palabra es propio de la cultura semítica y del próximo Oriente. La palabra (*dabar*) no es mera metáfora o concepto abstracto, sino acontecimiento y hecho histórico, de ahí que los relatos bíblicos expliquen la creación del cosmos a partir de la acción del Verbo, del Logos.

Para el cristianismo, el mundo proviene de un acto creador y libre que introduce una cesura entre quien crea y el mundo creado. Supone un "contenerse de Dios" para que el mundo y el ser humano existan.[28] Por la creación tiene consistencia y tiene sentido. Según la teología clásica, este vaciamiento o retirada amorosa de Dios para dejar espacio no supone ninguna reducción de su naturaleza y, en cambio, permite la diferenciación, la posibilidad de existencia y respuesta distinta por parte del ser humano. Así la imagen y semejanza presupone a la vez capacidad de actuar con amor y con libertad, es decir, la posibilidad de dejar espacio al otro para que sea en dignidad y plenitud. Reconocer esta relación siempre cambiante y novedosa, cuyo origen es el Dios Amor y creador, nos une al resto como iguales, como hermanas y hermanos. Desde la neuroteología podríamos afirmar que la realidad movilizadora del Amor altera la estructura de nuestro cerebro permitiéndonos sentir amor y superar los límites del miedo.

El pensamiento cristiano sostiene que las personas tenemos libertad y que somos responsables de nuestras vidas. Esto supone tener que dialogar con determinadas corrientes neurocientíficas que afirman que la libertad humana es un constructo o bien que el libre albedrío no es más que el resultado de una cadena de órdenes del cerebro.[29] Sin embargo, desde la experiencia creyente nos referimos a situaciones como la de aquella mujer samaritana (*Jn* 4, 1-30). Ella fue al pozo a buscar agua y quedó afectada por la transgresión cultural, religiosa y de género de Jesús al dirigirle la palabra siendo ella mujer, pagana y samaritana. El resultado fue que esta experiencia cambió la orientación definitiva de su vida, la empujó a desear un agua diferente de la que apaga la sed fisiológica y la indujo a transmitir una experiencia de liberación a los demás.

---

[28] En el judaísmo se usa el término *tzimtzum* (proveniente del hebreo *simsum*) para referirse a la "contracción" o "retirada" que Dios hace para dejar espacio a la creación. Según la teoría de Isaac Luria se trata de un espacio conceptual para que el mundo físico y la libertad puedan existir (ver http://encyclopedia.thefreedictionary.com/tzimtzum). También es un concepto utilizado por Simone Weil, "Formas de amor implícito a Dios," en: Simone Weil, *A la espera de Dios* (Editorial Trotta: Madrid 1993), 87-98.

[29] Cf. Daniel Dennet, *La libertad de acción* (Gedisa: Barcelona 1992).

La comprensión cristiana del ser humano, pues, evidencia que las personas somos y nos conformamos en "relación", porque también la imagen del Dios trinitario de la teología clásica es "relación" en un plano de igualdad entre las tres personas. Este es el concepto de Dios que muestra Gregorio Nacianceno[30] (padre capadocio del siglo IV). Rompió con las categorías aristotélicas preeminentes e incluyó el concepto de relacionalidad como substancia del ser de Dios. Sin embargo, para Aristóteles el movimiento y la relación eran accidentes que no podían formar parte de la sustancia o esencia del ser. Por otra parte, el movimiento pericorético continuo del amor entre el polo creador y el polo receptor de "Dios madre/padre-espíritu Amor-Hijo" son el movimiento analógico que nos constituye como un seres capaces de amar y de responder libremente frente al dolor y al sufrimiento de los demás.

La relación entre las tres personas de la trinidad es de igualdad y no jerárquica, como ya había descrito poco tiempo antes el también padre capadocio Basilio de Cesarea (siglo IV) con el concepto de *koinonia* (comunión de iguales).[31] La plenitud de la unidad reside en el movimiento pericorético del amor entre iguales, y así acontece también en la comunidad humana. La plenitud del "ser persona" necesita cumplirse al mismo tiempo que la plenitud en las relaciones de amor e igualdad entre los seres humanos. Así, la teología trinitaria clásica aporta una noción de libertad que no puede desunirse del amor y la transcendencia hacia el otro. Según estos autores, cada persona está llamada a la plenitud personal en comunión con los demás para constituir unas relaciones fraternas y fructíferas en una comunidad diversa y unida.

En relación a la noción de libertad y de "ser persona", Hannah Arendt,[32] en su reflexión sobre la banalidad del mal a raíz de describir el juicio a Eichmann, plantea el fundamento del sujeto en la capacidad de pensar y de ser crítico en el contexto de un marco epistemológico, cultural e histórico concretos. Lo que distingue, pues, el ser propiamente un "sujeto" es la conciencia crítica y el gesto de libertad para con los demás que rompa la cadena causal de obediencia a la ley y a la autoridad del momento.

---

[30] Estos conceptos están explicados en la tesis publicada por Teresa Forcades, *Ser persona avui: estudi del concepte de persona en la teologia trinitària clàssica i de la seva relació amb la noció moderna de llibertat* (Publicacions de l'Abadía de Montserrat: Barcelona 2011), 16-67. Existe un artículo en castellano que contiene un resumen al respecto: Teresa Forcades, "Hacia una sociedad de iguales," en: *Iglesia Viva* 239 (2009), 31-48.

[31] Cf. Forcades, *Ser persona avui*, 16-67.

[32] Cf. Hannah Arendt, *Eichmann en Jerusalén* (Debolsillo: Barcelona 2006).

A finales del siglo XX e inicios del XXI, las aportaciones del movimiento feminista crítico, del movimiento LGTBI y las teorías *queer* sobre la performatividad del sujeto "en relación" con los demás, conectan de nuevo con estos conceptos de "persona" y "subjetivación" humanas ligadas a la práctica de la libertad y el amor, más que con la identificación en alguna de las categorías de binarismo sexual que la heteronormatividad patriarcal ha impuesto. Estos movimientos críticos han cuestionado los prejuicios y las categorías de género que pretenden limitar la autocomprensión de cada ser humano y que pretenden esencializar las diferencias sexuales.[33]

Deconstrucción de categorías epistemológicas y amplitud de visión
De la aportación de una imagen y concepción de Dios uno y trino, no piramidal ni jerárquico, se deduce una antropología liberadora que contempla al ser humano capaz de tener una conciencia propia, con capacidad de amor y de relación al mismo nivel tanto con los demás como hacia Dios. De ahí también se deduce la tradición subversiva de una teología crítica y de la liberación, cuyo objetivo es derribar fronteras, prejuicios sociales y normativos, sean estos de género, de etnia, de prestigio y estatus social o económico, por razones de salud/enfermedad, capacidad/discapacidad, etc., que pueden ser impuestos en un marco social y cultural determinado.

Desde el feminismo y las teologías *queer*, se aboga por la necesidad de deconstruir las categorías de conocimiento y de interpretación de la realidad que eviten abusos y marginalizaciones de todas aquellas personas que no se reconocen en las categorías identitarias como "hombre", "mujer", "inmigrante", "pobre" o "negra". Estas etiquetas ejercen violencia sobre las otras personas. Se nos invita a ser sujetos únicos con capacidad de acción más allá de los prejuicios, asunciones y normas sociales que nos empequeñecen y limitan.

Las teologías formuladas desde la perspectiva *queer* y postcolonial, pues, están llamadas a contribuir a la formación de este sujeto personal y a promover comunidades de iguales en comunión. Están llamadas, a su vez, a desvelar la capacidad de acción e intervención en el espacio público-político que se alinee totalmente con las luchas por una sociedad que pretenda la justicia, el bien común, la dignidad y el respeto por cualquier persona.

---

[33] Cf. Judith Butler, "Performatividad, precariedad y políticas sexuales," en: *AIBR, Revista de Antropología Iberoamericana* 4.3 (2009), 321-336. Conferencia en la Universidad Complutense impartida en Madrid, el 8 de junio de 2009.

En este objetivo común, el concepto de capacidad de "agencia" del yo, libre y encarnado al que se refiere la teoría *queer*,[34] confluye con la plasticidad y la necesidad de responsabilizarnos ante nuestros cerebros y que reconoce la neuroteología.

Seguramente, deconstruir la epistemología o el sistema de categorías con que se nos educa, nos permitirá ser más críticos con los fundamentalismos y el pensamiento único que pretenden imponer las élites del poder económico y político o las instituciones religiosas. Se trata de un reto liberador para construir una democracia real basada en proyectos sociales incluyentes y que busquen el bienestar de todas y de todos.

El pueblo *yoruba* del África occidental usa el concepto de *ilaju* (literalmente "ojo abierto", en el sentido de tener "amplitud de visión") para referirse a "civilización" o "cultura".[35] Mientras que el pueblo romano consideraba "civilización" todo aquello "urbanizado" (*civis* en latín significa "ciudad"), la cultura yoruba considera "civilizado" el pueblo capaz de "mirar alrededor", de tener una "visión amplia" hacia la realidad y hacia sus congéneres. El movimiento feminista africano ha recuperado esta imagen potente del término *ilaju* para resistir la colonización blanca europea y para ejercitar la apertura de conocimiento y visión donde quepan unas nuevas relaciones de respeto, dignidad, libertad y armonía con la naturaleza y con los demás.

Las teologías desde la perspectiva *queer* y postcolonial están llamadas a fecundar el espacio público y a fortalecer el espacio democrático. Éstas son algunas de sus tareas prioritarias. Pero para que esto suceda es necesario que las distintas teologías se pregunten por cuáles son los modos de producir conocimiento y sus regímenes de verdad. En la actualidad, las neurociencias están revelándose como un ámbito apropiado en el cual poder pensar desde otras perspectivas al ser humano, tanto en el ámbito individual como en el social. La neurobiología nos muestra que las estructuras neuronales del cerebro junto a las estructuras socioculturales modelan nuestro comportamiento y las creencias morales, éticas y religiosas. Por ello, parece

---

[34] Cf. Gracia Trujillo, "Del sujeto político *la Mujer* a la agencia de *las (otras) mujeres*: El impacto de la crítica *queer* en el feminismo del Estado español," en: *Política y sociedad* 46.1-2 (2009), 161-172.

[35] Cf. Desiree Lewis / Elaine Salo / Joanne Henry / Tara Turkinton / Fakara Fainké / Margo Okazawa-Rey / Samy Nja Kwa / Renée Mendy Ongoundou / Gnimdéwa Atakpama / Upenyu Makoni Muchemwa (interviewers), *Africana. Aportacions per a la descolonització del feminisme: Entrevistes amb Amina Mama, Molara Ogundipe, Fatma Aloo, Fatima meer, Ayesha Imam, Fatoumata Maiga, Yasmin Jusu-Sheriff, Aminata Traoré, Ken Bugul i Tstsi Dangaremgba* (Oozebap i Espai Àfrica-Catalunya: Barcelona 2010).

pertinente que cuestionemos, a la luz de las neurociencias y de la noción de "persona" de la teología cristiana clásica, los fundamentos epistémicos sobre los que se apoya nuestro conocimiento de la realidad. De esa manera podremos interrogarnos, éticamente, por las posibilidades transformadoras que surgen para que todas las vidas humanas encuentren posibilidades de florecimiento.

Queer and postcolonial theologies are meant to fill the public space and to strengthen the democratic space. These are, indeed, some of their main tasks. Yet, for this to be possible, the various theologies have to analyse the way in which they produce knowledge and truth. Nowadays, neuroscience is becoming an appropriate way to consider the human being from another perspective, both on the individual and social level. Neurobiology clearly shows that our behaviour and our moral, ethical and religious convictions are not only determined by our sociocultural structures, but also by our neuronal structures. Therefore, with the insights of neurosciences and the Christian classical theology of the concept of "subject" we should question the epistemic pillars sustaining our perception of reality, and at the same time try to think of the possibility of making each and every human life better.

Queere und postkoloniale Theologien sollen den öffentlichen Raum füllen und die Demokratie stärken. Dies sind in der Tat ihre hauptsächlichen Aufgaben. Aber damit das möglich wird, müssen die diversen Theologien die Art analysieren, wie sie Wissen und Wahrheit produzieren. Heute sind die Neurowissenschaften ein angemessener Weg, um den Menschen auf individuellem und sozialem Niveau aus einer anderen Perspektive zu betrachten. Die Neurobiologie zeigt deutlich, dass unser Verhalten und unsere moralischen, ethischen und religiösen Überzeugungen nicht nur von unseren sozio-kulturellen, sondern auch unseren neuronalen Strukturen determiniert sind. Auf dem Hintergrund der Erkenntnisse der Neurowissenschaften und der klassischen christlichen Theologie zum Konzept des Subjekts sollten wir daher die epistemischen Säulen hinterfragen, die unsere Wahrnehmung der Realität tragen, und gleichzeitig nach Möglichkeiten suchen, jedes einzelne menschliche Leben besser zu gestalten.

Montserrat Escribano-Cárcel es licenciada en Ciencias Religiosas y Máster en Teología por la Facultad de Teología de San Vicente Ferrer, València. También licenciada en Humanidades y Máster en Ética y Democracia por la Universitat de València. Es miembro de la Asociación de Teólogas Española (ATE) y desde agosto de 2013 forma parte del Board de la Asociación Europea de Mujeres para la Investigación Teológica (ESWTR) como tesorera. Forma parte del Grupo de Investigación en Bioética de la Universitat de València (GIBUV). Sus ámbitos de investigación son: Neuroteología, hermenéutica feminista crítica y éticas aplicadas. Actualmente, prepara su doctorado en la Facultad de Filosofía y Ciencias de la Educación Moral y Política en la Universitat de València (España) en el Departamento de Filosofía del Derecho, Moral y Política.

Neus Forcano i Aparicio es licenciada en Filología y Máster de Estudios Históricos de las Mujeres-DUODA, ambos títulos obtenidos en la Universitat de Barcelona (Catalunya-España). Se dedica a la enseñanza de lengua y literatura en Secundaria y Bachillerato. Está cursando actualmente el grado en Ciencias Religiosas en el Instituto de Ciencias Religiosas de Barcelona y participa en colectivos de mujeres de base (*Col·lectiu de Dones en l'Església*; *Escamot Magdala*) que organizan cursos de formación y de estudios bíblicos desde una perspectiva crítica feminista. Es miembro de la Asociación Europea de Mujeres para la Investigación Teológica (ESWTR) desde el 2007, y formó parte del equipo de preparación y coordinación del XIV Congreso Internacional de la ESWTR titulado "La teología feminista: escuchar, comprender y responder en un mundo secular y plural", celebrado en Salamanca (España) en el año 2011.

Journal of the European Society of Women in Theological Research 22 (2014) 215-226.
doi: 10.2143/ESWTR.22.0.3040800

BOOK REVIEWS – REZENSIONEN – RECENSIONES

Jenny Daggers, *Postcolonial Theology of Religions: Particularity and Pluralism in World Christianity*, London and New York: Routledge 2013, 256 pages, ISBN 978-0-415-61043-8.

This creative and learned book develops an original postcolonial theology of religions, which is highly needed in the globalised, neoliberal and postcolonial empire, with enhanced movement of peoples and knowledge and the meeting of different worldviews. This is also a time when theologies and religious studies are still too often suffering from universalist postcolonial and patriarchal heritages. Understandings of "religion" are on the one hand torn between religious and secular fundamentalisms, and on the other hand the notion of "religion" gains new and different public interest with the post-secular turn. Furthermore, postcolonial (feminist and queer) scholars and activists underline their understanding of "religion" as a category which enables agency.

Daggers presupposes that interreligious engagement is enhanced by a renewed attention to the particularity of religious traditions. She starts with a criticism of Christian theology of religions as entangled with European colonial modernity. In her historical overview, she puts the emphasis on the violent essentialisations of "religion" in modernity. However, she later elaborates her own approach on feminist and especially Asian philosophies and theologies which try to disentangle Eurocentrism from the study of religion and the notion of "religion" itself.

The book consists of two parts. Part I lays the basis for Jenny Daggers's constructive model. She undertakes a theological investigation of the generic category "religion" and of the study of "the religions", which emerge in response to the Enlightenment and along with colonialism, and critically assesses the formation of Christian perceptions of other religions. The author also focuses on the attitudes toward other religions in the modern missionary movement, and analyses how they are influenced by other faith traditions. The first part concludes with a discussion of the twentieth-century discourse of the Christian "theology of religions", which is marked by missionary debates and Eurocentric priorities.

Part II shows the postcolonial disentangling of theology and of the study of "religion" concurrent with an undoing of the notion of "religion". Daggers scrutinises the relationship of Euro-American feminist theology with Christianity, and in relation to interreligious diversity. She then analyses Asian women's feminist and postcolonial theologies of religion and other important and distinctive Asian perspectives on religious pluralism. On this basis, Daggers constructs her particularist model for a postcolonial theology of religions using elements from George Lindbeck, Jeannine Hill Fletcher and Kathryn Tanner.

Finally, Daggers situates her own project within the recent trinitarian turn in Christian theologies in dialogue with Asian and feminist theologies. She argues that

> the trinitarian core of Christian faith is fully congruent with the determined pursuit of gender justice. Trinitarian theologies that have been deployed to underwrite injustices to women are distortions: the "turn to religious particularity" in recent Christian theology of religions invites articulations of trinitarian Christian faith in dialogue with partners from other religious traditions; this is an opportunity to present the rich gendered economy of Christian faith, rather than its narrow patriarchal defacement (5).

Jenny Daggers's book covers her subject horizontally and vertically because it looks at vast areas of theory, is historically sound, and is therefore a real achievement in the field which could only be enhanced by a stronger epistemological scrutiny of the category "religion". This excellent, theologically innovative study is not only important for scholars of theology of religions but for all those who search for an appropriate Christian theology which respects the integrity of Christianity and of other religious traditions and practices in the light of postcolonial and poststructuralist investigations. These methods of analysis underline the discursive character of the notion of "religion" and try to abandon violent definitions of "religion", which feed "Eurocentric", "western", "white", "male", "heterosexist", "able bodied", etc., and Christian universalist presumptions.

Ulrike Auga (New York – USA)

Catherine Keller, *Über das Geheimnis: Gott erkennen im Werden der Welt: Eine Prozesstheologie*, übers. von Angelika Reichl, Herder: Freiburg i. Brsg. 2013, 282 Seiten, ISBN 978-3-451-33263-0.

> Kein Geschöpf, nicht einmal ein Eremit im Himalaja oder ein Sauerstoffmolekül kilometerweit über unseren Köpfen ist von dem gesamten Lebensprozess auf der Erde unberührt. (50)

In ihrem Werk *Über das Geheimnis* (deutsche Übersetzung des 2008 bei Fortress erschienen Originals, *On the Mystery: Discerning Divinity in Process*) führt uns die US-amerikanische Prozesstheologin und Feministin Catherine Keller mit ihrer alternativen, progressiven "Theo-Logik" auf einen "dritten Weg" (22, 78 u.ö.), den Weg des Werdens in Beziehung. Dieser alternative Weg ist kein Kompromiss zwischen dem Spannungsfeld von Omnipotenz und Impotenz, Absolution und Dissolution, Absolutismus und Relativismus, Agape und Eros, sondern ein neuer, resolut offener Weg, der sich auf das "omniamouröse" (164) Abenteuer des lockenden Gottes einlässt, und die eigene Mit-Verantwortlichkeit der Geschöpfe im Werden der Welt radikal ernst nimmt. Keller stellt sich hier häufig vorgebrachten Vorurteilen und Anfragen an die Prozesstheologie (wie etwa: Was ist denn an Gott noch göttlich, wenn diese Gottheit nicht all-mächtig ist?) und zeigt sowohl die biblische Verwurzelung als auch die höhere Theo-Logik einer relationalen Theologie auf. Biblische Zitate werden hierbei stets in ihrem Kontext gelesen und als dialogeröffnend und auf das unendliche Geheimnis verweisend interpretiert. Scheinbar "nebenbei" räumt sie dadurch mit tradierten Missverständnissen auf; so verweist sie auf die Fehlübersetzung von "El Shaddai" mit "der Allmächtige" anstatt, wie es korrekt heißen müsste, "die Bebrüstete" (12, 115). Keller ruft sich hierbei immer wieder die Vorläufigkeit einer jeden Theologie – so auch ihrer eigenen – vor Augen. Wir können von Gott nur in Metaphern oder Analogien sprechen, Gott bleibt das Geheimnis schlechthin: "Die Wahrheit zu besitzen, bedeutet, sie zu verlieren" (64). Mit aus dem Leben gegriffenen Beispielen führt sie uns eindringlich die Notwenigkeit einer Theologie der Beziehung vor Augen, die sich einem Dasein in absoluter Relationalität und konspirierender, verkörperlichter Interaktivität öffnet ("anything flows" statt "anything goes" [39], "[w]eil die Frage danach, wer wir sind, untrennbar mit den offenen Prozessen der Interaktion verbunden ist, brauchen wir eine radikal relationale Theologie" [35]).

Eine resolute Theologie des Werdens sieht Keller bereits in den Anfängen aller Theologien, in der Schöpfung der Welt aus der "bodenlosen Tiefe Gott" (81), dem *tehom*, grundgelegt. Genesis bedeutet "Werden", jedoch kein amaterielles Werden, sondern der Geist Gottes wirkt permanent und zu aller Zeit in Materie (81-97). Eindrücklich zeigt sie auf, dass eine solche Interpretation von Gen 1 weder Raum lässt für eine homo- noch eine tehomophobe Interpretation. Ebenso wenig lässt sie eine Anti-Egalität der Geschlechter oder einen missverstandenen Herrschaftsauftrag zu, mit dem wir unsere Ausbeutung der Schöpfung zu rechtfertigen suchen (104f). Das Werden der Welt wird als kontinuierlich-kooperierender Prozess verstanden:

Im Gegensatz zur Vision eines linearen Designer-Universums wird die Schöpfung in der Genesis nicht als Gottes Solo-Auftritt dargestellt. Dort kann man nur von einem Prozess kosmischer Zusammenarbeit lesen. Keine dinghafte Schöpfung, sondern ein komplexer interaktiver Prozess wird geweckt: Nennen wir ihn doch das *Genesis-Kollektiv*. […] Die zunehmende Zusammenarbeit entfaltet sich wie ein Rhythmus, eine kosmische Liturgie: göttliches Locken, geschöpfliche Improvisation und göttliches Empfangen – welch ein Genuss! (101).

Die Interaktion von Gott und Welt wird als reziproke Ko-Kreativität verstanden, ein Wechselspiel zwischen der leidenschaftlich lockenden "schöpferische[n] Liebe Gottes" und der "erwidernde[n] Liebe Gottes" (151ff). Hierbei verschleiert die Autorin das (kreative) Risiko des ganzen Prozesses nicht. Eine Erlösung der Welt kann nicht garantiert sein, wenn die Mitverantwortlichkeit der Geschöpfe am "Commenwealth of God" (John B. Cobb) in letzter Konsequenz ernst genommen wird. Ihre deutliche Beschreibung der gut begründeten Annahme einer eschatologischen Fortsetzung der pluralistischen Verwobenheit allen Seins ist ein Höhepunkt der Lektüre:

Nichtsdestotrotz bleibt die Frage: Was hat es nun mit dem Endgericht nach dem Leben auf sich? Ich denke so darüber: Wenn wir den Übergang in ein größeres Liebesleben nicht vollziehen können, wenn wir uns eisern an dem festhalten, was wir haben, oder uns mit Bitterkeit nach dem sehnen, was wir nicht haben können – dann würden wir ohnehin nicht in diesem "Himmel" sein wollen! Wir würden dort nicht hingehören. Der falsche Verein, die falsche Nachbarschaft, das falsche Altenheim. Denn welche Bilder bietet uns die Bibel von diesem Reich Gottes an, von der neuen Schöpfung oder vom "Himmel" – außer intensiv relationale Metaphern vom Feiern, der Annahme, der Hochzeit, von einer endlos singenden und tanzenden *Gemeinschaft*. Mit diesen Anderen, die wir ignoriert haben, die wir spirituell unbedeutsam, uninteressant, abstoßend oder einfach nur unwirklich in unserer tatsächlichen Existenz fanden? Sollten wir jetzt auf Ewigkeit mit ihnen verstrickt sein? In einem subtileren Leib, der mich nicht mehr von ihnen abschirmt (wie meine Haut, meine Kleidung und meine Kirche es getan haben)? Igitt! (211-212).

Inhaltlich verständlich und sprachlich kreativ bietet *Über das Geheimnis* eine überaus gelungene Einführung in die Prozesstheologie für all jene, die den Mut haben, sich in das Abenteuer des Geheimnisses einer Theologie im Werden, eines Gottes im Prozess hineinzubegeben (Achtung: Open End!). Durch die gute Aufbereitung der jeweiligen Kapitel mittels tiefgreifender und teils persönlicher Leitfragen am Ende des Buches und dem weitgehenden Verzicht auf technische Begriffe und Fachtermini eignet es sich ebenfalls für (Lektüre-)

Seminare mit Studienanfänger_innen. Kellers charakteristische Theopoetik, die dem Werk eine ganz eigene, narrative Sprache verleiht, verliert ein wenig aufgrund der Übersetzung ins Deutsche, kann aber dennoch als echte Meisterleistung bewertet werden. Dass es sich bei *Über das Geheimnis* um eine Übersetzung der bereits 2008 erschienenen Originalausgabe *On the Mystery* handelt, erklärt, warum keine aktuelle(re) Literatur berücksichtigt wurde.

Keller gilt derzeit als Avantgarde der zweiten Welle der Prozesstheologie. Ihr Werk *Über das Geheimnis* ist in jeder Hinsicht eine Lektüre wert, denn "[e]s gibt keine Theologie, die die Wahrheit über unsere radikale relationale Abhängigkeit voneinander früher oder besser aufgenommen hätte als die Bewegung der Prozesstheologie." (50)

Julia Enxing (Münster – Germany)

Saba Mahmood, *Politics of Piety: The Islamic Revival and the Feminist Subject*, Princeton: Princeton University Press 2012 [2005], 233 pages, ISBN 978-0-691-14980-6.

The second edition of Saba Mahmood's ethnographic and anthropological analyses of the women's mosque movement in Cairo in 1995-1997 develops an elaborate critique of normative secular-liberal accounts of politics and understandings of agency after 9/11. Mahmood challenges dominant concepts of feminist theory including the binary of resistance and subordination as well as their relation to critical terms of authority, women's agency, freedom and the human subject. Furthermore, this study argues the inalienable need of involving issues of ethics and embodiment into debates on the emergence of political and social imaginaries. Mahmood's research emphasizes the significance of academic investigations into politics and religion. The implication of her argument on Islamic piety cannot be overestimated for contemporary debates on modern religiosity, resistance, and the importance of moral reformation movements to the regime of oppression.

In the preface to the 2012 edition Mahmood places the politics of the piety movement within the context of the coalition that led to the transformation of Egyptians' political consciousness toward a new sense of collective agency, revolutionary mobilization, and brought down the dictatorship of Hosni Mubarak in February 2011.

The author later responds to critical notes in the perception of her work since 2005, in particular to feminist critics, by underlining the aim of developing an analytical language that constitutes and enables modalities of agency going beyond liberatory feminist, leftist or liberal alliances. Mahmood elaborates on two central issues constructing her new model of thinking about resistance: "(a) The kinds of capacities – embodied, rational, technical – these various modalities of agency require; and (b) the conceptions of the body, personhood, and politics these capacities presuppose, enable, and construct" (x). Furthermore, Mahmood replies critically to characterizations of the piety movement as a "hermeneutical exercise" indifferent to political issues, and comments on critics of her work claiming the neglectfulness of the semiotic processes.

Mahmood develops her argument in five chapters. At the beginning the author discusses the reference of various historical and cultural contexts to feminist movements against the theoretical background of Michel Foucault's and Judith Butler's notions of agency. Mahmood scrutinizes Butler's concept of the primarily socially constructed agent before her/his bodily constitution, and claims the understanding of norms as not only consolidated, but also inhabited, individually experienced, and multiply performed.

The second chapter focuses on the history, the aims, and the genealogy of the women's mosque movement. Its emergence is traced back to the reaction against an increasingly secular government and the processes of westernization. Even though patriarchal structures still exist, Mahmood puts the emphasis on new developments within the movement such as new social spaces for female agents within educational reforms of Islamic non-profit organizations.

Next, Mahmood examines the women's mosque lessons, and in particular the practices of dealing with sexual norms in order to analyze the possibility of a shift in authority. Here, she uses a discursive concept that acknowledges that the macrolevel limits the possible horizon of acting at the level of micropractices. Consequently, the Islamic cultural tradition is regarded as a mode of engaging with the religious texts and enabling agency within the tradition's limits rather than predefining people's "identity".

In chapter four she discusses subject formation in the context of an Aristotelian ethic that configures the ethical subject through actions. Mahmood uses the example of ritual to argue how external action constitutes the internal self and concludes that ethical norms are a model of potentiality. Consequently, it is the autonomous agent who is responsible for her/his individual subject formation. However, the multiplicity of bodily practices represents symbolic acts which are actively related to the subject's exteriority as well as interiority: both enable and express the individually constituted subject.

220

In conclusion, Mahmood outlines new modalities of agency that go beyond resistance. Based on an examination of Butler's concept of performativity, the author positions the piety movement as a new emergent form, even though it includes the elements of iterant performance for subjects' self-formation and the creation of agency.

This outstanding analysis of the women's piety movement proposes an alternative perspective on the transformative potential of piety in contemporary Egyptian society in terms of establishing a new ethics of care and solidarity, of the creation of distinct political and social creative imaginaries, and of developing new understandings of gender norms. The nexus between bodily performative religious practices, the ethics of politics and agency, critical approaches to liberalism, secularism and feminist theory makes Saba Mahmood's *Politics of Piety* one of the central new approaches not only for anthropologists, feminists and cultural theorists, but also for scholars of theology and history of religions. It is an innovative approach with theoretical potential for scholars working on visuality and performativity, as well as on the emergence of new resistances and ethics in the context of intercultural, social and political transformations.

(Elisaveta Dvorakk, Berlin – Germany)

Jane Schaberg, *La resurreción de María Magdalena: Leyendas, apócrifos y testamento cristiano*, trad. Pilar Flórez Martín, Estella (Navarra): Verbo Divino 2008, 620 pages, ISBN 978-84-8169-773-5.

Among the many books, both academic and fictional, written about Mary Magdalene, Jane Schaberg's book is remarkable in her effort "hacer de ella fuente de autoridad para cambios de orden eclesiástico tanto en el siglo anterior como en el presente" (55).

Schaberg is conscious of the danger involved in making iconic images, as this has been known to produce legends or half-truths. But she takes the risk because she knows that rethinking the past is a way to help to define the future. To imagine Mary Magdalene, to study her social, ecclesiological and historical exclusion, is a way to see her as an ancestor and an inspiration for numerous women. She may help them to be freed from the "oppressive power" present throughout history.

For this study, and this represents an element of novelty, the author is inspired by Virginia Woolf's work. Her imagination and irony provide a pool of elements encouraging Schaberg's academic work. Analyzing Woolf's legacy will provide a source of revitalization to religious studies, Schaberg's own field of research. Following the pathway that Woolf opens, Jane Schaberg strives to explore what she knows may be controversial.

The start of her study concerns geography. Schaberg travels to Migdal, the hometown of Mary Magdalene, and in the first chapter, she describes the character of the Magdala in general terms. From this city, which Schaberg visits every year, she establishes the link between its oversight and ruin, as it seems to suffer from the same ecclesiastic and cultural dismissal as the woman carrying the name of the town.

Next, Jane Schaberg moves on to canonical texts, the work of the Fathers of the Church and the Christian literature of the first century. In these texts she finds confirmation of the process of censorship and distortion surrounding the image of Mary Magdalene that we have received. Without forgetting the contribution of novels, films and other cultural elements, the author corroborates how this woman was excluded from patriarchal succession, in a process that was based mostly on legends.

The daunting situation in which she finds Mary Magdalene's image motivates Schaberg's review of the Nag Hammadi Library. There she finds a new Magdalene. A woman who very well understood and transmitted her experience of the resurrection to everybody who wanted to listen, and who had to face the apostles' intolerance. Schaberg makes use of a comprehensive analysis of the different apocryphal texts to better defend her arguments, including the preeminence of Mary (217), her role as a leader surrounded by men (239), and her defense by Jesus himself (275). The knowledge of apocryphal and gnostic traditions regarding Mary Magdalene, Schaberg writes, "puede enseñarnos a leer estos textos de nuevas maneras, y también a trabajar para transformar las estructuras de opresión" (338).

The next step is to build a feminist reconstruction of Mary Magdalene through an analysis of the misuse and erasure of her memory in the Christian Testament (339-344). In this chapter the author reviews the different gospels and the academic contributions of François Bovon, Robert M. Price, Antti Marjanen, Karen King and John D. Krossan. For this, she draws on Elisabeth Schüssler Fiorenza, who established the grounds for a feminist theological reconstruction of the Christian origins.

This analysis allows Jane Schaberg to focus on the apocalyptic readings of the death and resurrection of Jesus, their explanation of the empty tomb, and their presentation of the first appearance to Mary Magdalene. In the conclusion

Schaberg presents this woman as Jesus's successor and develops a historical and imaginative reconstruction in the context of early Jewish mysticism.

Schaberg is aware that "mi tratamiento del tema no convencerá a todo el mundo" (p. 586). She finishes her book with a brilliant reiteration of her desire to provide new lines of research, different and innovative approaches to texts that have remained unattended for too long, thus opening novel and encouraging venues for others to follow.

Carmen Picó Guzmán (Madrid – Spain)

Adrian S. van Klinken, *Transforming Masculinities in African Christianity*, Farnahm: Ashgate 2013, 234 pages, ISBN 978-1-4094-5114-3.

Gender studies in Africa is a relatively new discipline, and this book is an important contribution to the study of African Christianity, the study of men, masculinities and religion. The author attempts to answer central questions about how Christian traditions, identities and practices change in social, cultural and religious contexts in the modern world.

The author points out that World Christianity can be regarded as many "local theologies". In Africa, many people are writing local theologies in order to translate the universal (mostly western) theology into their particular contexts, and to apply the Christian faith to all spheres of human life.

The author did research into two African churches in Zambia, a Roman Catholic and a Pentecostal one, which represent two different local theologies and how they affect the masculinities of their members.

The rapid spread of HIV in Zambia is said to be caused primarily by the irresponsible sexual behavior of men in the country. According to traditional views of masculinities it is accepted that married men have many sexual partners due to the believed strength of their sexual drive. Young unmarried men also have many sexual partners. More than anything else, this behavior has led to the spread of HIV and resulted in many social problems. About 60% of AIDS victims are women and some say that the AIDS epidemic has a female face.

Constructionist insights have shown that it is possible to deconstruct tradional views, and that men can reshape their identities.Thus it is worth noticing the changes in masculinities that have taken place.

The book looks at two ways of approaching masculinities, from the point of view of theology and from the life of local churches. African feminist theologians, especially the Circle of Concerned African Women Theologians, take experiences of women as their starting point and "engage in the paradigm of an HIV liberation theology" (39). They study the concepts of *gender* and *patriarchy* and find in them the root causes of most injustices, not least structural, against women both in society and the Church. Their aim is to work towards "equal shares of power between women and men in order to guarantee autonomy and mutuality in sexual and wider gender relations" (47).

The Catholic congregation that the author studied, did not have any intention of transforming the hegemonic masculinities of its congregants. However, in an organization for men within the congregation, Saint Joachim is promoted as "the model Catholic husband and father" (65). Here men are taught not to engage in extramarital affairs, to use their income for the well-being of their family, and to care for their wives and children. The ideal man is responsible, shows self-control and is financially independent. He nurtures his faith. The men of this organization aim at following their role model although the general public and many of the ordinary congregants do not. Wives contribute to changing the masculinites of their husbands by insisting that they attend the meetings of St. Joachim. The reality and danger of AIDS has contributed to responsible sexual behavior of many men as well as to their awareness of divine judgement and accountability to God.

In the Pentecostal church the author studied the importance of individual sexual chastity is emphazised. In his preaching the pastor of the church maintains that Jesus can change men as individuals when they meet him personally in their faith. The reality of AIDS and the awareness of divine judgement also contribute to changes in the sexual behavior of men. In conclusion, the author draws attention to the different approaches of theologians and churches to the changes of masculinities. Theologians contribute through structural analysis, but the churches "seek to transform masculinities within an ideological frame that can be considered patriarchal, while the theologians aim at the liberation of men from patriarchy in order to achieve gender justice" (172). Religion can enable men to contribute to changes through their own agency. Theologians are criticized for hardly defining any specific positive ideal of masculinity and for not being "sensitive to the subtle changes in gender relations and gender identities taking place in local religious contexts" (181).

This book is a valuable contribution to gender studies and takes theology out of the ivory tower. The way it shows how masculinities can change in imperfect social settings is very valuable and applies to contexts all over the world.

Kjartan Jónsson (Hafnarfjordur – Iceland)

Marta Zubía Guinea, *Para nuestra memoria histórica: Las mujeres en la voz de los papas*, Estella: Editorial Verbo Divino 2011, 288 pages, ISBN 978-84-9945-205-0.

Para nuestra memoria histórica: Las mujeres en la voz de los papas contributes to the recovery of the historical memory, something important nowadays, especially for those who are marginalized, as a person or group. Specifically, people who have been silenced and are invisible, without a place in the history that has been told. Women occupy an outstanding place in this group. Different religions are responsible because they have laid foundations to maintain this situation even by law.

This volume is a survey that denounces what the popes have said about women from the middle of the 19th century until today. These pontiffs have used the name of God in vain, and we can discover obvious patriarchal hermeneutics. This ideology associates the rejection of women with God's will. Thus, this survey unmasks pontifical perversions and the ecclesially sanctioned sexist structures of power and supremacy that have driven women out of history and motivate the continued exclusion and suffering of women. Through the systematic investigation of papal documents which refer directly to the popes' thoughts about women, it is possible to sufficiently deduce clues about the patriarchal power structure and ideology that exists in religion, according to the writer, even though they tried to ground their theories theologically.

Para nuestra memoria histórica is structured in three chapters. The first contextualizes the socio-political and cultural environment for each period and the characteristics of each pontificate, and provides a summary of their thoughts about women. Consequently, it is possible to understand and distinguish what the influences of each time are. Their patriarchal slant leads to a distorted hermeneutics that has rejected women in religious contexts. The second chapter presents a large selection of papal texts, organized according to topics which the author considers meaningful and recurrent. In the third chapter, the author underlines the implicit theological clues in these documents and offers a critical presentation of some deviations or perversions that point to the theological principles of the Christian faith. It also shows how popes are continuing to follow them. The most important one, which is the root of all of them and their own misogynist tendencies and expositions, is the statement – sometimes explicit and sometimes not – that women, for being women, are not made in God's image.

This book is for a scholarly audience who will find a lot of information and interesting, well-organized material for a survey of theological gender subjects.

It is also of interest for a general public. The ultimate purpose of this work is to better understand how this doctrine about women has been developed as theological by the popes, and the reality that it cannot be the will of the God but represents a patriarchal androcentric construction and ideology.

It is a serious and rigorous work resulting from detailed research, an analysis that is founded in solid academic background and excellent documents. However, although it is a rigorous survey, at the same time the reader will find it interesting and lively to read and will be invited to have hope and faith in the Holy Spirit and to make a commitment to the freedom of the Church so that she will become a true community called by Jesus.

Mª Belén Brezmes Alonso (Murcia – Spain)

EUROPEAN SOCIETY OF WOMEN IN THEOLOGICAL RESEARCH

EUROPÄISCHE GESELLSCHAFT FÜR THEOLOGISCHE FORSCHUNG VON FRAUEN

ASOCIACIÓN EUROPEA DE MUJERES PARA LA INVESTIGACIÓN TEOLÓGICA

Journal of the European Society
of Women in Theological Research

1 **Luise Schottroff, Annette Esser**, *Feministische Theologie im europäischen Kontext – Feminist Theology in a European Context – Théologie féministe dans un contexte européen*, 1993, 255 p., ISBN: 90-390-0047-6 [out of print]

2 **Mary Grey, Elisabeth Green**, *Ecofeminism and Theology – Ökofeminismus und Theologie – Ecoféminisme et Théologie*, 1994, 145 p., ISBN: 90-390-0204-5 23 EURO

3 **Angela Berlis, Julie Hopkins, Hedwig Meyer-Wilmes, Caroline Vander Stichele**, *Women Churches: Networking and Reflection in the European Context – Frauenkirchen: Vernetzung und Reflexion im europäischen Kontext – Eglises de femmes: réseaux et réflections dans le contexte européen*, 1995, 215 p., ISBN: 90-390-0213-4 23 EURO

4 **Ulrike Wagener, Andrea Günter**, *What Does it Mean Today to Be a Feminist Theologian? – Was bedeutet es heute, feministische Theologin zu sein? – Etre théologienne féministe aujourd'hui: Qu'est-ce que cela veut dire?*, 1996, 192 p., ISBN: 90-390-0262-2 23 EURO

5 **Elisabeth Hartlieb, Charlotte Methuen**, *Sources and Resources of Feminist Theologies – Quellen feministischer Theologien – Sources et resources des théologies féministes*, 1997, 286 p., ISBN: 90-390-0215-0 23 EURO

6 **Hedwig Meyer-Wilmes, Lieve Troch, Riet Bons-Storm**, *Feminist Pespectives in Pastoral Theology – Feministische Perspektiven in Pastoraltheologie – Des perspectives féministes en théologie pastorale*, 1998, 161 p., ISBN: 90-429-0675-8 23 EURO

7 **Charlotte Methuen**, *Time – Utopia – Eschatology. Zeit – Utopie – Eschatologie. Temps – Utopie – Eschatologie*, 1999, 177 p., ISBN: 90-429-0775-4 23 EURO

8 **Angela Berlis, Charlotte Methuen**, *Feminist Perspectives on History and Religion – Feministische Zugänge zu Geschichte und Religion – Approches féministes de l'histoire et de la religion*, 2000, 318 p., ISBN: 90-429-0903-X [out of print]

9   **Susan K. Roll, Annette Esser, Brigitte Enzner-Probst, Charlotte Methuen, Angela Berlis**, *Women, Ritual and Liturgy – Ritual und Liturgie von Frauen – Femmes, la liturgie et le rituel*, 2001, 312 p., ISBN: 90-429-1028-9   23 EURO

10 **Charlotte Methuen, Angela Berlis**, *The End of Liberation? Liberation in the End! – Befreiung am Ende? Am Ende Befreiung! – La libération, est-elle à sa fin? Enfin la libération*, 2002, 304 p., ISBN: 90-429-1028-9   23 EURO

11 **Elżbieta Adamiak, Rebeka J. Anić, Kornélia Buday with Charlottte Methuen and Angela Berlis**, *Theologische Frauenforschung in Mittel-Ost-Europa – Theological Women's Studies in Central/Eastern Europe – Recherche théologique des femmes en Europe orientale et centrale*, 2003, 270 p., ISBN: 90-429-1378-9   23 EURO

12 **Charlotte Methuen, Angela Berlis, Sabine Bieberstein, Anne-Claire Mulder and Magda Misset-van de Weg**, *Holy Texts: Authority and Language – Heilige Texte: Autorität und Sprache – Textes Sacrés: Autorité et Langue*, 2004, 313 p., ISBN: 90-429-1528-X   23 EURO

13 **Valeria Ferrari Schiefer, Adriana Valerio, Angela Berlis, Sabine Bieberstein**, *Theological Women's Studies in Southern Europe – Theologische Frauenforschung in Südeuropa – Recherche théologique des femmes en Europe Méridionale*, 2005, 255 p., ISBN: 90-429-1696-6   23 EURO

14 **Sabine Bieberstein, Kornélia Buday, Ursula Rapp**, *Building Bridges in a Multifaceted Europe. Religious Origins, Traditions, Contexts, and Identities – Brücken bauen in einem vielgestaltigen Europa. Religiöse Ursprünge, Traditionen, Kontexte und Identitäten – Construire des ponts dans une Europe multiforme. Origines, traditions, contextes et identités religieux*, 2006, 257 p. ISBN 978-90-429-1895-5   23 EURO

15 **Hanna Stenström, Elina Vuola, Sabine Bieberstein, Ursula Rapp**, *Scandinavian Critique of Anglo-American Feminist Theology – Skandinavische Kritik angloamerikanischer feministischer Theologie – Critique scandinave de la théologie féministe anglo-américaine*, 2007, 292 p. ISBN 978-90-429-1974-7   23 EURO

16 **Sabine Bieberstein, Christine Gasser, Marinella Perroni, Ursula Rapp**, *Becoming Living Communities – Construyendo comunidades vivas –*

All volumes of the Journal of the ESWTR can be ordered from Peeters Publishers, Bondgenotenlaan 153, B-3000 Leuven
Fax: +32 16 22 85 00; e-mail: order@peeters-leuven.be

The volumes of the Journal of the ESWTR are also available online at
http://poj.peeters-leuven.be